Memoirs of the Nuttall Ornith

MW01614170

No. VII

THE BIRDS

OF

NEWFOUNDLAND LABRADOR

By OLIVER LUTHER AUSTIN, Jr.

WITH MAP

CAMBRIDGE, MASSACHUSETTS

PUBLISHED BY THE CLUB

SEPTEMBER, 1932

PREFACE

This work was undertaken more than six years ago. Its progress has been interrupted all too frequently by unavoidable circumstances which it is needless to enumerate here. Its successful culmination in this volume would never have been possible, even at this late date, had it not been for the generous assistance I have received from many persons whose knowledge and experience have been invaluable to me. To Dr. Glover M. Allen, under whose immediate supervision most of the researches were carried on, and who gave me much sage council and advice, and to Mr. Charles F. Batchelder, whose painstaking and careful editing of the manuscript and proof has put my efforts into publishable form, I am especially indebted. Mr. Francis H. Allen, Mr. Outram Bangs, Dr. Thomas Barbour, Professor M. L. Fernald, Dr. Herbert Friedmann, Mr. Gower Rabbitts, and Mr. James Lee Peters have also given me much valuable assistance. To them, and to still others whose names appear on the following pages, especially those true altruists, the Moravian Brethren, the Rev. Mr. W. W. Perrett, Dr. Paul Hettasch, and the Rev. Mr. B. Lenz, I am sincerely grateful.

The form and contents of this volume are self-evident. I have endeavored to incorporate herein all the information available regarding the avifauna of Newfoundland Labrador, and have paid particular attention to the systematic status, the present distribution, and the probable origin of its component parts. I trust that the work may prove to be of some use to students of distribution in general, and to those interested in Labrador birds in particular. Above all I hope that it is meritorious enough to justify the efforts of all those who have contributed so materially to its completion, and to repay them in some small way for their kindness and assistance to me.

OLIVER L. AUSTIN, JR.

North Eastham, Cape Cod, Massachusetts
August, 1932

INTRODUCTION

TITLE to the Labrador Peninsula is held by two separate units of the British Empire. By far the greater part of this immense tract, all the territory extending westward from the height of land, lies in the Province of Quebec. As it is within the jurisdiction of the Dominion of Canada, it is generally known as 'Canadian Labrador.' The section of the Peninsula covered by this work is the portion owned and exploited by Newfoundland, which is Great Britain's oldest colony and has a government of its own distinct from that of Canada.

Bounded on the north by Hudson Strait, on the east by the North Atlantic Ocean, on the south by the Straits of Belle Isle and the Gulf of St. Lawrence, and on the west by Canadian Labrador, 'Newfoundland Labrador' is thus the northeasternmost corner of the continent of North America. The western boundary line extends from the north shore of the Gulf of St. Lawrence at Blanc Sablon (lat. 51° 24′ N; long. 57° 09′ W.) northward along the height of land to MacLelan Strait. I have included in this treatise the Cape Chidley Islands and the Button Islands, which, while they belong politically to Canada, are faunally an integral part of the coastal region. Thus we may define the territory roughly as that part of the Labrador Peninsula east of the height of land between the Straits of Belle Isle and Hudson Strait.

That part of the coast line fronting the Straits of Belle Isle from Blanc Sablon to Cape Charles is characterized by low hills and cliffs of soft red sandstone in horizontal strata, seldom rising over three or four hundred feet. From Cape Charles north the coast is low, though bold, bluff and rugged, as far as Port Manvers. There the Kiglapait Mountains loom several thousand feet up, just back from the shore. From Cape Mugford north, the ragged Torngat range (where Torngat, the evil spirit of the Eskimos, was supposed to dwell) rears its lofty peaks four thousand feet out of the sea.

The coast is cut by many deep bays which extend varying distances inland, and is dotted with a veritable maze of islands. In the interior the region rises abruptly to the top of the high Laurentian plateau, down which many torrents rush to the sea, most of them entering at the heads of the fiords. The tops of the hills and mountains are barren rock, but the valleys boast an interesting flora.

To classify the southern two thirds of Labrador faunally is almost impossible, so mixed and scattered are the elements of the various zones. South of Hamilton Inlet the wooded regions back from the coast are mainly Canadian in type, as is evidenced by the presence of such species as the Hermit Thrush, Olive-backed

Thrush, White-winged Crossbill, Slate-colored Junco, White-throated Sparrow, Yellow Warbler, Myrtle Warbler.   North of Hamilton Inlet the sparsely forested valleys are seemingly more Hudsonian, and are populated by such birds as the Gray-cheeked Thrush, Pine Grosbeak, Tree Sparrow, Fox Sparrow, Wilson's Warbler, and Blackpoll Warbler.   However, many Canadian forms are to be found in the bays as far north as Port Manvers, and Hudsonian elements reach down the coast from Saglek Bay to Belle Isle.   The barren northern third of the coast is definitely Arctic.   Its vegetation is low tundra, and Snow Buntings, Lapland Longspurs, and Gyrfalcons comprise the dominant land avifauna.   Owing to the influence of the icy Labrador current, a treeless strip of pseudo-arctic tundra, somewhat Arctic in type but containing many Canadian and Hudsonian species, extends in a belt from five to ten miles wide along the entire outer coast. In it Pipits, Horned Larks, Redpolls, and White-crowned and Savannah Sparrows are the most prevalent birds.

ORNITHOLOGICAL EXPLORATIONS IN NEWFOUNDLAND LABRADOR

THE BIRDS of Newfoundland Labrador have received considerable attention in literature.   Many ornithologists have visited the region for the sole purpose of studying its avifauna.   Not a few adventurers, explorers, and sportsmen have traveled along the coast and in the interior and have published, incidentally, random notes on a few of the birds they encountered.   In spite of this, our knowledge of the ornithology of Labrador is still somewhat one-sided and unbalanced. The region is accessible from the southward only during July and August.   Pack ice prevents navigation usually until the end of June, and by this time the spring migration has ended and the nesting period is well under way.   If one does not wish to have to remain on the coast until the following summer, it is necessary to leave it by the middle of September, before the autumn migration is ended. Most ornithologists are unable to spend a full year in the region, and consequently most of the few data we have on spring and fall migrations and on the winter birds, have been garnered by men whose main interests have not been ornithological and who, wintering on the coast for other reasons, have found time to make a few bird notes.   Of the birds of the interior little is known.   In a short summer the ornithologist in Labrador naturally confines his activities to the outer coast, where the bird life is more profuse, and where working conditions are much easier than in the insect-infested interior.

The earliest writings on the ornithology of Labrador are to be found in the diary of Captain Cartwright, an English trader and adventurer who established the settlement bearing his name at the mouth of Sandwich Bay.   It was published in three ponderous quarto volumes at Newark, England, in 1792, under the self-explanatory title "Journal of Transactions and Events, during a Residence of Nearly Sixteen Years on the Coast of Labrador; Containing Many Interesting Particulars, both of the Country and its Inhabitants, Not Hitherto Known. Illustrated with Proper Charts." The Captain came to Labrador in 1770, and left it for the last time in 1786. Most of his time was spent in the vicinity of Cape Charles and Sandwich Bay, and his observations are hence limited to those localities. Regarding the birds he encountered he made many notes, most of which are of value today, because the species are perfectly identifiable and the exact localities and dates are mentioned in each case. The Captain used local vernacular names which, distinctive as they are, are still widely used by the English-speaking people on the coast today. He called the Red-throated Loon the 'Whabby'; the Loon the 'Loo'; the Golden-eye the 'Pie Duck'; the male and female Harlequin the 'Lord and Lady'; the Old-squaw the 'Hound'; the Razor-billed Auk the 'Tinker'; the Pine Grosbeak the 'Mope.' He gives us good pictures of the abundance of wild-fowl in his day, which are interesting and instructive when contrasted with the present status of those species that have been persecuted by men of more recent times.

Audubon, on his Labrador trip in 1833, visited only the southern Canadian sections on the north shore of the Gulf of St. Lawrence. While he worked there for over two months, he did not voyage as far east as the western boundary of Newfoundland Labrador, and hence wrote nothing on the birds of the region we are considering.

Elliott Coues was the first man to visit Newfoundland Labrador for the sole purpose of studying its bird life. At the age of eighteen he accompanied an expedition in charge of J. W. Dodge, which sailed along the coast in a fishing-schooner in 1860 "in order to procure for the Smithsonian Institution specimens of the birds to be found there, together with their nests and eggs, and to study their habits during the breeding season." He arrived on the north shore of the Gulf of St. Lawrence on July 1, and spent a week at Sloop Harbor outside our territory. He left there July 6, and proceeded north through the Straits of Belle Isle to Esquimaux Bay (now called Hamilton Inlet), where he spent most of the remainder of the summer. He left Hamilton Inlet August 15 and went to Henley Harbor on the Straits of Belle Isle, where he worked on the migrating shore birds until September 1. One cannot read the excellent and voluminous notes Coues made on the bird life of the region without gaining an immense amount of respect for the man, or rather the boy, who was able to amass such an amount of pertinent and valuable data in so short a time under very adverse and trying conditions.

In 1866 the Reverend S. Weiz, one of the Moravian Brethren, published a short list of the birds occurring at Okkak. Although he had spent many years on the coast as a missionary, his list is mainly nominal, and contains several doubtful identities.

W. A. Stearns spent a year and two summers on the north shore of the Gulf of St. Lawrence, about 1880. He penetrated Newfoundland Labrador only as far east as Red Bay, during a short trip by dog-team. His writings were evidently intended for the layman, and hence are of little value from a strictly scientific viewpoint.

In 1877 Ludwig Kumlien sailed north to Baffin Island from Newfoundland. Although he did not land in Labrador, he made a few notes on the birds he observed as he skirted the coast.

Lucien M. Turner worked in Labrador from June 15, 1882, to October 3, 1884. He spent most of his time at Fort Chimo in Ungava, but collected at Hamilton Inlet and Davis Inlet and sailed along the entire eastern coast. His full manuscript notes have never been published, but are on file at the National Museum in Washington. He wrote a short list of the birds of the region, which was first published in 1885. This same list, slightly altered by Dr. J. A. Allen, was republished by A. S. Packard in 1891.

A. S. Packard, who spent the summer of 1864 exploring the coast from Henley Harbor to Hopedale, wrote but little about the birds. His interests were mainly the geology and the marine invertebrates of the region, to which he devoted most of his time.

Dr. Robert Bell, on the Canadian Geological Survey Expedition, sailed past the coast of Labrador from Belle Isle to Cape Chidley during the summer of 1884, and published a short list of the birds he observed.

Then, in the summer of 1891 an expedition from Bowdoin College explored the coast from Red Bay to Hopedale between July 13 and September 7. Two of the members pushed up the Hamilton River to Grand Falls. The ninety-five specimens of birds, representing thirty-two species, which they brought back were studied, and the results published, by Arthur H. Norton in 1901.

J. D. Sornborger spent much time in Labrador from 1892 to 1897, collecting birds and mammals. He died in 1929 without having published anything on his ornithological work, which is a great misfortune. All evidences show that he amassed a collection of birds on the coast, and he probably garnered much valuable information which is now irretrievably lost to science. A few skins he procured from the Moravian missionaries are to be found in the Museum of Comparative Zoölogy, but these are only a small fraction of what he probably collected. Mr. Perrett gave him most of his collection of skins, eggs, and nests, but nothing of them was found among Sornborger's effects after his death.

In 1899 and 1900 Ernest Doane, a fox farmer living at Loup Bay on the Straits of Belle Isle, collected birds and mammals for Outram Bangs, most of which are now in the collection of the Museum of Comparative Zoölogy. Some of these specimens have been commented on in literature by Bangs and others. (Among the birds is the type of the Labrador Savannah Sparrow, described by Howe in 1901.) Doane spelled the locality on his specimen labels 'Lance au Loup,' which is evidently a corruption of 'L'Anse au Loup,' the old French name which is still used locally for the place on occasion. He is still living at Loup Bay, and, I understand, has recently begun collecting birds again.

A. P. Low, of the Canadian Geological Survey, explored the interior of the Labrador peninsula between 1892 and 1895. He gives, in his report of 1896, the only published records from the interior, most of them made on the upper Hamilton River. He did not publish a list of his specimens, nor are his manuscript notes complete. Many of the latter, however, found their way into Macoun's 'Catalogue of Canadian Birds,' published between 1900 and 1904.

Dr. Henry B. Bigelow accompanied the Brown-Harvard Expedition to Labrador in the summer of 1900. The expedition was held up by pack ice in the region of the Straits of Belle Isle for a short time, and then went on to Port Manvers. Here Dr. Bigelow remained from August 13 to September 11, while the rest of the party pushed north to Nachvak. He published the results of his findings in the 'Auk' for 1902, and in slightly amended form later the same year in the Proceedings of the Philadelphia Academy of Natural Science.

The Reverend C. W. G. Eifrig wrote in 1905 a report on the 'Ornithological Results of the Canadian 'Neptune' Expedition to Hudson Bay and northward, 1903-1904,' based on specimens and notes furnished by A. P. Low and A. Halkelt, who accompanied the expedition. Most of the data pertain to the Ungava region and Southampton Island, but there are a few records for Port Burwell.

In 1906 Dr. Charles W. Townsend and Dr. Glover M. Allen made a trip along the coast of Labrador on the Newfoundland Government mail boats. They skirted the southern coast in the 'Home' from Blanc Sablon eastward to Battle Harbor, and spent four days early in July in the neighborhood of St. Lewis Inlet. On July 15 they took the 'Virginia Lake' to Nain; they returned to Battle Harbor on July 26. They stopped at about forty-five ports of call, and were able to spend a week at Rigolet and Cartwright, where they collected a few specimens. They kept complete notes on all the birds observed. In their 'Birds of Labrador,' published in 1907, besides recounting their own experiences on the coast, they reviewed the literature for the whole Labrador peninsula, described its topography and faunal areas, and commented aptly on the egg destruction and other pertinent local ornithological problems. This report has been the standard work on Labrador birds to date.

Another excellent ornithologist visited Labrador in 1906, but confined his activities to the extreme northern section of the coast. Bernhard Hantzsch came over from England in the old Moravian Mission ship 'Harmony' (the smallest steam vessel ever to cross the Atlantic Ocean) and landed at Port Burwell on August 4. He explored the mountainous Chidley region until the middle of September and then, in the company of several Eskimos, ventured southward to Nain and Hopedale. Early in October he accompanied the 'Harmony' back to Europe. His report, published in German in 1908 (translated by R. M. Anderson and published serially in English in the 'Canadian Field Naturalist' in 1928 and 1929), is the most complete that ever has been written on the bird life of the northern third of the coast. In addition to his own most thorough and painstaking observations Hantzsch included many notes by the Reverend Walter W. Perrett.

Dr. Townsend published a few short records regarding the birds of Newfoundland Labrador between 1909 and 1929, some of them furnished him by Dr. (now Sir Wilfred) Grenfell. Although he made several trips along the north shore of the Gulf of St. Lawrence, he did not visit Newfoundland Labrador again until 1928, when he spent a few days at Battle Harbor.

Clarence W. Birdseye lived at Battle Harbor and at Cartwright from 1912 to 1915. He made notes on the arrival and departure of many of the common species, which were edited and published by Professor W. W. Cooke in 1916.

In 1921 Mr. A. C. Bent accompanied Donald B. MacMillan in a small launch along the coast from Battle Harbor to Cape Mugford. He has included many of his copious notes on the birds he observed in his 'Life Histories of North American Birds,' but most of them have hitherto been unpublished. He has most generously turned his field notes over to me, with permission to incorporate them here.

There have been no other publications of importance on the bird life of Newfoundland Labrador. However, in addition to the published records referred to above and in the bibliography, I have had, besides my own experiences, several other sources of information. The most important of these are the observations of the Reverend Walter W. Perrett, who has been a missionary on the coast since 1894. Though primarily engrossed with his altruistic duties among the Eskimos, he found time, especially during his earlier years on the coast, to keep a few records of the birds he encountered. He collected many nests and eggs and made a few bird-skins, most of which he gave to Sornborger and which now are lost. However, he preserved his rather sketchy notes, and while Hantzsch and Bent have printed a few of them, the bulk of them, especially the arrival and departure dates, have never been published. He gave me his old field book in 1928 (it is a possession which I prize most highly) and asked me to use whatever I wanted of the information it contained. Many of the nests and eggs he collected furnish the only breeding records for the region. For the past twenty years Mr. Perrett has been working on an Eskimo-English dictionary, a task which has consumed almost all his leisure time. He furnished the Eskimo names included herein for the birds of the region (some of which were published by Hantzsch) together with the English translation.

In 1925 Walter Koeltz accompanied Donald B. MacMillan on his trip to Greenland and Baffin Island. He collected along the Labrador coast, but has never published the results of his work there, and many of his specimens are now scattered among various museums throughout the country.

During the summers of 1926, 1927, and 1928 MacMillan carried with him a staff of scientists from the Field Museum. A few birds were collected, a list of which the Field Museum has kindly forwarded to me. In 1927 he established a permanent station in Anaktalak Bay near Nain, and he wintered there. Inasmuch as there was not an ornithologist in the party, there was no systematic work done on the avifauna. However, the ethnologist of the expedition, Dr. W. D. Strong, made several trips into the interior to study the Nascopie Indians, and made a few observations on the birds. He carried with him the pocket edition of 'Reed's Bird Guide,' which he showed to the Indians in order to learn their names for the birds, a list of which, together with his own observations on birds, is included here through his courtesy.

I have a few random notes given me by various inhabitants along the coast. Two of the Moravian missionaries, Dr. Hettasch at Nain and Mr. Lenz at Makkovik, have contributed items of importance. Mr. John Keats, the factor of the Hudson's Bay Company Post at Davis Inlet, has written to me several times of unusual birds he has taken, and has also furnished several arrival and departure dates. He talks the Indian language fluently, and besides giving me another list of Nascopie names for some of the common species, he obtained for me some of the Indians' observations on the birds of the interior.

In 1927 Dr. E. P. Wheeler, 2d, accompanied us north to Nain, where he launched his canoe, and traveled inland up the Fraser River alone, on geological exploration bent. He spent the winter of 1927-1928 at Nain, and made a few trips into the interior by dog-team with the Eskimos. He started northward from Nain as soon as the ice broke up in 1928 and explored the Kiglapait Mountains, and returned to the United States late in the autumn. He went back again to the coast in 1930, stayed another winter and summer exploring the region between Nain and Okkak, and returned in the autumn of 1931. He kept a record of the birds he saw, and he very generously sent me a transcription of the bird notes from his diary for inclusion here.

In company with my father, Dr. Oliver L. Austin, who has aided and abetted me in all my work on the Labrador birds, and without whose assistance and encouragement this work could never have been completed, I have made three trips to Labrador. In 1926, with two Newfoundland fishermen as pilots, in a little thirty-two-foot motor launch, we sailed northward, July 12, from Battle Harbor to make a general reconnaissance of the region, in order to lay plans for future work. We cruised along the coast as far as Nain, investigated many of the bird islands, and went into Sandwich, Turnavik, Nain, and Tikkoatokok Bays. We reached Battle Harbor again September 1, and, encouraged by our experiences, decided to return the next year properly equipped for work.

Accordingly, in 1927, we sailed north from New Rochelle, New York, in the fifty-five-foot auxiliary schooner 'Ariel' with a complement of seven men, and reached Battle Harbor July 10. We had planned to explore the Button Islands off Cape Chidley, and hoped, if fortune permitted, to get to Baffin Island. But the fates were against us, and we were delayed all along the coast. Motor trouble held us up for ten days at Indian Harbor, and fog kept us bound in Saglek Bay and Nachvak Bay for an additional valuable two weeks. When we finally reached Cape Chidley on August 20 the season was already well advanced. We attempted to land on the Button Islands, but were unable to approach them because of threatening weather. We put into an uncharted harbor just north of Cape Chidley, to take shelter, but on August 21 the schooner was driven ashore by the furious tail of a West Indian hurricane. This so damaged the vessel that it was deemed unwise to proceed farther north or to waste more time trying to land on the Buttons, and we reluctantly turned southward with a badly cracked foremast and several smashed planks. We encountered high easterly gales most of the way south, but finally managed to limp into Battle Harbor on September 21. There it was decided that the 'Ariel' was not sound enough for the voyage back to the United States. We ran her up into the head of St. Lewis Bay, left a native in charge of her, and allowed her to freeze in for the winter.

Yet in 1927, despite adverse weather conditions and the series of mishaps, we managed to accomplish considerable ornithological work during the summer. On our way north we stopped for a day at the Bird Islands and the Gannet Islands, where the nesting of the colonial alcids was just beginning. A full day was used at the Red Islands in Turnavik Bay for banding five hundred juvenal Arctic Terns. We were able to spend some time collecting in the wooded areas at Nain and in Tikkoatokok Bay. The most important part of the summer was the three weeks spent on the arctic northern third of the coast. The tree growth stops at the Kiglapaits, and our fog-bound days at Saglek and Nachvak Fiords afforded us an opportunity for investigating the fauna of this barren, arctic country, with its bare rocky mountains where the Gyrfalcons breed, its hanging valleys, and snow-filled cirques. In the treeless valleys we trudged over a soft carpet of grassy, mossy tundra ablaze with the yellows and reds of arctic poppies, and hunted Lapland Longspurs and Snow Buntings amid the lichen-covered rocks of the talus slopes at the bases of the cliffs. North of Nachvak we visited and collected at Bay of Seven Islands, Ryan's Bay, Joksut, and Port Burwell. On our way south we were able to do some work in the Nain region, but landing on the outside islands was impossible.

In 1928 we caught the first mail boat north, took the 'Ariel' out of her winter quarters, and ran her under canvas to St. John's, Newfoundland, where she was dry-docked and repaired. We sailed north again July 5, and reached Battle Harbor six days later, to begin our most successful summer's work. There we stayed only overnight, just long enough to take aboard water and fuel. The next day a head wind forced us to find shelter in Petty Harbor, twelve miles farther on. Here, only three miles inland, a marked difference from the barren pseudo-arctic coastal tundra could be noted. In the bottom lands are heavy, thick stands of spruce, larch, and fir, fifteen to twenty feet tall, tenanted by Lincoln's Sparrows, Blackpoll Warblers, and Ruby-crowned Kinglets. The Canadian faunal element was represented by several families of Juncos and a single White-throated Sparrow.

On July thirteenth we advanced through Squasho Run, a series of sheltered, rocky 'tickles' bordered by wooded islands, out past Cape St. Michael, where the Eiders were still winging northward, to Caplin Bay, and anchored for the night. The following day we proceeded on to Gready, stopping for a few hours on the Bird Islands to inspect the alcid colony. On July fifteenth we sailed in to the head of Sandwich Bay, and three miles up Paradise River. Here, far in from the ocean, the heavy forest is that of the upper Canadian zone. The firs and spruces run to sixty feet in height, and on the richer, wetter soils there is not a little paper birch and balsam poplar. The trees grow more closely together than in the Hudsonian forests, and there is a thick underbrush of deciduous shrubs present, which is frequently impenetrable, and which furnishes splendid cover for avian species more southern in type, such as the Olive-backed Thrush, the Northern Water-Thrush and Wilson's Warbler. I found Yellow Warblers playing about in the alder and willow scrub bordering the streams, as I had observed them on the nearby Eagle River in 1926, and over the broad stretches of fresh water a Kingfisher rattled, a few Tree Swallows darted after insects, and a pair of Ospreys hunted fish for their young. In back-water swamp along the river we collected toads (*Bufo americanus*) and frogs (*Rana pipiens*) (Mr. Hettasch told me he found frogs as far north as Webb's Bay!).

We stopped at the Hudson's Bay Post at Cartwright on our way out of Sandwich Bay, July sixteenth, and were surprised to find a decided concentration of birds near the human dwellings, lured there, no doubt, by the richer insect fare which must accompany the more varied vegetation in the man-made clearings. In less than an hour two Fox Sparrows, two Lincoln's Sparrows, two Savannah Sparrows, two White-crowned Sparrows, and a Robin were collected. In the scrubby evergreen growth there Yellow and Blackpoll Warblers were common.

On the next day we went across Hamilton Inlet to Indian Harbor, where the year before a broken oil-pump had caused us so much delay. We remained there overnight, and journeyed on to Holton Harbor, about fifteen miles northward, the following morning. Holton Harbor is on the very edge of the pseudo-arctic coastal belt; in its bordering stretches of open moor, with its mats of bear-berry and bake-apple and clumps of Labrador tea, are many low, thick patches of stunted spruce, dwarfed to a height of three feet by the prevailing high, cold, salty winds. Tree, Savannah, and White-crowned Sparrows nest abundantly in these spruce copses, as do Redpolls, while on the open, rolling tundra, besides the usual Horned Larks and Pipits, we found about fifty pairs of Semipalmated Plovers, and ten of Phalaropes, showing the excited behavior characteristic of breeding birds.

Two days later we rounded Cape Harrison and anchored at nightfall in a convenient harbor behind Manak Island. Here the small open forests of fir, spruce, and larch are truly Hudsonian in character. The trees are seldom over twenty-five feet high, they are well spaced, and deciduous underbrush is almost entirely lacking. Occasionally in wind-swept places impenetrable thickets of dwarfed evergreens are encountered, but for the most part one can walk through the forests on the soft sphagnum and caribou moss as on a well-kept lawn.

On the twenty-second we advanced past Makkovik and Ailik to one of our main objectives, the Red Islands in Turnavik Bay. Two days were spent there, photographing and banding in the Arctic Tern colony, and investigating the Eiders, Gulls, and Phalaropes that also nest on these islands.

In Turnavik Harbor we were informed that the best Tern rookery in the vicinity was 'Paytrick Island,' a sizable one lying twelve miles out to sea (it is charted as Nanuktok). Visiting it, we found Eider Ducks and Black Guillemots abundant, but only three nesting pairs of Terns.

On July twenty-fourth we arrived at Hopedale, to find Blackpoll and Myrtle Warblers, Labrador Jays, and Pine Grosbeaks in the Hudsonian forest growing in the valley behind the mission, and to renew our esteemed friendship with Rev. Walter W. Perrett. Leaving Hopedale the next day, we were weather-bound for two days at Windy Tickle, where the sparse evergreen country teemed with Redpolls of the year on the wing.

We reached Davis Inlet on the twenty-eighth, after passing Entry Island, a splendid little Gull and Guillemot rookery situated at the southern portal of Davis Inlet. Although I have sailed by it six times, often not farther away than two hundred yards, the exigencies of travel never afforded time for landing. This day, for instance, a bank of threatening fog rolling in, with darkness only an hour distant, warned us to make harbor at Davis Inlet as quickly as possible. The evening was spent recording the competent ornithological observations which had been made for us by John Keats.

In spite of continued bad weather, we went on the next day through the maze of islands to the northward. It having become too rough for navigation even in these sheltered waters, we took refuge in a poor harbor behind barren Achpitok Island, where the fog shut us in for two more days while the easterly gale blew itself out.

We reached Nain on July thirty-first and, accompanied by Dr. Hettasch, sailed the following morning into Anaktalak Bay, to spend a day with Commander MacMillan at his permanent station. The larch and spruce forests in the lowlands between the bare rocky hills almost swarmed with Chickadees, largely in family groups. On our way back to Nain the next day we stopped to band young birds at a nearby Gull cliff. At Pitsiulak Island, a Black Guillemot rookery, as its Eskimo name implies, we found the eggs just commencing to hatch.

On the third of August we entered Nain Bay, and, as every ornithologist who ever goes there must do, stopped at Perkalujak (or Iceberg) Island, a little castle of rock at the entrance of the bay. Having made it a point to visit it each year, we were happy to find the same Herring and Glaucous Gulls on its cliffy sides, the same pair of 'Saddlers' on its grassy top, the same Guillemots just hatching their young under the rocks of the talus slopes around its base.

In 1926 at the head of Nain Bay I had observed Rusty Blackbirds for the first time. Here I now found them again, and collected a pair in the swampy border of the Fraser River which flows through a larch-covered stretch of glacial fill to empty into the bay. In this same patch of woods were a mother Spruce Partridge with a brood of young, White-crowned and Tree Sparrows, Juncos, Pine Grosbeaks, Blackpoll and Myrtle Warblers, Gray-cheeked Thrushes, Chickadees, and Robins. In the estuary where the river joins the bay a single adult Red-breasted Merganser herded an enormous flock of downy ducklings, undoubtedly playing foster-mother to several other broods besides her own. August fifth, in our flat-bottomed skiff propelled by an outboard motor, we explored about ten miles up the gorge of the Fraser, through recurrent stretches of dead-water, each dammed back by a transverse fill of glacial gravel and boulders. Bare rock walls rise precipitously on each side of the chasm which stretches indefinitely into the blue, fading distance. Between the stream and the walls of the mountains, on the infertile gravels of the former stream bed, grows a scant, open larch-spruce forest. Many of the dead trees showed signs of Woodpecker work, but not one member of this group was seen. Labrador Jays abounded in small family groups, always assembling in curiosity after a shot had been fired.

The following day we sailed into the next bay north, Tikkoatokok. There are two streams emptying into this bay by a series of rapids in which Harlequin Ducks delight to play. In swampy tracts in the bordering forest were fresh caribou tracks, the water still trickling into them. Tracks on the shore of the bay, below the level of the last high tide, showed where a black bear, alarmed by our approach, had retired hurriedly.

The waning of summer halted further exploration northward, so we turned back and on August eighth headed outward from Nain through the maze of islands to the outside rookeries. Unusually calm weather favored us, and that night we anchored in an uncharted tickle between some small, flat, low rocky islands, bare of vegetation, where Black Guillemots were nesting. The next day we managed to land on and explore Negro, Kidlit, and Nunarsuk Islands. The innumerable icebergs which slowly drifted by were so dazzlingly white that the Kittiwakes perched on their pinnacles looked black.

Nunarsuk, which in Eskimo means 'lovely little island,' so attracted us we spent an extra day there. It is the most interesting and least disturbed alcid rookery we found on the Labrador. Isolated well out to sea, an almost continuous heavy ground-swell secures it immunity from the landing of marauding fishermen. Hidden behind a boulder on the top of one of its cliffs, with a long-handled net, Eskimo fashion, I scooped Puffins for banding out of the enormous flocks which flew by continuously.

On August thirteenth a final inspection was made of the Arctic Tern colony on the Red Islands. The fourteenth was spent with Mr. Lenz at Makkovik, where again the concentration of birds around human dwellings was particularly notable. Here, in a superb stand of Hudsonian forest, I found Water-Thrushes and Tennessee Warblers. The White-winged Crossbills were still in full song, and in the little swamp behind the Moravians' gardens I encountered several pairs of Wilson's Snipe.

It was difficult to leave the sincere hospitality of the altruistic Moravian missionaries, whose keen interest and ornithological knowledge had been invaluable to us. Hurrying homeward, we anchored on the night of August fifteenth in a cove behind Manak Island. The next day a hurricane overtook us. We sought shelter behind one of the Ragged Islands, but lost our anchors and were forced to ground the Ariel on a nearby and comparatively sheltered ledge. The hurricane abated during the night, and we were able to proceed on the seventeenth. We reached Gready August eighteenth, and remained there three days to make a final examination of the rookeries on the Gannet and Bird Islands. Proceeding onward to Battle Harbor, we made our final departure from Labrador on September first.

I shall desire, always, to return to the Labrador, to see again the Kittiwakes flying through the rigging as my vessel rounds northernmost Cape Chidley, to slide down treacherous slopes to Murre ledges, and to glean some of the ornithological secrets that yet remain hidden among its little-explored islands and fiords and in the all but impenetrable interior.

THE ORIGIN AND HISTORY OF THE LABRADOR AVIFAUNA

THE greater part of Labrador was denuded during the Pleistocene epoch by an ice sheet that covered many places where we find birds living today. Hence we know that the bird life of the region has not always existed there as at present. Is it possible, then, from an analysis of the data here to be presented to tell how the more or less artificial groups we term genera, species, and subspecies came into being? An analysis of the present distribution of the forms known to inhabit Labrador may at least indicate where and when they had their origin.

It is a commonly accepted view with many students of distribution that during the periods of maximum glaciation every living thing inhabiting the areas covered by the ice was suddenly driven southward, to be pushed into a fierce competition (rather unsuccessful) with the established local forms of the tropical and subtropical regions.

The atmospheric change from cold to warm and *vice versa* was in reality extremely gradual. There was nothing cataclysmic about it. It took thousands of years for the glaciers to form, and it required additional thousands for them to disappear. It has been estimated, through the varve-clay studies, that the ice needed more than twenty thousand years to retreat from its maximum advance back to northern New England alone (Antevs, 1922). The faunal evacuation and reoccupancy of the devastated areas must have been equally gradual. Many of the northern forms probably were pushed southward, but they could not have remained there except at the expense of those species already occupying the region. That boreal birds were able to live farther south indicates that environmental conditions there were suitable for them, and it follows that the cooler climate was, in a like degree, unsuitable for the warmth-loving species that now inhabit it.

It is difficult to imagine a more active competition for territory than exists among many of our birds today. Habitable areas appear to be occupied to the full limit of their capacity at all times, and Grinnell has shown (1928) that even in apparently sedentary species fully seventy-five or eighty per cent of the annual increase in population is wasted in trying to acquire new lands. When the glaciers advanced, there was undoubtedly a wholesale southward shifting of life zones, and there may have been a slight increase in activity in the peripheral belts where the climatic change was most rapid. But the southern areas could hardly have been more crowded than they are now. The species deposed from their homes by the ice either were able to occupy other areas at the expense of the forms already inhabiting them, or else perished. When the ice retreated, the lands it had covered were repopulated immediately when they became habitable. No more impetus for dispersal was needed than is in force throughout the avian kingdom today.

It has been shown but comparatively recently that, widespread though the glaciers were, they did not by any means cover all the northern lands. The average man, who knows that the ice came south as far as northern New Jersey, assumes that from there it extended northward to the pole. This was not so, even during the maximum height of glaciation. In Alaska and the Arctic Archipelago there were a few local valley glaciers in the mountains, but there was no mammoth continental ice-mass such as now covers the interior of Greenland. The greater parts of Alaska, the Arctic Archipelago, northern Siberia, and even northern Greenland have never been subjected to glaciation. The reason advanced for this phenomenon is that, whereas the temperature may have been low enough, the precipitation was insufficient. Precipitation is quite as important as low yearly temperature as a factor of moment in the forming of glaciers, and certain it is that many of the northern lands ice-free today would even now be covered by glaciers were there snowfall enough.

And even though the average yearly temperature may have been lower, there is no evidence to indicate that these far northern lands were any colder in summer during the Pleistocene than they are now. The seasons ran their courses then as they do today, and even now reproduction and growth, the only absolutely essential stages in the life cycles of all species, are limited in boreal forms to the few short months of summer. It is well within the realm of probability that the present flora and fauna of the arctic tundra persisted in large part through the Pleistocene on these unglaciated lands in the north. That such was the case, is indicated by the high percentage of boreal species that are circumpolar in their distribution. The long non-stop flights made by such birds as the Snow Geese and many of the Limicolae from their breeding grounds in the unglaciated north to their wintering areas south of the maximum advance of the ice, may very well have had their origin in a forced migration over the intervening ice barrier.

In addition to these ice-free lands north of the continental glaciers there were many nunataks, areas untouched by the ice, well within the boundaries of the territory supposedly covered by the ice-sheets. The Gaspé Peninsula, the Magdalen Islands, the long range of western Newfoundland, as well as certain islands in James Bay and in the Great Lakes, were ice-free throughout the Pleistocene. Fernald has shown conclusively (1925) that a flora persisted through the glacial period on these nunataks, and there are no reasons why an accompanying fauna could not have lived there with it. (See systematic discussion under *Perisoreus canadensis*.)

Newfoundland Labrador received one thorough scouring from Pleistocene ice, probably during the early part of the glacial epoch. This ice advance covered the whole district with the exception of the tops of the Torngat Mountains in the northern third of the region and possibly some of the outside islands. The later advances visited the northeast coast mainly as local valley glaciers, and it is probable that several avian species existed in the region contemporaneously with them. Certain it is, however, that a fair percentage of the present Labrador avifauna, including most of the land birds, has entered the area comparatively recently, since the retreat of the last ice-sheet. Whence did they come?

I have listed as known or believed to occur in Newfoundland Labrador one hundred and seventy-seven species and subspecies of birds of one hundred and twenty-two genera. The evidence for the presence in our territory of twenty-eight of these species and subspecies, and of fourteen of the genera, is faulty and unreliable. It cannot be shown to be in error, but it leaves ample room for doubt. Inasmuch as their occurrence in the region cannot be proved beyond question, we must eliminate them from further consideration as integral parts of its avifauna.

HYPOTHETICAL LIST

1. Gavia arctica pacifica
2. Morus bassanus
3. Branta leucopsis
4. Anas americana
5. Spatula clypeata
6. Camptorhynchus labradorius
7. Lophodytes cucullatus
8. Mergus merganser americanus
9. Haliaeëtus albicilla
10. Rallus limicola limicola
11. Pelidna alpina sakhalina
12. Catharacta skua
13. Larus kumlieni
14. Larus philadelphia
15. Plautus impennis
16. Scotiaptex nebulosa nebulsosa
17. Archilochus colubris
18. Dryobates villosus
19. Dryobates pubescens
20. Riparia riparia riparia
21. Sitta canadensis canadensis
22. Regulus regulus satrapa
23. Mniotilta varia
24. Dendroica virens virens
25. Dendroica castanea
26. Acanthis hornemanni exilipes
27. Spinus pinus pinus
28. Loxia curvirostra

Of the remaining one hundred and forty-nine species and subspecies and one hundred and eight genera there are twenty-seven species and twenty genera which are only casual in occurrence. There are specimens on record to prove their presence, but they do not occur regularly, and hence cannot be regarded as integral parts of the avifauna. They neither breed in, migrate through, nor spend the non-breeding season in Labrador. Their normal ranges lie well outside its boundaries, and their visits may be traced either to extraordinary meteorological disturbances, or to exceptionally lengthy post-nuptial wanderings. They are all of very recent origin so far as their entry into the avifauna is concerned, and not one of them has been able to gain a foothold. They are of importance, however, in that they indicate how far and in what direction species may be dispersed, and whence we may expect invasions into our territory from outside. They fall into three groups, according to the direction of their normal ranges and breeding grounds from Labrador, as follows:

Southwest

1. Podilymbus podiceps podiceps
2. Florida caerulea caerulea
3. Anas crecca carolinensis
4. Porzana carolina
5. Fulica americana americana
6. Totanus flavipes
7. Zenaidura macroura carolinensis
8. Chordeiles minor minor
9. Sphyrapicus varius varius
10. Tyrannus tyrannus
11. Hirundo rustica erythrogaster
12. Setophaga ruticilla
13. Dolichonyx oryzivorus
14. Spinus tristis tristis

East

1. Anas penelope
2. Anas crecca crecca
3. Fulica atra atra
4. Vanellus vanellus
5. Capella gallinago gallinago
6. Lymnocryptes minimus

West or Northwest

1. Cygnus columbianus
2. Anser albifrons gambelli
3. Chen hyperborea
4. Chen caerulescens
5. Nyroca marila nearctica
6. Limnodromus griseus griseus
7. Tryngites subruficollis

The relative numbers of these three groups indicate that, as might be expected, casuals occur in a region according to the laws of chance. The percentages are in inverse ratio to the distances they must come and the effectiveness of the natural barriers they must cross. Thus 78 per cent occur normally elsewhere in continental North America, and only 22 per cent are from distant Europe. Four of the six European accidental visitors were blown across the Atlantic by an exceptionally violent easterly gale that happened while they were on migration and forced them out of their usual course, and another occurs fairly regularly elsewhere in North America. Of the North American species two thirds evidently entered Labrador by following up the coast from the

southwest, a comparatively easy route to traverse.   Only one third are forms
that dwell on the other side of the high Laurentian plateau, and possibly some
of these may have voyaged around rather than over it.

There now remain one hundred and twenty-two species and subspecies of
eighty-eight genera that occur more or less regularly in Labrador, either as breeding birds, as migrants, or as non-breeding visitors.   These are the forms which
have established themselves definitely as integral parts of the Labrador fauna,
and it is with their origin that our problem lies.

The fossil record shows us that a few of our present-day genera (Aquila,
Bubo, Grus) were established by Eocene time, and that many more (including
Uria, Larus, Puffinus, Sula, Buteo, Phalacrocorax, Charadrius) were in existence
by the end of the Miocene.   It is considered by most authorities that practically all our genera were established by the advent of the Pliocene.   Many
present-day species are known as fossils from the Pleistocene, and the avifauna
of this epoch was evidently essentially that of today.   Hence we may safely
assume that even if our Labrador species were not in existence by Pliocene time,
they were at least represented then by an ancestor of the same generic line.
And thus, keeping in mind that during the early Pliocene the Holarctic continent
existed in the form of one large land-mass, we may look to the present distribution of the Labrador genera to tell us something of their distribution then.

If we classify the eighty-eight genera according to their occurrence in the
Nearctic and Palearctic regions, we find that sixty, or 68 per cent, of them are
Holarctic in distribution.

1. Gavia	21. Charadrius	41. Sterna
2. Colymbus	22. Pluvialis	42. Bubo
3. Fulmarus	23. Squatarola	43. Nyctea
4. Phalacrocorax	24. Arenaria	44. Surnia
5. Botaurus	25. Capella	45. Asio
6. Branta	26. Phaeopus	46. Cryptoglaux
7. Anas	27. Actitis	47. Picoides
8. Bucephala	28. Tringa	48. Otocoris
9. Clangula	29. Totanus	49. Perisoreus
10. Somateria	30. Calidris	50. Corvus
11. Melanitta	31. Arquatella	51. Penthestes
12. Oidemia	32. Pisobia	52. Turdus
13. Mergus	33. Crocethia	53. Oenanthe
14. Astur	34. Phalaropus	54. Anthus
15. Buteo	35. Lobipes	55. Lanius
16. Aquila	36. Stercorarius	56. Pinicola
17. Haliaeëtus	37. Larus	57. Acanthis
18. Pandion	38. Pagophila	58. Loxia
19. Falco	39. Rissa	59. Calcarius
20. Lagopus	40. Xema	60. Plectrophenax

The relative amount of specific differentiation in each hemisphere indicates that a few of these genera are of Palearctic origin and entered the Nearctic probably (with one exception) previous to Pliocene time. Anthus, Oenanthe, and Lanius show extensive development in the Old World and comparatively little in the New. Oenanthe seems to have come to North America but recently, probably in late Pliocene or even in Quaternary time. Its two subspecies, one of which must have come eastward from Siberia to Alaska, the other westward from Europe to Labrador (*via* Iceland and Greenland), apparently still migrate back through the Palearctic to their wintering grounds, along the route by which their ancestors entered the country. The other two genera, as their strong specific differentiation on this continent indicates, are the remnants of ancient conquests.

The remaining fifty-seven genera show equal speciation in each hemisphere. To hypothesize that they are of Holarctic origin seems logical, and in the absence of an adequate fossil record we cannot attempt to attribute their ancestry to either of the subdivisions. The close of the Pliocene must have seen these genera widely dispersed throughout the Holarctic realm, which was a solid land-mass.

Entirely Nearctic in distribution are twenty, or 23 per cent, of the Labrador genera.

1. Histrionicus	8. Hylocichla	15. Passerculus
2. Canachites	9. Corthylio	16. Junco
3. Bonasa	10. Vermivora	17. Spizella
4. Ereunetes	11. Dendroica	18. Zonotrichia
5. Megaceryle	12. Seiurus	19. Passerella
6. Colaptes	13. Wilsonia	20. Melospiza
7. Iridoprocne	14. Euphagus	

Three of these genera—Canachites, Ereunetes, and Corthylio—are borderline cases, and are so closely related to Eurasian genera that they might also be considered with the circumpolar group as members of the ancient Holarctic avifauna of Miocene or Pliocene time. They have branched from it, but whether they did so very early and have had more time to differentiate, or whether they developed more rapidly than other less plastic groups, we cannot tell.

The rest, however, are southern in their affinities, and may have had their origin in the American tropics or sub-tropics. A few of them, Hylocichla and Histrionicus for example, have extended their ranges into northeastern Siberia, no doubt comparatively recently.

We still have eight genera remaining, nine per cent of the whole, for which we have not accounted. These are all oceanic, more or less pelagic, genera which are difficult to assign to continental masses. Oceanites breeds in the southern hemisphere and spends its winters in the northern oceans during the summer.

Oceanodroma and Puffinus are of cosmopolitan distribution in both the North Atlantic and the North Pacific. Fratercula, Cepphus, Uria, Alca, and Alle are all representatives of an ancient boreal family, the Alcidae, which doubtless had its origin somewhere in the northern Pacific, where it has its greatest development. Some members of the family, such as Alle, Uria, and Cepphus, may have lived in the ancient land-locked polar sea. All of them must have entered the Atlantic from the Pacific *via* the Arctic Ocean, and probably did so either before or early in Tertiary time. Their generic lines are very marked, strong, and clear, and denote great antiquity. Nor is there any reason for us to imagine that the glaciers ever drove them entirely from their present breeding grounds.

The amount of specific divergence between the American and Eurasian forms of the circumpolar genera is variable, for some groups evidently differentiated more rapidly than others. In general the water birds show less variation than the land-inhabiting forms, which may be explained by the fact that theirs is the more stable environment. Since no two species react to the same environmental conditions in precisely the same manner, it is difficult to group them. Nevertheless, certain broad lines are evident.

The sixty circumpolar genera are represented in Labrador by eighty-three species. Of these twenty-five are entirely American in distribution. Some of them, such as *Pisobia minutilla*, *Phaeopus hudsonicus*, and *Perisoreus canadensis*, have Eurasian homologues, together with which they form ancient units, the descendants of common ancestors which were circumpolar in distribution. Others such as *Bucephala islandica*, *Phaeopus borealis*, and *Picoïdes arcticus*, have no Palearctic equivalent of any sort, and their genera are circumpolar through other distantly related species. They are unquestionably descended, however, from the same widely dispersed boreal stock, but for reasons not yet clear either developed in the Nearctic alone, or else were unable to survive in the Palearctic. The origin of all these American species of boreal ancestry goes back at least to the time when the connections between the Holarctic continental masses were broken down at the close of the Pliocene, and probably is much earlier.

AMERICAN SPECIES OF CIRCUMPOLAR GENERA

1. Gavia immer
2. Phalacrocorax auritus
3. Botaurus lentiginosus
4. Branta canadensis
5. Anas rubripes
6. Bucephala islandica
7. Melanitta perspicillata
8. Haliaeëtus leucocephalus
9. Phaeopus hudsonicus
10. Phaeopus borealis
11. Actitis macularia
12. Tringa solitaria
13. Totanus melanoleucus
14. Pisobia melanotos
15. Pisobia fuscicollis
16. Pisobia minutilla
17. Crocethia alba
18. Larus delawarensis
19. Bubo virginianus
20. Picoïdes arcticus
21. Perisoreus canadensis
22. Penthestes hudsonicus
23. Turdus migratorius
24. Lanius borealis
25. Loxia leucoptera

Three species—*Larus leucopterus, Larus marinus,* and *Sterna hirundo*—are limited in their dispersal to the shores of the North Atlantic Ocean and the adjacent Arctic Sea, thus paralleling somewhat the distribution of certain of the Alcids. It is difficult to trace their ancestry beyond the fact that they are of boreal origin, for they are ancient species, and occupy ranges strangely unconformable to those of their nearest relatives.

CIRCUMPOLAR SPECIES

1. Gavia stellata
2. Colymbus griseigena
3. Fulmarus glacialis
4. Phalacrocorax carbo
5. Branta bernicla
6. Anas platyrhynchos
7. Anas acuta
8. Bucephala clangula
9. Clangula hyemalis
10. Somateria mollissima
11. Somateria spectabilis
12. Melanitta fusca
13. Oidemia nigra
14. Mergus serrator
15. Astur gentilis
16. Buteo lagopus
17. Aquila chrysaëtos
18. Pandion haliaëtus
19. Falco rusticolus
20. Falco peregrinus
21. Falco columbarius
22. Lagopus lagopus
23. Lagopus mutus
24. Charadrius hiaticula
25. Pluvialis dominica
26. Squatarola squatarola
27. Arenaria interpres
28. Capella gallinago
29. Calidris canutus
30. Arquatella maritima
31. Phalaropus fulicarius
32. Lobipes lobatus
33. Stercorarius pomarinus
34. Stercorarius parasiticus
35. Stercorarius longicaudus
36. Larus hyperboreus
37. Larus argentatus
38. Pagophila alba
39. Rissa tridactyla
40. Xema sabini
41. Sterna paradisaea
42. Nyctea nyctea
43. Surnia ulula
44. Asio flammeus
45. Cryptoglaux funerea
46. Picoides tridactylus
47. Otocoris alpestris
48. Corvus corax
49. Oenanthe oenanthe
50. Anthus spinoletta
51. Pinicola enucleator
52. Acanthis hornemanni
53. Acanthis linaria
54. Calcarius lapponicus
55. Plectrophenax nivalis

These species (with the exception of *Oenanthe oenanthe*) show no very definite partiality to either the Palearctic or Nearctic regions. Not a few of them exhibit in different portions of the territory they occupy subspecific variations which in some cases may be correlated with the probable shifting of ranges during Pleistocene glaciation. Geographical races are apparently not the result of rapid changes in the germ plasm, but seem to be very slow and gradual reactions to a constant environment over a very long period. Geographical separation is necessary for their consummation, as well as the time element (see *Perisoreus canadensis*). The last time the ranges of the species they represent were continuous, unbroken by any natural barriers, was toward the close of the Pliocene. Hence most of them trace their ancestry back to the early part of the Quaternary.

Nor has it ever been necessary for the barren-ground inhabitants to evacuate much of their present range since the Pliocene. That some of the boreal species were driven southward by the glaciers, especially the forest-dwelling types, there can be no doubt. But the birds that breed in the true arctic tundra, for all that can be shown to the contrary, could have nested where they do now all through the Pleistocene. If we postulate that they all retreated southward before the ice, we assume that all our previously circumpolar species were divided into two groups, a Palearctic and a Nearctic, separated widely for thousands of years by excellent natural barriers, the continental ice caps. If such radical changes in their distributions occurred, why was there not more specific differentiation then ? How could such a large percentage of our Nearctic boreal species remain identical with those of the Palearctic ? It seems far more probable that, while some of them found available territory to the southward below the glaciers or on nunataks within the glaciated areas, the bulk of the circumpolar species remained in the high north in practically their present ranges. I see no difficulty in assuming that the following species have bred on the barren grounds north of the glaciers ever since the close of the Pliocene, and have radiated from there since the retreat of the last ice-sheet, as well as from nunataks or southern centres of persistence, to occupy their present ranges in Labrador and elsewhere.

1. Gavia stellata	16. Falco rusticolus	31. Larus hyperboreus
2. Colymbus griseigena	17. Falco peregrinus	32. Larus argentatus
3. Fulmarus glacialis	18. Lagopus lagopus	33. Pagophila alba
4. Phalacrocorax carbo	19. Lagopus mutus	34. Rissa tridactyla
5. Branta bernicla	20. Charadrius hiaticula	35. Xema sabini
6. Anas platyrhynchos	21. Pluvialis dominica	36. Sterna paradisaea
7. Anas acuta	22. Squatarola squatarola	37. Nyctea nyctea
8. Clangula hyemalis	23. Arenaria interpres	38. Otocoris alpestris
9. Somateria mollissima	24. Calidris canutus	39. Corvus corax
10. Somateria spectabilis	25. Arquatella maritima	40. Oenanthe oenanthe
11. Melanitta fusca	26. Phalaropus fulicarius	41. Anthus spinoletta
12. Oidemia nigra	27. Lobipes lobatus	42. Acanthis hornemanni
13. Mergus serrator	28. Stercorarius pomarinus	43. Acanthis linaria
14. Buteo lagopus	29. Stercorarius parasiticus	44. Calcarius lapponicus
15. Aquila chrysaëtos	30. Stercorarius longicaudus	45. Plectrophenax nivalis

The following of our circumpolar species, although of boreal origin, probably retreated southward before the ice:

1. Bucephala clangula	6. Surnia ulula
2. Astur gentilis	7. Cryptoglaux funerea
3. Pandion haliaëtus	8. Asio flammeus
4. Falco columbarius	9. Picoides tridactylus
5. Capella gallinago	10. Pinicola enucleator

These are all species that are obviously more or less dependent on a forest growth for their nesting, and such an environment was certainly not to have been found north of the glaciers. It is possible that a few of them may have found a place to breed in nunatak areas, as for instance in the vicinity of the Gulf of St. Lawrence.

To return to the twenty genera of wholly American distribution: they are represented by twenty-five species as follows:

1. Histrionicus histrionicus
2. Canachites canadensis
3. Bonasa umbellus
4. Ereunetes pusillus
5. Megaceryle alcyon
6. Colaptes auratus
7. Iridoprocne bicolor
8. Hylocichla guttata
9. Hylocichla ustulata
10. Hylocichla minima
11. Corthylio calendula
12. Vermivora peregrina
13. Dendroica aestiva
14. Dendroica coronata
15. Dendroica striata
16. Seiurus noveboracensis
17. Wilsonia pusilla
18. Euphagus carolinus
19. Passerculus sandwichensis
20. Junco hyemalis
21. Spizella arborea
22. Zonotrichia leucophrys
23. Zonotrichia albicollis
24. Passerella iliaca
25. Melospiza lincolnii

With the possible exception of *Histrionicus histrionicus* and *Ereunetes pusillus* these birds lived south of the glaciers during the Pleistocene. They have invaded the territory they now inhabit in Labrador from the south since the retreat of the ice-sheet.

We may sum up the status, distribution, and origin of the species comprising the avifauna of Newfoundland Labrador as follows:

Of the one hundred and seventy-seven species and subspecies listed there are:

Hypothetical	28	15.8%
Casual	27	15.2%
Established	122	69%

The one hundred and eighteen species of the established avifauna (four species are represented in Labrador by two subspecies each) fall into the following groups:

Distribution	Origin	Number	Per cent
Holarctic	Boreal	55	46.5
Nearctic	Boreal	25	21.2
Nearctic	Southern	25	21.2
Pelagic	Boreal	9	7.6
Pelagic	Southern	3	2.7
Pelagic	Questionable	1	.8
		118	

Thus, though 23.9 per cent of these species trace their ancestry from stock probably inhabiting the American tropics or subtropics, the evidence indicates that 75.3 per cent are descended from the component parts of an avifauna which throughout Tertiary time was spread widely over the ancient polar land-mass

ANNOTATED LIST

Gavia immer immer (Brünnich)

COMMON LOON

Local vernacular: 'Loo.'
Eskimo: 'Tullik.' Hantzsch suggests that this name is possibly derived from the voice, but, according to Perrett, it is more likely a combination of 'took,' meaning 'tusk,' and 'lik,' 'having.'
Indian: 'Moke.'[1] B. G. B. and D. I. B.

The Common Loon breeds all over northern North America, as far west as the Aleutian Islands, north through the Arctic Archipelago, to Greenland, as far east as Iceland and Jan Mayen Land, and south to northern New England, migrating somewhat southward in winter. It is replaced on the southwestern border of its breeding range by *G. i. elasson* Bishop.

The bird is common during the breeding season at the heads of the bays from Cape Chidley to Battle Harbor, and on the larger lakes in the interior; it is to be seen occasionally along the outer coast, especially after the breeding season. A specimen in the Museum of Comparative Zoölogy was taken at Hamilton Inlet by C. H. Goldthwaite, August 5, 1895. Turner (1885, 253) lists specimens from Davis Inlet and Rigolet. Cartwright records the earliest date of arrival as April 14, 1775. Cooke (1916, 163) mentions a bird at Battle Harbor, May 15, 1913. Perrett noted the first arrivals at Makkovik, May 25, 1899, and at Killinek (Port Burwell) during the last week in May, 1906. The species seems to depart some time before the bays freeze over, the latest autumn records being October 2 at Davis Inlet (Bent, 1919, 60) and October 12, 1912, at Ticoralak (Cooke, 1916, 163).

It nests on islands in the calm waters of the inner bays and along the streams and lakes in the interior. Perrett found two eggs in a nest "of mud and moss,

---

[1] Unless otherwise designated, the Indian names have been supplied by Dr. Strong. 'B. G. B.' refers to the Barren Ground Band, and 'D. I. B.' refers to the Davis Inlet Band. When neither is given, as in most instances, the name was obtained from the Davis Inlet Indians alone.

about three feet away from a brook" at the head of Makkovik Bay, June 20, 1899. Coues (1861, 248) saw a pair at Hamilton Inlet with young "apparently but a few days old" on August 1, 1860. I watched two half-grown young swimming with their parents about the big dead-water at the mouth of the Fraser River, August 18, 1926. It is supposed that both sexes incubate, and the period of incubation is estimated at twenty-nine days. The young are highly precocial, but remain in the parents' care at least until the middle or last of September (Bent, 1919, 51).

The Loon eats mostly fish, which it pursues under water, swimming strongly with its wings as well as its legs. During the breeding season in Labrador it feeds usually at the heads of the bays, preferring especially the tidal river mouths where the sea trout gather. It is seldom seen on the outer coast, where food is certainly most abundant, before the young are well able to take care of themselves.

Though its meat is exceedingly tough, rank, and oily, this species is prized as a food bird by both whites and Eskimos. Before they adopted the white man's mode of dress the Eskimos made garments of the skins. Even today the beautiful plumage of the breast and throat is used extensively for ornamental purposes in trimming and decorating such articles as game-bags and tobacco-pouches.

[**Gavia arctica pacifica** (Lawrence). PACIFIC LOON. Indian: 'Wah peéte ah moke.'
Gavia arctica is almost circumpolar in its distribution, being divided into four geographical races as follows: *Gavia arctica arctica* breeding in northern Europe, *Gavia arctica sushkini* in central Siberia, *Gavia arctica viridigularis* on the coasts of northeastern Siberia, and *Gavia arctica pacifica* in northwestern North America, possibly as far east as Ungava, Baffin Island, and northwestern Greenland. There is adequate proof (Soper, 1928, 77) of the occurrence of the last form as an uncommon breeder in the extreme northwest portion of the Labrador peninsula and Baffin Island, but it has never been taken in northeastern Labrador.

This species may be a rare visitor, but there is not a single definite record within our strict boundaries. The Indians questioned by Dr. Strong recognized its picture in a 'Reed's Bird Guide,' gave it a name, and stated that it bred in the inland lakes. If it does so, there is no reason why it should not occasionally drop down to the northeast coast from the height of land, but it is yet to be taken there. H. F. Lewis ('Auk,' 1925, 279) records a specimen of this race from the south coast.]

Gavia stellata (Pontoppidan)

RED-THROATED LOON

Local vernacular: 'Whabby.'
Eskimo: 'Kaksaut'—from the *kak-kak-kak* of the bird's call.
Indian: 'Khâ shi kut'— probably from the call.

This is a widespread, completely circumpolar species, breeding in the summer throughout the northern parts of the northern hemisphere, and moving slightly southward in winter. It is non-plastic, breaks into no geographical races whatsoever, and has no close relatives.

It is a tolerably common summer resident throughout the region, both on the ponds in the interior and in the bays along the coast. Perrett gives as the earliest dates June 1, 1899, at Makkovik, and June 4, 1906, at Killinek. A specimen in the Field Museum was taken by the Rawson-MacMillan Expedition at Jack Lane's Bay, June 22, 1928.

I encountered a flock of ten birds, mixed adults and young, just south of Frenchman's Run, September 7, 1926, which is the latest autumn date recorded. The young birds seemed fully grown, but dived at my approach instead of flying off with the old birds.

It breeds on the fresh-water ponds inland and on the small sloughs in the tundra on islands and the mainland. Eifrig says (1905, 234), "In Labrador it nests on grass tussocks along the ponds or on little islands in them." It builds a rough, flat nest of sticks, grasses, and mud on the ground, often on a slight mound, always in the open and within a few feet of the water. Both sexes are supposed to take part in the incubation, the duration of which is unknown. A set of two eggs in the collection of the Museum of Comparative Zoölogy was taken at Nachvak, June 23, 1905, by George Ford. According to the Reverend Mr. Schmitt (Townsend and Allen, 1907, 302) it breeds at Nain early in July, but it is probable that most of the eggs are laid during the second and third weeks in June.

Both Bigelow (1902, 25) and Bent (1919, 77) record the caplin as the staple of diet. The small inland ponds where the Red-throated Loon breeds contain, in the way of fish life, usually but a few small sticklebacks, which do not exist in sufficient numbers to satisfy the bird's voracious appetite. Hence it frequently visits the salt water, where there is always an abundance of food. It pursues its prey under water, as is well known, swimming both with its heavily webbed feet and with its wings. It is noteworthy that this is the only Loon capable of rising straight up from the water.

The species does not occur in sufficient numbers to be of much economic importance either as food or as a consumer of food and game fishes. Hantzsch says (1928, 89) that the Eskimos like to kill it on account of its size, but "it is skinned before eating the flesh, which does not taste especially good." It is a wary bird and is not often killed by the native hunters.

Colymbus griseigena holböllii (Reinhardt)

HOLBOELL'S GREBE

Indian: 'Wey wee nuk a tey oh.'

Holboell's Grebe breeds from northeastern Siberia easterly across northern North America as far as northern Ungava and Hudson Strait, and south to northern Washington and northwestern New Brunswick; it winters south along both the Atlantic and the Pacific coasts as far as Georgia, southern California, Japan, and China. Allied subspecies replace it in most of the Palearctic Region.

It is a rare transient visitor in Labrador. The Indians told Dr. Strong that they had seen it occasionally at Bay of Seven Islands, but the only definite records rest on a specimen received by Perrett at Makkovik (Hantzsch, 1928, 87) and on a ragged skin a half-breed at Spotted Island showed me in July, 1926, of a bird he had killed early the preceding spring.

Podilymbus podiceps podiceps (Linn.)

PIED-BILLED GREBE

An accidental visitor. The normal northern limit of this species lies far to the south of Labrador, yet Hantzsch (1928, 89) records an individual killed in the Ramah region in the spring of 1901, which, he says, "passed through my hands, and is now in the collection of the Count Arrigoni degli Oddi in Padua."

Puffinus griseus (Gmelin)

SOOTY SHEARWATER

Local vernacular: 'Black Hagdown.'

The Sooty Shearwater is widely distributed over both the Atlantic and the Pacific Oceans, breeding only in the southern hemisphere, on islands near New Zealand and Cape Horn. It goes northward in the Atlantic as far as southern Greenland, where it was recorded off Cape Farewell on June 22 (Bent, 1922, 90).

It is a common summer visitor off the southern part of the coast, becoming rarer to the northward. The Sooty Shearwater is not quite so common as the next species, and, while it is seen occasionally with the large flocks of 'Greaters,' it usually occurs singly or in small bunches of three or four. Coues (1861, 243) saw "a few individuals of this easily recognizable species" in company with the Greater Shearwaters at Henley Harbor, August 19, 1860. Bigelow (1902, 27) found it "common, among the Greater Shearwaters." Townsend and Allen (1907, 320) "saw one in the Straits of Belle Isle and three in an immense flock of over 5000 of the greater species not far from Spear Harbor." Hantzsch (1928, 173) found none in northern Labrador, but records that "Perrett observed the species abundantly at Okkak in the summer of 1900 and secured verifying specimens at that place."

Bigelow says, "The shearwaters were the only sea fowl which proved to be totally inedible."

Puffinus gravis (O'Reilly)

GREATER SHEARWATER

Local vernacular: 'Hag,' 'Hagdown.'
Eskimo: 'Kakkordlungoak'—meaning 'image of the Fulmar.'

Known only from the Atlantic Ocean. Its range covers the area between western Greenland, Heligoland, Tierra del Fuego, and the Cape of Good Hope. Its breeding ground remained for a long time unknown, but one rookery has been found recently on Inaccessible Island of the Tristan da Cunha group in the South Atlantic.

The Greater Shearwaters are common summer visitors off the southern part of the coast; rarer in the northern portions. On calm days they rest in large rafts on the smooth water far from shore, coming close to the land only when driven in by inclement weather. I have seen large flocks in the Straits of Belle Isle each time I have gone through them in June or July. Hantzsch says (1928, 174) "Perrett observed the species abundantly at Okkak in the summer of 1900 and secured verifying specimens at that place," which is the northernmost record for Labrador. Coues (1861, 242) saw many near Henley Harbor, August 19, 1860, "resting on the water in companies." Kumlien (1879, 103) calls the species "abundant from Belle Isle to Resolution Island." Norton (1901, 149) lists a male and two females, taken near the Ragged Islands, August 9, 1891, by the Bowdoin Expedition. Bigelow (1902, 27) found it "common in large flocks off-shore . . . . They were very tame and would hardly take wing . . . ." Birdseye (Cooke, 1916, 163) saw the Greater Shearwater at Hawke Harbor, August 19, 1912.

I saw many small bunches, from two or three up to twenty-five in a flock, scattered over Lewis Bay, July 10, 1927. My earliest date is June 12, 1928, large flocks in the Straits of Belle Isle, and my latest a single bird seen off Cape Porcupine, September 11, 1927.

The Shearwaters, both Greater and Sooty, seem to be plankton feeders almost exclusively. I have never observed them with the Gulls and Jaegers. They are not often used for food because they seldom come within range of a gun except when a fishing-schooner is bowling along at a good clip, and then the mark offered by the swiftly sailing bird is not one to delight a fisherman. Besides, when his schooner 'has the wind' no skipper would stop to pick up a 'measly one or two birdses' for the table.

Fulmarus glacialis glacialis (Linn.)

ATLANTIC FULMAR

Local vernacular: 'Noddy.'
Eskimo: 'Kakkordluk,' meaning 'dirty white.'

This circumpolar species is divided into two races, *F. g. rodgersii*, occupying the North Pacific section of the range, and *F. g. glacialis*, breeding north to Spitzbergen and Franz Josef Land, east to Novaya Zemlya, and west to Melville Island and the western side of Davis Strait, where, in Cumberland Bay, Baffin Island, is located the southernmost rookery known in North America. It winters slightly southward, seldom going below the parallel of 43° north latitude.

A common summer visitor off the coast from Battle Harbor to Cape Chidley, there are many records in literature of the occurrence of the Fulmar on the Labrador, as practically every ornithologist who has voyaged along the outer coast has seen them at one place or another. Coues (1861, 242) says, "On the 19th of August, while at sea off Belle-Isle, many Fulmars were seen, mostly resting on the water in companies of about a dozen." Bell (1885, 54) took a specimen at Port Burwell, September 28, 1884, which was misidentified as *Puffinus tenuirostris* (see Townsend and Allen, 1907, 320). Turner (1885, 253) found them "excessively abundant from Cape Chidley to the Strait of Belle Isle. Thousands were seen in July near the former locality." Bigelow (1902, 27) noted the species as "rather common offshore among the flocks of shearwaters. Almost all were in the light phase." Townsend and Allen (1907, 319) saw eight off Cape Harrison, "of which but two were in the light phase." Hantzsch (1928, 173) observes that at Cape Chidley "from September on, flocks of Fulmars numbering up to hundreds, appeared often." He found "the dark variety was on the whole rarer than the light variety."

My own records, which show the white phase slightly predominant, are as follows: July 10, 1927, two off Cape St. Lewis; July 14, 1927, two off Hamilton Inlet; July 31, 1926, seven off Cape Harrison; August 20, 1927, two hundred and fifty individuals scattered through Gray Strait; September 4, 1927, two off Cape Harrison. The most furious of northeast gales fail to drive these hardy pelagic birds to the shelter of the land, and I have never seen them within five miles of shore.

There are no records for the breeding of this species in Newfoundland Labrador, though Hantzsch (*ibid.*) reports that it is said to nest on the Button Islands. On August 20, 1927, while sailing through Gray Strait, which separates these islands from the Chidley Peninsula, I observed more Fulmars than ever before at one time. The two hundred and fifty individuals I saw there were not gathered in small flocks, as I have always encountered them elsewhere along the coast, but were scattered loosely throughout the passage. Bad weather made it impossible for us to approach the islands closely enough to see whether or not the fabled rookeries are really there, but the large number of birds in the vicinity, their actions, and the precipitous nature of the islands, lend plausibility to the supposition. The known breeding places of the Fulmar elsewhere are on high, steep cliffs such as seem to abound on the Buttons.

Whether the two color phases, the dark and the light, represent immature and adult plumages, or are simply a case of dichromatism, is still a moot question. Whenever I have seen Fulmars, both varieties usually have been in evidence. Pleske (1928, 344) suggests the species does not breed until its second year, basing his argument on the fact that individuals are seen frequently during the breeding season far away from the nearest known rookery. If we assume the nesting starts during the latter part of April, the young can hardly be grown by the middle of August, for the incubation period supposedly lasts six or seven weeks, and several more must elapse after hatching before the young are able to fly away. Hence, the birds seen during July and August several hundred miles from the nearest rookeries must be non-breeding individuals, and as both color phases are usually represented, it suggests that dichromatism is probably the case.

One stomach I examined contained cod livers, evidently offal from the nearby fishing schooners.

This is one of the few large birds that are seldom killed for food. The peculiar musky odor of the Fulmar, which clings to the meat even after the skin and fat are removed, is repugnant to the least particular fisherman or Eskimo.

Oceanodroma leucorhoa leucorhoa (Vieillot)

LEACH'S PETREL

Local vernacular: 'Carey's Chicks' (*partim*).

This Petrel ranges throughout the North Atlantic and the North Pacific, and winters southward across the Equator. It breeds in the Atlantic in Great Britain, the Faroe Islands, and Iceland, and, on the American side, from Casco Bay, Maine, northward to southern Greenland, and in the Pacific from the Aleutian to the Commander and Kurile Islands. An allied race, *O. l. beali*, breeds on the coast of northwestern North America, from southeastern Alaska to Oregon, and another, *kaedingi*, breeds on Guadalupe Island.

Whereas Leach's Petrel is doubtless a common visitor just off the coast, the only actual specimen on record for the district is a skin sent me by Mr. Lenz, the Moravian missionary at Makkovik. This bird was shot near Turnavik during the great 'mild' just before Christmas, 1927. Turner (1885, 253) says, "Atlantic coast of Labrador; observed mostly in spring and fall, then abundant." Bigelow (1902, 27) found it "very common locally south of Hamilton Inlet. North of that they were rare."

Bigelow (*ibid.*) says, "We visited several islets where the turf was riddled with their holes, and the air reeked with their sharp, musky odor." Dr. Grenfell told Townsend and Allen (1907, 321) that Leach's Petrel "breeds at Peter's Island near Henley Harbor." This is probably one of the St. Peter Islands, which, according to the 'Newfoundland Labrador Pilot' (1917, Vol. I, page 286), are "a scattered cluster of low islets, with many rocks above and under water, the outer of which is situated 2¾ miles southward from Tablehead." On the same page of the invaluable 'Pilot Book,' however, is the following: "Peterel islands, so named because these birds breed upon them, are a group of low islets and rocks above and below water, the outer of which is situated 1½ miles southward from Tablehead." It has never been my good fortune to visit these Petrel rookeries, which are in all probability the northernmost ones on the North American coast, and though I have examined most of the important islands where sea birds are known to breed north of Battle Harbor, I have never seen any trace of Petrels there.

Oceanites oceanicus (Kuhl)

WILSON'S PETREL

Local vernacular: 'Carey's Chicks' (*partim*).
Eskimo: 'Kukkiliksoak'— having long claws.

Wilson's Petrel is known in all the oceans of the world except the North Pacific. It breeds in the Antarctic during our winter, and summers north in the Atlantic to Resolution Island.

Turner (1885, 253) says, "Atlantic coast of Labrador; observed mostly in spring and fall, then plentiful." Townsend and Allen, (1906, 321) record the finding of a pair of wings on Battle Island, August 1, 1906. There is no reason why Wilson's Petrel should not be a common summer visitor off the coast, but there are no other records.

[**Morus bassanus** (Linn.). GANNET. Although the Gannet breeds in Newfoundland and along the southern coast of Labrador, there is not a single shred of evidence to show that it has ever occurred north of the Straits of Belle Isle. The Gannet Islands, just off Gready and south of Hamilton Inlet, were, according to Gurney (1913, 312, 313), probably named for some other bird. Neither Cartwright nor Coues records the species at all, and surely one or the other would have mentioned it had the bird once been common there.

The Gannet is a non-plastic species that sticks closely to its ancestral breeding grounds, returning to nest on the same cliffs and islands year after year. Inasmuch as all the Gannet rookeries known today are in unglaciated areas, it is more than probable that they were established in Tertiary time, and have been occupied continuously ever since. The various ice advances in the Pleistocene never interfered with them on the islands and cliffs they inhabit at present, but possibly may have wiped out many other rookeries. The outer coast of Labrador is one of emergence, and the rate of its rise has been extraordinarily rapid. Beaches of late Pleistocene origin now exist three hundred feet above sea-level in places. Hence most of the suitable cliffs in our district are of too recent origin to have been populated as far back as the time when the Gannets were aggressively acquiring new territory.]

Phalacrocorax carbo carbo (Linn.)

European Cormorant

Local vernacular: 'Wapatigun' (*partim*), 'Shag' (*partim*).
Eskimo: 'Okaitok' (*partim*), meaning 'the one without a tongue.'

The European Cormorant formerly bred from western Greenland (God-haven, 69° north) and Baffin Island (Cumberland Sound) south to Newfoundland, the Gulf of St. Lawrence, and the Bay of Fundy, and, in the eastern hemisphere, from Iceland, through the Scandinavian and Russian coasts, east to the Kola Peninsula, and south to England, Ireland, and Wales. A few are still reported to breed in western Greenland and in the Gulf of St. Lawrence. It is replaced by allied races in China, Japan, Australia, New Zealand, Tasmania, Russia, Morocco, and western, southern, and northeastern Africa. The bird that once inhabited Newfoundland Labrador is undoubtedly this form, most closely related to the bird of Greenland, Iceland, and northern Europe.

Although formerly a fairly common breeder in localized areas, especially from Hamilton Inlet south, and a rarer visitor northward, it is now practically extirpated from Newfoundland Labrador. Turner (1885, 251) called it "plentiful and breed-ing along the eastern and southern coasts." Macoun (1900, 65) says it is "plenti-ful and breeding along the whole coast of Labrador." Hantzsch (1928, 174) mentions seeing one east of the Button Islands, July 23, 1906, and another in MacLelan Strait, September 5, 1906, where "a specimen was also shot a short time before." There are no other recent records. The innumerable 'Shag Rocks' to be seen on the chart between Battle Harbor and Hamilton Inlet doubtless gained their names from the colonies of this and the following species, that once inhabited them. Some still breed on the south coast, but the rigorous persecution that has been kept up for many years by the fishermen and the 'liveyeres'[1] has wiped out all the colonies from Newfoundland Labrador. It is one of those cases of sheer wanton killing for the sake of killing, as the birds were not considered fit to eat, even by a people as unparticular in their choice of food as Labradormen. This species, once the 'Common Cormorant,' evidently was extirpated before the Double-crested, and where the two occur together today, this is by far the rarer form. It is evidently the more staid and specialized of the two.

---

[1] The permanent white inhabitants are so called locally because they *live here.*

Phalacrocorax auritus auritus (Lesson)

DOUBLE-CRESTED CORMORANT

Local vernacular: 'Wapatigun' (*partim*), 'Shag' (*partim*).
Eskimo: 'Okaitok' (*partim*), meaning 'the one without a tongue.'

It breeds from central Saskatchewan, southern Keewatin, northeastern Quebec, and Newfoundland, south to northern Utah, South Dakota, southern Minnesota, and Penobscot Bay, Maine. It is replaced by related subspecies in the southeastern United States and on the Pacific Coast.

Formerly it was a common breeding bird in the southern part of Newfoundland Labrador, from Hamilton Inlet to Cape St. Charles and westward; now it is almost extirpated. The Double-crested Cormorant of late years has been by far the commoner of the two species known to have inhabited the region, but it, too, has fallen a prey to the vicious, wanton persecution of so-called 'civilized' man. The numerous barren 'Shag Rocks' on the Admiralty charts offer mute testimony to the past occurrence of the species. Coues (1861, 241) heard of a colony on the south coast "near Sloop Harbor, a short distance south of Little Meccatina," which Townsend and Allen (1907, 324) misinterpret as being the Sloop Harbor just north of Hamilton Inlet. The specimen from Groswater Bay that Coues mentions as presented to him by Captain Dodge is now in the American Museum of Natural History. Turner (1885, 251) calls the species "plentiful and breeding along the eastern and southern coast." Bigelow (1902, 27) saw a few near Belle Isle, and Perrett took a specimen near Kaipokok Bay in 1899.

A native, John Gowdy, who has lived in Hamilton Inlet for many years, but who in 1927 was working at the Hudson's Bay Company post at Davis Inlet, informed me that he knew the 'Shag' well, and described the bird to me so accurately that I consider his records valid. He said he saw them occasionally in Groswater Bay, probably about once every summer, and usually a flock of six or eight individuals. He knew of no place where they might breed today, and had never seen their breeding grounds. That the Eskimos have a name for these two Cormorants testifies in itself to their former range and abundance.

Its effect on the fisheries is nil, as proved by Taverner (1915); and not only is its flesh too rank, tough, oily, and fishy for eating, but its filthy nesting habits and its unappetizing appearance have long eliminated it as a possible food bird, even among unparticular and half-starving peoples. Yet man has driven it from its former haunts, where there is still an abundance of its food all through the summer months and there are plenty of islands adapted to its breeding habits.

Florida caerulea caerulea (Linn.)

LITTLE BLUE HERON

An accidental visitor. The only record is of a specimen obtained by E. Doane at Loup Bay, May 23, 1900, and recorded by Bangs (1900a, 386). The bird, which is now in the Museum of Comparative Zoölogy, is a "young male just emerging from the white plumage."

Botaurus lentiginosus (Montagu)

AMERICAN BITTERN

The Bittern breeds in North America from Florida and southern California north to British Columbia, Manitoba, Ungava (Fort George), and Newfoundland, and winters southward.

It is a rare summer resident in the southern part of Labrador. Coues (1861, 227) saw a wing in the possession of a native at Rigolet. Bigelow (1902, 28) "saw two or three at Cape St. Francis" during September, 1900. The only specimens I have been able to locate are a male and a female in the Museum of Comparative Zoölogy, taken by E. Doane at Loup Bay, May 16 and 30, 1899.

There is as yet no proof that the Bittern breeds in the territory, but it is highly probable that it nests sporadically and locally at the heads of some of the more southern bays. Birdseye (Cooke, 1916, 164) heard rumors of its breeding near Sandwich Bay, which is probably the source of the "northeastern Quebec, Paradise," quoted by Bent (1926, 82) as a part of the breeding range of this species. John Gowdy, an intelligent native, who has never been out of Labrador, described the Bittern to me so accurately I could not doubt the identity, and stated that it bred every summer at Hamilton Inlet.

Cygnus columbianus (Ord)

WHISTLING SWAN

Eskimo: 'Kogjuk.'
Indian: 'Wah pis shúe.'

Although this Swan formerly bred throughout the Nearctic region, across boreal America from Alaska to Baffin Island, nesting as far south as Southampton and Nottingham Islands in Hudson Bay, it is very doubtful that it ever bred on the Labrador peninsula. It is now exceedingly rare, and restricted in its range to the more favored and wilder parts.

In Labrador it is an accidental visitor. Weiz (1866) lists it from Okkak. Perrett records that six individuals were taken at various points along the coast during the autumn of 1918. Two of these were taken in Jem Lane's Bay, two were picked up dead at Lance Ground in Stag Bay, and two more were found frozen in the ice in a lake at the head of Jack Lane's Bay. Mr. Perrett kindly presented me with a pair of wings he had saved from one of the latter pair, which are now in the collection of the Museum of Comparative Zoölogy.

Branta canadensis canadensis (Linn.)

COMMON CANADA GOOSE

Local vernacular: 'Goose.'
Eskimo: 'Nerklek.'
Indian: 'Nis k.'

This species breeds throughout northern North America, from the edge of the Barren Grounds south to the northern United States, and winters southward throughout the United States. It is replaced to the north and west of its breeding range by allied subspecies.

The Canada Goose is a common summer resident in Labrador at the heads of the bays from the tree line south, and a common migrant in spring and fall along the coastal islands. Coues (1861, 238) says, "No Wild Geese were observed until the second week in August, when for several days we saw them fly southward in small flocks, keeping at a great height in the air, and always preserving a wedge-shape form." Low (1896, 324) says, "seen . . . at Grand Falls, Hamilton River, May 4th. From the journals of the Hudson's Bay Company, the average date of the first arrival at . . . Northwest River, is May 10th." Bigelow (1902, 28) calls the species "abundant in spring. Common in fall after August 1." Hantzsch (1928, 207) writes, "It may probably be the smaller subspecies of the Canada Goose [*hutchinsii*] which visits our neighborhood as a not rare spring and fall migrant. I got sight of a flock of four individuals only once, on 26th September, but there was such an exceedingly strong southwest wind that my stalking was unsuccessful." Cooke (1916, 164) says: "The first were noted at Battle Harbor May 1, 1913, and at Sandwich Bay April 30, 1915. These dates agree closely with those given by Cartwright, who records the first as arriving near this same locality on May 4, 1775, April 30, 1776, May 1, 1779, and May 8, 1786." Perrett gives arrival dates as May 12, 1899, at Makkovik; May 7, 1900, at Adlavik; and May 31, 1906, at Killinek. Wheeler found them in Tikkoatokok Bay, May 9, 1928, and again on May 9, 1931. They are almost never to be seen among the outside islands during the breeding season, but show a preference for the rivers and the bays. They start flocking during the last week in August, and from then on through September it is not unusual to see the flocks flying by, seeking berry country. I observed six on the Red Islands, September 3, 1927, and a flock of fifty in Table Bay, September 14, 1927. Hubbard and Wallace, on their ill-fated trip to Michikamau, saw geese flying southward and secured two September 24, 1902. Wheeler noted a large flock still lingering around Bart Island in Nain Bay, October 26, 1927.

The Canada Goose breeds in nearly all the deep bays along the coast south from the tree line at Webb's Bay. Weiz (1866) recorded it as a breeding bird at Okkak. No nests from Labrador have ever been described, but according to native say-so it lays its eggs late in May on islands in the bays and occasionally on the mainland. Pardee Island in Nain Bay, a long, low island covered with extensive bogs and grassy meadows, has long been known to the Nain Eskimos as a favorite goose breeding ground. Dr. Hettasche has told me that there are three or four broods hatched there every spring.

According to Bent (1925, 209) the incubation is performed entirely by the female and lasts twenty-eight to thirty days. The eggs usually are laid late in May. A female Wheeler killed near Nain, May 23, 1931, "contained a full-sized egg with a soft shell." The young are hatched toward the end of June, or at the latest early in July, but it is usually well toward the end of August before they are ready to take to wing. Dillon Wallace encountered a pair of adults with three young near Lake Nipishish, July 27, 1905. The "old ones had just passed through moulting, and their new wing feathers were not long enough to bear them, and the young ones, though nearly full grown, had not yet learned to fly." He and Hubbard found young still unable to fly August 18, 1902, in the Upper Hamilton region. Wheeler found a flock in Webb's Brook about five miles above the bay, August 16, 1928. "Some could not fly, and took to the underbrush on the bank. When I was too close to them while they were in the water they swam with their necks under water, or lay still by the bank in the same position. This hides the black on the neck, and the back looks surprisingly gray. The white on the face and rump is all that gives them away."

I surprised two parent Geese with four young ones, July 21, 1927, on the banks of a little stream not two hundred yards from salt water at the head of Ailik Bay. The young seemed to me to be about two weeks old, for they were still in down, and stood not over a foot high. As I came around a bend in the brook, the two adults immediately set up a dismal honking and fluttered heavily away upstream. The four goslings paddled furiously about fifty feet against the current and then tried to hide along the gravelly stream-bank. They crouched at the edge of the water, with their heads and necks out flat along the surface, and were astonishingly well camouflaged. When I walked them up and tried to catch them, they ran awkwardly, though rapidly, into the thick dwarf spruces that lined the brook, and soon disappeared from view.

The Canada Goose is primarily a vegetarian, and feeds on marine grasses, as Zostera, such algae as the sea-lettuce, and the tender young sprouts of grasses and sedges. In Labrador crowberries, bake-apples, blueberries, and blackberries form the major portion of the diet. A gander I shot out of a flock of fifteen, feeding five miles inland from Windy Tickle, August 24, 1926, was full of the seeds and crushed fruit of these four common berries.

It is highly prized as a food bird on account of its size and its delicious flavor. The Nain and Hopedale Eskimos catch the young in the bays during July, before they can fly, pen them up away from the dogs, and fatten them on grass for Christmas feasting.

Branta bernicla (Linn.)

BRANT

Eskimo: 'Nérklenak'—meaning another kind of goose.
Indian: 'Ah pis tisk.'

In its breeding range this species is practically circumpolar in the high north, and is not known to nest south of the Arctic Circle. It winters southward along both coasts of both oceans, and to some extent inland. There are three sub-species generally recognized, the white-bellied *B. b. bernicla* breeding in northern Europe and Asia from Novaya Zemlya to the Taimyr Peninsula, *B. b. hrota* breeding in Arctic North America from about Coronation Gulf eastward to Greenland and Spitzbergen, and *B. b. nigricans* breeding across northern Siberia from the Taimyr Peninsula eastward to Coronation Gulf. Birds between the 100° and 110° meridians of west longitude are supposedly intermediate between two races. In the absence of specimens I dislike to assign the Labrador transients definitely to any one race, but I assume that *hrota* is the logical subspecies to expect there.

The Brant is an uncommon transient visitor, fairly regular locally. Bigelow (1902, 28) says: "Reported as very rare. One specimen from Dr. Grenfell, Nain, October, 1899." This specimen is not in the Museum of Comparative Zoölogy with the rest of the material collected by Bigelow. Hantzsch (1928, 221) calls it a "not rare migrant, often in considerable flocks. At Killinek, I observed five individuals, apparently old and young, on 16th September [1906], as well as two old individuals with white under parts on 24th September." Cooke (1916, 164) says, "One is reported to have been taken at Ticoralak the fall of 1912 and the record is probably correct." John Keats wrote me from Davis Inlet that he "killed seven Brant Geese July 15, 1926, in Jack Lane's Bay. About two hundred or more were in the company. These birds are quite often seen traveling north in the spring, but are seldom observed going south in the fall." Both the Indians and the Eskimos know the bird well. The former told Dr. Strong they saw Brant on the George River frequently.

[**Branta leucopsis** (Bechstein). BARNACLE GOOSE. Weiz (1866) reports this species from Okkak, and there is little reason to doubt his record, for he was familiar with European birds. Hantzsch (1928, 221) says, "Moeschler offered for sale a specimen from northeastern Labrador in his catalogue of January 3, 1871." According to Bent (1925, 263) there were then eight other American records.]

Anser albifrons gambelli Hartlaub

TULE GOOSE

The specimen Bigelow (1902, 28) mentions as taken by Dr. Hettasche near Hopedale in May, 1900, still remains the only one recorded from the district. I have examined this specimen, which is now in the collection of the Museum of Comparative Zoölogy, and find that its measurements place it well within the limits of the larger race. Hantzsch (1928, 207) suggests that, in spite of the dearth of records, the species might probably occur in northern Labrador rather regularly as a migrant, but this seems unlikely.

Chen hyperborea (Pallas)

LESSER SNOW GOOSE

According to Kennard (1927, 85) the breeding range of this species extends across Arctic America from Baffin Island to Point Barrow, and to northeastern Siberia; and its winter range, while a few may straggle east to the Atlantic, lies generally west of the Mississippi River from Louisiana to Texas, and on the Asiatic coast south to Japan.

In Labrador it is an accidental visitor. Cooke (1916, 164) sums up its status in the district as follows: "Snow Geese are only stragglers on the Labrador coast; indeed a single doubtful record at Okkak [Weiz] is the only one for the whole coast. One was shot at Independent Harbor [at the entrance to Sandwich Bay] about October 1, 1914, where none of the inhabitants could remember seeing a white goose. Its skin is now in the U. S. Biological Survey collection."

Chen caerulescens (Linn.)

BLUE GOOSE

An accidental visitor. There is but a single record. The Eskimos brought to Perrett for identification one they shot at Jack Lane's Bay during the autumn of 1922. Unfortunately the skin was not preserved, nor was the exact date noted.

Anas platyrhynchos conboschas Brehm

GREENLAND MALLARD

The Mallard, *A. p. platyrhynchos*, breeds in the northern parts of the northern hemisphere from Iceland across Eurasia and western and central North America as far as the western side of Hudson Bay. No Mallards are known to breed in the Labrador peninsula nor on the islands of the Arctic Archipelago immediately to the northward. *A. p. conboschas*, which is readily separable from the Eurasian and North American bird, breeds on the south and west coasts of Greenland, where it is supposedly a permanent resident. However, there are indications that it occasionally strays southward, at least as far as Labrador.

It may be considered a rare visitor in the northern portion. The only traceable occurrences of Mallards in Labrador are more definitely referable to this form than to the bird of the rest of North America. Hantzsch examined a male taken at Okkak during the autumn of 1905 which he says (1928, 175) inclines to this race, as also in my opinion does a female in the collection of the Museum of Comparative Zoölogy, taken at Nachvak in October, 1904 (see Townsend, 'Auk,' 1909, 201). The latter lacks the rufous markings on the back, has the heavy speckling on the belly, and possesses a singularly small, thin bill. Hantzsch (*vide supra*) records the fact that Perrett noted a Mallard at Makkovik; Turner (1885, 249) mentions specimens from Davis Inlet; Coues (1861, 238) saw a pair offered for sale by one of the natives, where, he does not say; and Bent (field notes) tells of seeing a native-made skin at Okkak.

Anas rubripes Brewster

BLACK DUCK

Eskimo: 'Mítterluk'—meaning 'the slight, mean, or bad Eider.'
Indian: 'In i ship.'

The Black Duck breeds throughout northeastern North America from the west side of Hudson Bay to Cape Chidley, and south to Virginia and the Great Lake region; it winters southward along the Atlantic coast from Nova Scotia to Florida. There are two races recognized, *A. r. rubripes* Brewster and *A. r. tristis* Brewster, of which the former is the more northern and western breeder. Both races occur as summer residents on the northeast coast of Labrador, but there are as yet too few data to permit more than an approximate fixing of the dividing line between them. Hantzsch (1928, 176) assigns a Black Duck taken at Tuppertalik, near Chidley, to *A. r. rubripes*, which probably occupies the northern third of the coast. Brewster (1902, 187) refers to a bird taken by Sornborger at Okkak, July 8, 1896, as being "intermediate in certain respects" between the two races. The northern race has been taken in the southern two thirds of the district only as a migrant. A typical red-legged specimen in the Museum of Comparative Zoölogy was collected by W. Koeltz at Red Bay, October 3, 1924, obviously a flight bird. A skin I have examined, that was obtained by Townsend and Allen from the Hopedale Eskimos in 1906, is beyond question the southern race, which they (1907, 326) recognize, as is also a female in the Museum of Comparative Zoölogy, collected by Doane at Loup Bay, April 25, 1900.

The species, represented by one or the other of its geographical races, is a common summer resident throughout the territory. It is seldom seen on the outer coast during the breeding season, for at that time it keeps to the rivers and ponds farther inland, where it nests. The earliest spring record is the Loup Bay specimen (*vide supra*) taken April 25, 1900. Low (1896, 323) gives an arrival date on the Hamilton River as May 1. Perrett saw the first ones on May 26, 1899, at Makkovik, while Cooke (1916, 163) records their first appearance at Battle Harbor, May 1, 1913; and at Sandwich Bay, May 2, 1915. Wallace in 'The Lure of the Labrador Wild' gives the late autumn date of October 2, north of Hamilton Inlet. The Red Bay specimen (*vide supra*) on October 3, 1924, is the latest fall record. There seems to be a tendency for the birds to gather in small flocks and to venture farther out into the open bays after the breeding season is over. My own records show only scattered birds wherever I met them during July and August, but in Hawke Bay, on September 6, 1926, I saw a flock of eight, and September 14, 1927, I found a flock of thirty at Table Bay.

The Black Duck lays its eggs late in May or early in June. Cartwright shot a female in Sandwich Bay, containing a hard egg, May 28, 1778. Low (*loc. cit.*) records the eggs as laid May 23 on the Upper Hamilton, but does not describe the nest. The Black Duck is known to vary exceedingly in its choice of a nesting site, sometimes breeding on the ground in the open, as often under cover, and occasionally in trees, but there are no descriptions in literature of a nest from Labrador. The young usually hatch in July. Sornborger found ducklings at Okkak, July 8, 1896; Coues observed nearly half-grown young at Rigolet, August 1, 1860; Bent (field notes) mentions seeing a female with a brood of young near Davis Inlet, July 26, 1912; and I found a mother with five youngsters that were certainly not two weeks old, July 27, 1926, at Alleuk Bight. There is some evidence that the males go off by themselves in small bunches during the breeding season but do not leave the country. I saw a scattered flock of fifteen adults, July 15, 1926, in Sandwich Bay, two old birds flying over the tundra at Holton, July 30, 1926, a flock of twenty in Adletok Bay, August 7, 1926, and three more, August 11, 1926, at Davis Inlet. On August 4, 1927, three adults rose out of a chilly little uncharted harbor among the islands near Okkak as we came to anchor.

According to McAtee the food of this species is made up of 24.09 per cent animal matter and 75.91 per cent vegetable matter, depending greatly on the season of the year and the locality. The animal food consists of over 50 per cent mollusks, with crustaceans and insects next in importance. The bulk of the vegetable food (75 per cent) is made up of pondweeds, eelgrass, and wild celery, the grasses and sedges coming next in importance. Thus the preference shown by this bird for fresh-water habitats, except during the winter, can be readily understood.

This is one of the finest eating of the Labrador waterfowl, but not plentiful enough and too wary to be an important item in the local diet. Because of its wariness and its secretive method of nesting, man has affected it very little in the north.

Anas penelope Linn.

EUROPEAN WIDGEON

The European Widgeon breeds across northern Eurasia, in Iceland, and occasionally in Greenland. It winters in southern Europe, northern Africa, southern Asia, and British Columbia and California. It occurs less frequently, but regularly, in the upper Mississippi Valley and along the Atlantic coast of North America.

The bird may occur regularly in Newfoundland Labrador, but at present it can be regarded only as a casual visitor there. The only record is of a specimen Perrett shot at Seal Cove, just south of Makkovik, in October, 1900.

[Anas americana Gmelin. BALDPATE. Turner (1885, 249) says, "Mr. John Ford assures me that the Widgeon is common in Hamilton Inlet and on the southeast shore of Labrador." This record is of very doubtful value, for, as Townsend and Allen (1907, 326) remark about it, " ' Widgeon ' is a name . . . loosely applied to various species of ducks. "]

Anas acuta tzitzihoa Vieillot

AMERICAN PINTAIL

Eskimo: 'Jvugak.'

The Pintail has been separated into two weak geographical races, *D. a. acuta,* breeding from Iceland across northern Eurasia to eastern Siberia, and *D. a. tzitzihoa,* breeding in western North America from Alaska to California and from Keewatin to Illinois. The American form winters southward through the southern United States and Mexico, and on the Atlantic coast from Delaware south to Porto Rico and Panama. It occurs infrequently but regularly on the north-eastern Atlantic coast in migration. The occurrence in Labrador of the smaller-billed European race is always a possibility, but I have referred the three Labrador specimens I have examined, none of which is marked definitely enough for ac-curate subspecific determination, to the American form, which is more likely to occur there.

It is an uncommon transient visitor in Labrador. A few individuals drop into the bays along the middle part of the coast fairly regularly. Turner (1885, 249) mentions an adult from Davis Inlet; Townsend and Allen (1907, 328) saw two skins at Hopedale that were supposed to have been taken the preceding autumn; Hantzsch (1928, 177) records an immature male, taken in September, 1904, at Hopedale; Townsend (1909, 201) lists an adult male taken at Nachvak, June 1, 1905, and sent to him by Dr. Grenfell. Perrett collected a specimen December 3, 1899, at Makkovik, and has also taken the species in Jack Lane's Bay, where he says it "comes often in the spring." John Gowdy told me he saw them occasionally in Hamilton Inlet and in Jack Lane's Bay, and that he could almost count on seeing a few every year.

I saw a male and two females at Tikkerasuk, September 2, 1927, but, as luck would have it, I had nothing ashore with me at the time but a .410 gun and no. 12 shot, which tells its own story of futility. The three birds alighted in a tundra pool and started feeding. I stalked to within twenty-five yards of them and observed them with my glasses for several minutes before they flew. I can, however, add to the record the skin of a young male sent to me by Mr. Lenz, the Moravian missionary at Makkovik. It was killed near Turnavik during the autumn of 1928, and the Eskimo who brought it in said he shot two such birds out of a flock of Eiders, but kept only that one.

Anas crecca crecca Linn.

EUROPEAN TEAL

The European Teal is almost entirely confined to the Old World and is of only casual or accidental occurrence in North America.

In Labrador it is an accidental visitor, known from two definite records. Coues (1861, 283) obtained a "well characterized specimen" on July 23, 1860, but does not mention the locality. Norton (1901, 149) records the skin of a male in nearly full nuptial plumage, which was purchased of a half-breed near Eskimo Island, Hamilton Inlet, in 1891 by the Bowdoin Expedition.

Anas crecca carolinensis Gmelin

GREEN-WINGED TEAL

The Green-winged Teal breeds in north-central and northwestern North America, migrating southward in winter through the United States.

It is an accidental visitor in Labrador, known from four records. Coues (1861, 238) saw a skin in a collection at Rigolet; Perrett took one at Makkovik in 1900, the skin of which was sent to Sornborger; Hantzsch (1928, 176) took a young male, September 8, 1906, at Opingevik, near Cape Chidley; and Cooke (1916, 163) reports Birdseye's seeing the wing of one that had been shot near Ticoralak.

[**Spatula clypeata** (Linn.). SHOVELLER. The only record for the occurrence of this species in Labrador is a somewhat doubtful one. Townsend and Allen (1907, 327) say regarding the Shoveller, "We are enabled to add this species to the list of Labrador birds on the evidence of Dr. W. T. Grenfell, who stated that he shot two specimens near Cartwright in September, 1901."]

Nyroca marila nearctica (Stejneger)

GREATER SCAUP DUCK

The Greater Scaup breeds in northern North America from the western side of Hudson Bay westward, and winters to the southward along both Atlantic and Pacific coasts. It is replaced in Iceland and Eurasia by two allied subspecies.

Its status as an accidental visitor in Labrador rests on three specimens. Bigelow (1902, 27) records one shot near Nain in October, 1899, and Cooke (1916, 164) lists two young males that were taken at Ticoralak, October 11, 1912. Hantzsch (1928, 201) found Scaups breeding near the Labrador border in northeastern Ungava, but he was unable to collect specimens for specific determination.

Bucephala clangula americana (Bonaparte)

AMERICAN GOLDEN-EYE

Local vernacular: 'Whistle-diver,' 'Pie Duck,' 'Pie Bird,' (*partim*).

Eskimo: 'Kabjitok'—meaning a piece of skin with the hair off, or the fat off the inside of the skin, referring to the 'eye-spot' on the head (*partim*).

Indian: 'Mis o kwisk' (*partim*).

This is a circumpolar species breeding usually just south of the tree line. Two subspecies are recognized, *B. c. clangula* in the Palearctic, and *B. c. americana* which nests from Alaska to Labrador and winters southward to California and the middle Atlantic States.

The American Golden-eye is a not uncommon summer resident from Port Manvers south, common locally at the heads of certain bays. Turner (1886, 250) notes it as an abundant fall migrant on the coast. Low (1896, 323) saw a few flocks on the upper Hamilton River during June. Bigelow (1902, 27) observed a single individual near Port Manvers, August 11, 1900.

On August 17, 1926, I found two large flocks at the head of Nain Bay, one of fourteen, the other of thirty-seven adults, and on revisiting the same locality August 3, 1928, I noted two smaller flocks feeding on the tidal flats among the boulders at the river mouth, one group of three males, and the other of nine males and three females. An adult male with two immature males flew by the 'Ariel,' July 29, 1928, among the islands north of Davis Inlet.

Since the nest is usually built in a hollow tree, the species is rarely found north of the tree line, and during the breeding season in Labrador it is limited to the more heavily wooded valleys. Perrett told me he found Golden-eyes breeding in a tree in Jack Lane's Bay during the summer of 1900, and saw the young leave the nest, but he has no written record of the fact. Two members of the Bowdoin Expedition found a female with young on the Grand River, August 9, 1891 (see Dutcher, 'Auk,' 1894, pp. 11, 175-176, and Norton, 1901, 150).

Bucephala islandica (Gmelin)

BARROW'S GOLDEN-EYE

Local vernacular: 'Whistle-diver' (*partim*).
Eskimo: 'Kabjitok' (*partim*).
Indian: 'Mis o kwisk' (*partim*).

Barrow's Golden-eye breeds in Iceland, southwestern Greenland, northern Labrador, and from south-central Alaska and northwestern Mackenzie to southern Oregon and Colorado. It winters southward along the Atlantic and Pacific coasts as far as Massachusetts and California.

In Labrador it is an uncommon summer resident in the north, probably common locally in migration along the coast. Turner (MS.) obtained specimens from Davis Inlet, and (1886, 250) found it "plentiful along the coast in autumn." Hantzsch (1928, 202) collected "a young male in the first plumage" at Killinek,

August 30, 1906. Anderson told Bent (field notes) that the species migrates past Hopedale in May and October.

The only breeding notes for the district are those of Hantzsch, who says (*ibid.*): "Somewhat north of the mission station Killinek there is a narrow, deep inlet which widens at the end like a lake. This species bred at that place as also at some similar, neighboring places, in considerable numbers up to six or eight years ago." He goes on to say that "at the end of August when the young were about ready to fly and the females were moulting their wing quills" the Eskimos were in the habit of going there and shooting them. Of course this soon depleted the colony, and probably extirpated them locally. He visited the place August 10, 1906, and saw only "six to eight birds, an old female and several young ones, which were moulting so that they were not suited for preparation."

Clangula hyemalis (Linn.)

OLD-SQUAW

Local vernacular: 'Hound,' 'Coc-caw-wee.'
Eskimo: 'Aggek' (pronounced 'A-angik')—from the voice.
Indian: 'Hów ish ish'—from the voice.

This is a non-plastic circumpolar species, breeding in the high north. It winters southward along both coasts of both oceans to approximately the latitude of New England, but some individuals stay as far north as open water is to be found.

It is an uncommon summer resident in Labrador north from Davis Inlet, but a common spring and fall transient visitor all along the coast. Though Old-squaws are occasionally seen in the inland ponds, their usual habitat is the wide waters of the larger bays, and they are especially fond of dabbling in the drift ice off shore. Cartwright gives May 16, 1776, as an arrival date at Sandwich Bay. Cooke (1916, 164) records the first autumn migrant at Pleasure Harbor (near Chateau Bay) on September 16, 1912. Perrett heard the 'Hounds' baying in the drift ice at Makkovik, May 25, 1899, and records their arrival at Killinek, May 23, 1906. He killed one at Ailik, November 14, 1899, which is at present the latest autumn record. Keats wrote me he killed four at Davis Inlet, May 20, 1928. Wheeler noted "Old-squaws calling on the small fresh-water ponds on Kikkertaksoak," June 5, 1928.

The Old-squaw builds its nest on the ground near the edges of small fresh-water ponds in the tundra, often under bushes. The eggs are laid during the middle of June, and the incubation period is said to be about three and a half weeks. Hantzsch (1928, 202) calls it "a well-known, even if in no way abundant, breeding bird on freshwater ponds. At Killinek in August, I only observed some females with their young a few times, drakes not at all. According to the reports of the Eskimos the drakes are said to assemble during the summer on large lakes farther in the interior of the mainland and not to collect with the females and the offspring until considerably later, after the end of the autumn moult." He lists in his collection a breeding pair with their eggs that Perrett collected for him at Ramah, July 1, 1907. Bent (1925, 50) gives three egg dates for Labrador as June 16, 17, and 27. When I reached Davis Inlet in 1926, John Keats told me he had surprised a mother 'Hound' with six downy ducklings in a small pond on a nearby island two weeks previously, on August 1.

Histrionicus histrionicus histrionicus (Linn.)

EASTERN HARLEQUIN DUCK

Local vernacular: 'Lord' (male) and 'Lady' (female).

Eskimo: 'Ingiuliksiut' (male)—meaning 'the one that is fond of strong current.' 'Tuglerunak' (female).

Indian: 'Nut vá ah stuk ah ish' (male), 'Kow ah pá me heh' (female). The latter name was given by the Indians to the picture of the Ruddy Duck, which does not occur in Newfoundland Labrador. To the untutored eye, however, there is a striking resemblance between the Ruddy and Harlequin females in the field. Both birds are of the same general size, both have the same drab coloring, and both cock their tails straight upward on occasion. Inasmuch as both the whites and the Eskimos give separate names to the two sexes of this species, it seems logical that the Indians should do so also.

The Harlequin breeds in Iceland, Greenland, and northern Labrador, and winters southward along the Atlantic coast to New England. A closely allied race occupies the territory from eastern Siberia, Alaska, British Columbia, and Mackenzie southward in the mountains to Colorado and central California.

It is a common summer resident in Labrador from the Hopedale region northward, and a common migrant along the entire coast. Turner says (1885, 250), it is "plentiful on the eastern coast of Labrador." Townsend and Allen (1907, 331) saw "an immature specimen swimming among the cakes of pack ice near Makkovik [July 23, 1906]. As the vessel passed, it dove several times, opening its wings as it went under. In swimming it cocked its tail slightly up." Hantzsch (1928, 203) lists an adult male taken at Okkak during the spring of 1905. An adult male in the Field Museum was taken by the Rawson-MacMillan Expedition at Bowdoin Harbor, Anaktalak Bay, June 4, 1928. Perrett recorded the first arrival at Makkovik on May 9, 1899. Bent (field notes) shot a specimen on a river in Mitchell's Bay, July 18, 1912.

I saw a flock of six males and two females swimming about in the surf at the Gannet Islands, July 14, 1926, and encountered three females, of which I collected two, at the head of Tikkoatokok Bay, August 6, 1928. As I followed up the rapids of the river that enters on the north side of Tikkoatokok, August 7, 1928, I found eight adults and three almost fully grown young sitting on boulders out in the middle of the white water. As I loomed on the horizon, they waddled calmly into the foam and swam upstream against the stiff current, around the bend, to be seen no more.

They breed commonly along the banks of the wild streams in the interior. Bent (1925, 58) gives two Labrador egg dates as June 3 and 10. Wheeler encountered Harlequins in the Kiglapait range, just north of Port Manvers Run, where he records them as "very common on some of the inland ponds, the young hatched out and swimming with their mothers, August 2, 1928." He found many broods about the rapids at the lower end of Angutausugevik, August 15, 1928, and on the next day found a young one feeding all alone "on a very small brook flowing into the second lake of Angutausugevik, about a half mile above the lake. Many falls and bad water below. He could shoot very nearly sheer falls and very rough water, but walked around if he had a chance." On August 27, 1928, he found them abundant in the lower reaches of Webb's Brook in Webb's Bay. On August 2, 1928, a lone duckling but a few days old came swimming boldly into Bowdoin Harbor in Anaktalak Bay. I caught it with a landing-net, photographed it, banded it, and released it.

[Camptorhynchus labradorius (Gmelin). LABRADOR DUCK. Now extinct, and while, according to Dutcher, there are three specimens extant which purport to come from "Labrador," there are none which we may be certain were taken within the boundaries of our territory. Coues (1861, 239) was informed in 1860 that "though it was very rarely seen in the summer, it is not an uncommon bird in Labrador during the fall." Townsend and Allen (1907, 331) mention the several references Cartwright made to killing "pied-ducks" or "pied-birds." The local names for the common waterfowl in use on the Labrador coast today date back to Cartwright's time, and there is nothing to indicate that he was not referring to one of the Golden-eye Ducks, which are the species to which these vernacular names are now applied.]

Somateria mollissima (Linn.)

EIDER DUCK

Local vernacular: 'Shore Duck,' 'Sea Duck,' 'Laying Duck.'
Eskimo: 'Mittek'—Eiders in general. The males may be referred to as 'Amautik,' meaning 'having a hood on the back of the head.' The 'amaut' is the hood on a woman's 'dicky' or 'parka.'
Indian: 'Pe ship,' D. I. B. and B. G. B.

The species breeds circumpolarly in practically all the lands of the high north and as far south along the coasts of the Atlantic and the Pacific as the Aleutian Islands, Kamchatka, eastern Maine, and Scotland; it winters slightly southward along the coasts of both oceans. It has been broken into many geographical races, of which five are accepted by Peters in his 'Check-List of Birds of the World.' Of these races two breed in Labrador and intergrade there. These are *S. m. borealis* (Brehm), the Northern Eider, and *S. m. dresseri* Sharpe, the American Eider. The sharp dividing line between these two races is supposed to be at Hamilton Inlet, all to the north being *borealis* and all to the south being *dresseri*, but, as might be expected, no such hard-and-fast line can be drawn, and it should be recognized that many birds taken north of Hamilton Inlet are not typical *borealis*, and likewise many taken south of there are not typical *dresseri*. These intermediate forms have been found breeding as far north as southern Baffin Island and as far south as the north shore of the Gulf of St. Lawrence.

The Eider is a common summer resident all along the coast, and stays all winter during the mild years when there is open water. Coues (1861, 239) calls it "the most abundant Duck throughout the extent of Labrador . . . Labrador, from the peculiar nature of its coast, seems a country especially adapted to its wants," a statement which is just as true today as when Coues made it seventy years ago. Bigelow (1902, 27) found it still "abundant" when he visited the coast in 1900, but Townsend and Allen (1907, 335) observed that by 1906 "constant persecution of these birds by the liveyers, summer fishermen, and Eskimo dogs has sadly thinned their ranks." Hantzsch (1928, 203) says in regard to its status in the northern part of the coast: "Abundant resident on the sea-coasts and in some places a breeding bird, which nests in colonies; by far the most frequent representative of the Anatidae. It is true that the slow diminution of the species is affirmed by the natives, but the exceedingly sparsely inhabited districts of neighboring Baffin Island . . . will yield for a long time sufficient fresh supply in case there should be too much destruction in our district."

The date of the Eider's arrival in the spring depends somewhat on the season, whether or not there is much open water, but the large flocks from the southward usually reach the coast about the first of May. Cooke (1916, 164) says: "A flock of not less than 400 was seen at Rigolet March 14, 1913. The first northward migrants were noted at Battle Harbor May 1, 1913, and on May 23, they passed by the thousand in companies of a hundred or more." The flight keeps on for over a month, the rafts passing northward until the end of June. I have seen large flocks of mixed males and females, averaging about a hundred to a flock, going northward past Battle Harbor as late as July 12 (1926). Perrett records the first Eiders at Ailik on April 15, 1899, and Wheeler notes from Nain, May 26, 1928, that "they have been passing northward along the edge of the ice by the outer islands just south of Nain in large flocks, and have probably been doing so for a good many days past." Cooke (*ibid.*) writes: "In the fall of 1912 the Eider Duck shooting began near Battle Harbor on September 20, but at that time the birds were scarce and only a few were obtained. Even a month later, October 24, the gunning season had not yet reached its height, and seven men in one day killed only about eighty birds. Later the numbers increased and the birds remained as long as they could find any open water. At West Bay on January 31, 1913, after the simultaneous discharge of six guns, one hundred and forty eiders were picked up and many more were lost." Perrett states that they remained all through the winter of 1905-1906 at Killinek, but his latest date farther south is one killed at Ailik, November 14, 1899. Wheeler writes me that "Eiders wintered during 1930-31 among the outer islands off Nain, but many were caught in the freezing pools, and they died in great numbers."

My field notes are full of sight records all along the coast and contain almost daily references to the species. The prevalent sex one sees during the summer is the male. During the breeding season the drakes band together and fly about aimlessly among the islands in long lines, staying, however, fairly close to the breeding grounds.

Coues (*ibid.*) says, "The Eiders choose for their breeding places the low, rocky, barren islands that stud the Labrador coast, generally giving preference to those which are more or less covered with grass and low scrubby juniper." Their favorite sites are the small offshore islets, but I have found small colonies thriving as far in the bays as Egg Island at the entrance to Sandwich Bay, and Black Island at the head of Turnavik Bay. This choice of an insular breeding site is evidently an attempt to escape the persecutions of such enemies as foxes and weasels.

The immediate nesting site varies considerably. Coues (*ibid.*) continues: "The nests are always placed on the ground; often a tuft of grass is selected, or the nest is hidden beneath the spreading boughs of juniper. The grassy crevices between flat strata, and the soft beds of moss at the foot of over-shadowing rocks are also favorite situations." Nests are very rarely found absolutely in the open. I have found many nests tucked under old stumps and behind large pieces of driftwood, as well as under small junipers and overhanging dwarf spruces. On the outside islands, where such heavy cover is lacking, the bird is partial to the thick clumps of the coarser sedges (*Scirpus caespitosum* being especially favored) that grow in the fault cracks and eroded diabase dikes.

Coues (*ibid.*) goes on: "The nest is of rather bulky construction, formed of moss, lichens, and dried grasses and seaweed, loosely matted together, and the whole fabric sunk as deeply as possible into the ground. The down is seldom, I think, added until the full complement of eggs is made up." The down, which is plucked from the breast of the female, is never pure, but is entangled with bits of twigs, moss, and grass. A large, fluffy bed of it is laid on top of the foundation described by Coues, and the female pulls it over the eggs when she leaves the nest to feed. However, when flushed from the nest by the sudden appearance of a man, she perforce leaves the eggs uncovered.

Between two and seven eggs are laid, the average being five when the rookeries are not disturbed. The incubating is done entirely by the female, and, according to Bent (1925, 99), lasts twenty-eight days. Under normal conditions the eggs may be laid at any time from early June to early July. Cartwright found the first eggs June 4, 1778, but on June 12, 1779, writes: "The ducks had only scraped out their nests," which indicates that there may be somewhat of a seasonal, as well as an individual, variation in the laying date. Lenz found the birds just starting to lay at the Metic Islands, June 16, 1916. Perrett notes the incubation as well advanced July 12, 1899. Wheeler found eggs "fairly well developed," June 22, 1918, on the outer islands at Kikkertaksoak.

The young hatch out during a period which varies from early in July to the middle of August. I found Eider's eggs just hatching on the Red Islands, July 22, 1927, and July 23, 1928, and noted some still being incubated as late as August 9, 1928, at Sandy Island near Ford's Harbor. I observed young of the year on the wing in MacLelan Strait, August 19, 1927, and found them still in down and evidently less than a week old, August 26, 1926, at Tikkerasuk. Many of the late dates are probably second or third layings after persistent nest-robbing by the natives.

The eggs frequently are laid several hundred feet from the water, but the young birds are led from the nest by their mother the moment their down is dry. On Nanuktok, a small islet thirty miles off the mainland at Turnavik, I found several broods just hatched, July 23, 1928, and many nests still being brooded by the parents. I counted seventy-eight nests on the island (and there were probably a few more that I missed), most of which were two hundred yards or more back from the water. Swimming around the island was a compact little raft of about forty downy young which appeared to be but a few days old. Eight females danced worried attendance on them and coaxed them out of the way of our approach.

Hantzsch (1928, 204) recorded four stomachs examined to contain "in four cases small stones, one time splinters of mussel-shell, remains of mussels, little black snails, crustaceans, unidentifiable remains of creatures, and feathers (Rörig)." Wheeler mentions killing two Eiders at Nain, November 1, 1927, each of which had in its crop "a single gastropod shell about three inches long, and nothing much else." The food of the species in general consists mainly of mollusks, crustaceans, and echinoderms, vegetable food taking very little place in the diet.

The Eider is the most important food bird on the coast, both for its flesh, and for its eggs. The flesh of the old birds, which is very rank, tough, and oily, is not considered good food even by the Labrador natives, and generally is not used unless there is nothing else to be had. The young birds, however, up to several months of age, are considered a delicacy. On July 28, 1928, I saw a native with two females and two half-grown young he had just shot. He fondled the young birds tenderly, and dwelt for a moment on their tastiness, and then volunteered the information that this was the best time of the year to kill Eiders, for they lie close and can be easily pursued in a motor-boat, and, as the females refuse to leave the young, they are easy to shoot. The greatest damage is done, however, by robbing the nests of their eggs. In this the whites are the worst offenders. The Eskimos do not go egging often, and when they do, they usually take but one set of eggs from a bird. It makes no difference how far advanced in incubation the eggs are,—it's either egg or bird to them,—and they eat them just the same. But the whites, and especially the Newfoundland fishermen, refuse to eat incubated eggs, and if the eggs in a rookery are advanced in incubation, they will break all they find so that they can come back later and be assured of fresh ones. The birds will lay a second, and even a third clutch, but the later clutches are always fewer in number, usually of only one or two eggs.

The famous down, which brings such a revenue to Iceland, where the industry is well developed and the birds rigidly protected, is not commercialized in Labrador. The natives occasionally gather some for their own use in lining quilts and comforters, but they make no attempt to market it, which, under the circumstances, is perhaps just as well.

Probably the most famous and certainly the largest colonies of breeding Eiders in Labrador are those on the Metik Islands, lying about ten miles off Eclipse Harbor, just south of Cape Chidley. Townsend and Allen (1907, 332) say): "Dr. Grenfell tells us that north of Nain, where the summer or 'green' fishermen rarely penetrate on account of the ice, the Eider, undoubtedly the Greenland Eider, still breeds in great numbers. On the Metik Islands between three and four thousand Eider's eggs were taken off by a man in 1905. He stated that the man could hardly find a place large enough free from eggs, to place his sleeping bag. Dr. Grenfell is anxious to employ a keeper for these islands, and says that the down alone would pay his salary. He fears, and with reason, that the advent of steam trawlers would allow the fishermen to penetrate to these regions and that the birds would be doomed." Neither the steam trawlers nor the keeper for the islands has ever materialized.

Hantzsch (1928, 204) says of these same islands: "The only breeding place of importance in our district is located on several small islands northwest of Aulatsivik on the Labrador coast, where thousands of pairs are said to nest. In former times eggs were brought from there occasionally, but since the trade in down has paid so well several families from Killinek journey annually to the island, and also some from Aulatsivik, in case weather and ice conditions permit. They then disturb the birds, not only by taking away the down, but also by vigorous shooting. The possibility will therefore have to be faced, that the creatures will sometime desert their breeding place. Quiet behaviour on the part of visitors and most practicable avoidance of every shot near the nests, might be impressed upon the natives with all firmness, in order that the advantage of collecting down and obtaining eggs might not be lost. The European settlers should make use of the experience which the Icelanders, for example, have obtained with the eider-birds and have formulated properly in this respect through their shooting regulations."

The Reverend Mr. Lenz, now in charge of the Moravian mission station at Makkovik, gave me the following notes concerning a visit he made to these islands while stationed at Killinek in 1916: "The Eiders breed there in thousands. We went on the islands on the 16th of June, and were a little early, for the birds were just starting to lay. Many nests were still empty, some had two, one three eggs, while most contained one apiece. We collected four hundred eggs in almost no time, slept on the islet that night, and, working over the same ground in the morning, got three hundred more that were laid during the night."

The wholesale robbery and destruction has undoubtedly reduced the numbers of birds greatly. The people are wantonly killing the goose that lays the golden egg with no attempt whatsoever to establish what might be developed easily into a profitable industry. Much has been written on this topic, especially by Dr. Townsend, who gives (1914, 14-21) a very excellent summary of the whole case. The Eider owes its present prevalence, in spite of persecution, to the rapid depopulation of the coast. The only sizable rookeries are in the far north, where few fishermen penetrate to bother them. Without doubt such large rookeries once existed farther south along the coast, and it is not yet too late to bring them back again in their former numbers by judicious legislation and protection.

Somateria spectabilis (Linn.)

KING EIDER

Local vernacular: 'Passing Duck,' 'King Duck,' 'King-bird.'
Eskimo: 'Kingalik'—meaning 'the one with a nose.'

The King Eider breeds circumpolarly in the high north, seldom south of the parallel of 65°. It winters as far north as open water is found, but some individuals migrate southward along both coasts of both oceans, as far as Long Island, N. Y., the British Isles, and the Aleutian Islands. There are a few records for the interior of North America and of Eurasia.

In Labrador it is a common spring and autumn transient, a rare summer resident, and a common winter visitor during the open years. The King Eider stays on the outer coast and almost never comes deep into the bays, which explains why there are comparatively few records for so common a bird. Coues (1861, 241) says, "I saw no individuals of the King Eider . . . during my stay; but was informed that in the fall they are not infrequently met with." Townsend and Allen (1907, 336) say: "The King Eider is generally an earlier arrival in the spring than the American Eider . . . Under date of April 7, 1775, at Charles Harbor, Cartwright records: 'Also one flock of King-ducks, which are the first I have heard of this year.' . . . We saw only two King Eiders on the Labrador coast. The first was an adult male on the shore at the mouth of St. Louis Inlet on July 13th . . . The second bird, apparently in immature plumage, was seen between Fanny's Harbor [at Cape Harrigan] and Nain." Hantzsch (1928, 205) lists an adult female August 20, 1906, and a female young of the year September 20, 1906, both taken near Killinek. I have never seen the bird on the coast, but I found that all the natives knew it well as a migrant and winter visitor.

Turner (1886, 250) calls the King Eider "abundant on the Atlantic coast of Labrador, where it is reported to breed." Macoun (1900, 108) lists a rather doubtful set of three eggs "taken at Nachvak, Labrador, by Mr. S. Forde, in 1897." Hantzsch (*vide supra*) calls it "only a sporadic breeding bird. It is also firmly established . . . that all of the specimens observed in our district by no means breed. Macoun certainly may be right when he assumes that the King Eider breeds on the Atlantic coast (I, p. 107); whether, however, eggs collected really belong to this species, must be proven in every single case. As far as my inquiries correspond to the facts, the King Eiders have no special breeding colonies in northeastern Labrador, but keep in the company of *Somateria mollissima*

... According to the assurance of the Killinek people, one meets this species in the midst of the large eider-duck colony north of Aulatsivik."

Hantzsch (*ibid.*) says, "The flesh and the somewhat darker down are prized just as much as those of the ordinary eider-duck."

Melanitta fusca deglandi (Bonaparte)

WHITE-WINGED SCOTER

Local vernacular: 'Brass-winged Diver.'
Eskimo: 'Pitsiulakpak'—meaning a large guillemot (Cepphus).
Indian: 'Mah muhk.'

This Scoter breeds in northern North America west of Hudson Bay. It does not occur in either Greenland or Iceland, but is represented in Eurasia by closely allied races. It winters southward along both coasts of both oceans.

In Labrador it is a common summer visitor. Large flocks, composed almost entirely of male birds, appear in the spring and spend the summer frequenting the quieter bays, fiords, and 'runs.' As their food is mainly molluscan, they seldom penetrate deeply into the bays, but stay near the outer coast, where there is more of their particular fare. Turner (1886, 250) terms the White-winged Scoter "abundant" in migration along the east coast, as also does Bigelow (1902, 28). Townsend and Allen (1907, 339) "found this the most abundant of the three scoters," and record seeing large flocks, especially near Hopedale. Hantzsch (1928, 205) did not see the bird on the northern third of the coast at all, but Wheeler found it "abundant" near Kikkertaksoak, June 21, 1928.

I have in my field notes a multitude of records of the occurrence of this species, which show it to be second in point of numbers only to the Surf Scoter. My observations of it range from Battle Harbor north to Port Manvers, the earliest being two I saw shot by a native July 9, 1926, at Battle Harbor, and the latest a flock of about two hundred at Davis Inlet, September 1, 1927. White-winged Scoters are especially numerous among the islands between Hamilton Inlet and Port Manvers during the summer months. They evidently do not undergo so severe an eclipse moult as do the Surf Scoters, for though I have observed them constantly throughout the moulting period, I have never seen them unable to fly.

Cooke (1906, 61) says, "This Scoter breeds along the north shore of the Gulf of St. Lawrence and north to Nachvak Bay, Labrador," a statement which is yet to be verified. There has never been any adequate, positive proof brought forth that the species nests anywhere on the Labrador peninsula. Since the nearest known breeding ground is west of Hudson Bay, it is most likely that the large flocks summering on the Labrador coast are the males (post-mating or impotent) accompanied by a few non-breeding females. (See also notes on *Oidemia nigra americana*.)

Melanitta perspicillata (Linn.)

SURF SCOTER

Local vernacular: 'Bottle-nosed Diver.'
Eskimo: 'Sorlotok'—meaning 'it has a cold in the head,' from the swollen nostrils.
Indian: 'Mét suk atáh gin.'

Though the Surf Scoter wanders occasionally to western Europe and is known to summer in eastern Siberia, it is typically a non-plastic Nearctic species. It breeds only in the boreal regions of northern North America, and chiefly from Hudson Bay west to the Mackenzie region. It winters southward along the Pacific coast to Lower California and down the Atlantic to the Carolinas.

It is a common summer visitor in Labrador. Coues says (1861, 239): "The Surf Duck is an abundant bird along the coast of Labrador . . . They are seen in flocks of considerable extent, especially during the renewal of their feathers, at which time they collect in great numbers along the shores of the bays and inlets. On the 3d of August, while sailing up Esquimaux Bay, the shore for nearly a mile was lined with these Ducks, and the succeeding species [*M. f. deglandi*]. They were all in deep moult, and most of them unable to fly." Turner (1886, 251) found it "abundant on the eastern coast of Labrador." Low (1896, 324) says, "Common on Hamilton River during migration, May and June; seen May 26th." Bigelow (1902, 28) writes, "Abundant, in about equal numbers [with the White-winged Scoter]." Townsend and Allen (1907, 338), contrary to most other observers, saw but a few, and classify it as the least abundant of the three Scoters. Though Hantzsch (1928, 206) lists an adult male taken at Okkak during the spring of 1905, he saw none himself in the northern region. Bent (field notes) found it "the most abundant of the three scoters, occurring in large flocks, predominantly males, north as far as Nain," during July and August, 1912. Wheeler found it "abundant about the bay east of Tessiajak," August 8, 1928. John Keats writes me that he killed two "Bottle-nosed Divers" at Davis Inlet, May 22, 1928.

I found this species the commonest of the three Scoters on the coast, though closely approached in numbers by the White-winged; but though I have observed

a good many thousand, I have seen very few females.   My earliest record is July
12 (1927), at the Gannet Islands, where I saw a flock of twelve birds, and my
latest, several flocks of over a hundred each, south of Hopedale, September 2,
1927. Surf Scoters are commonest in the quiet runs among the islands from
Turnavik to Port Manvers, where they spend the entire summer undergoing their
moult.   Indeed, during the latter part of July and the first two weeks in August
they are quite flightless, and escape pursuit by diving.   When they try to fly,
they can only patter along the surface of the water like a Puffin.

While there is no positive evidence of the breeding of any of the Scoters in
Labrador, there are circumstances indicating that this species may nest in the
nearby interior.   Coues (*ibid.*) says, "A good many breed," and Turner (*vide
supra*) says, "It breeds sparingly."   Cooke (1906, 62) asserts that it breeds from
southern Labrador and Newfoundland "north as far as Hudson Strait."   Harrison Lewis, however, assures me he has seen young of the year in the interior of
southern Labrador, which is the nearest definite record.   Dr. W. D. Strong
writes me: "Henderson and I saw two large flocks of Surf Scoters about 25-30
miles up Hunt's River [inland from Jack Lane's Bay] on one of the big ponds.
Apparently they were moulting as they were hard or impossible to raise.   Farther
up (forty miles northwest of Jack Lane's Bay) we saw several pairs of this species
swimming in the lake close to the shore.   They acted as though they might have
had nests in the vicinity, but mosquitoes were in clouds, and we didn't find
them. (This was in late June, 1928)."   Bent (1925, 146) sums up the situation
as follows: "On the northeast coast of Labrador, however, or rather a few miles
inland, they probably still breed regularly and abundantly.   We saw large numbers of males in the inner harbors and in the mouths of rivers at a number of places
all along the coast in July and August, which suggested that probably the females
were incubating sets of eggs or tending broods of young on the inland ponds or
marshes.   We hunted for nests in many suitable places, but never succeeded in
finding one.   Samuel Anderson, an intelligent observer and collector of birds at
Hopedale, told me that surf scoters breed about the inland ponds and lakes, making their nests in the grass or under bushes close to the edge of the water."   The
Labrador set of eggs he mentions, taken on Akpatok Island, is doubtless from the
island in Ungava Bay, and hence outside our territory.

Oidemia nigra americana Swainson.

AMERICAN BLACK SCOTER

Local vernacular: 'Butter-nosed Diver.'
Eskimo: 'Uvingiajok.'
Indian: 'Kwís kwis á patuk.'

The American Black Scoter breeds in northeastern Asia, the Aleutian Islands, and western Alaska, and winters southward along both coasts of the Pacific and on the western coast of the Atlantic from Newfoundland to the Carolinas. It is replaced in Iceland and in the northern Palearctic as far east as the Taimyr Peninsula by *O. n. nigra*. The species is not known to occur in either Greenland or Baffin Island, and its nesting grounds in North America east of Alaska (if there are any) have yet to be discovered.

In Labrador it is an uncommon summer resident, but a common transient visitor. It frequents the 'runs' between the islands and the wide bays, and has its centre of abundance with the two other species in the region between Hopedale and Port Manvers. Turner (1886, 250) states that it is abundant on the east coast in migration. Low (1896, 323) says, "Common on Hamilton River, May and June, in migration; seen May 26th." Bigelow (1902, 28) calls it "common; less so than the other scoters." Townsend and Allen (1907, 338) saw a few between Cape Charles and Hopedale, and found the bird more common than the Surf Scoter, though not nearly so abundant as the White-winged. Hantzsch (1928, 205) did not see a single individual in the northern section of the coast in 1906. Bent (1925, 120) says, "We did not observe this species on the south coast of Labrador, except as a migrant, but on the east coast we found it fairly common . . . as far north as Hopedale."

My own records show the Black Scoter to be the least common of the three species. I have observed it infrequently, usually in small bunches of four or five, from Cape St. Lewis to Hebron. My earliest record is of a flock of sixteen seen off Cape St. Lewis, July 10, 1927, and my latest, of four small flocks, of five, three, eight, and eight individuals, among the islands between Nain and Davis Inlet, September 1, 1927.

This species is not known to breed on the Labrador, and, in my opinion, does not do so. Audubon's breeding record for southern Labrador is extremely doubtful. Turner (1886, 250) was told that it breeds on the eastern coast, which is an equally unreliable record. The breeding of none of the Scoters has yet been proved for the district, and the American Scoters in Labrador are the farthest of the three from their known breeding grounds (which probably accounts for their comparative rarity). Bent (*ibid.*) says, "Flocks made up entirely of males were seen in many of the inner bays and in the mouths of rivers in July and August [1912]; probably their deserted mates were incubating on their eggs or tending broods of young about the inland ponds a few miles back from the coast." He gives the vastness, impassability, and difficulties of the country as the probable reason why definite breeding evidence has not been found there. The Indians told Dr. Strong that "these birds never breed in the interior; many drakes come in the spring, and a few ducks, but they have no eggs there."

The food of all the Scoters is much the same, consisting almost entirely of mollusks, both univalve and bivalve. They rarely eat any vegetable food.

[Lophodytes cucullatus (Linn.). HOODED MERGANSER. This species is not known to breed north of southern Nova Scotia, New Brunswick, and the Gulf of St. Lawrence, nor are there any definite records of its occurrence in the Labrador peninsula. Hantzsch (1928, 175) says, "According to the statements made to me by Missionary Perrett, this is an infrequent migrant and possibly a breeding bird on freshwater lakes." Perrett has never mentioned this species to me, nor does he refer to it at all in his notes. Neither the Eskimos nor the Indians know the bird, and its possible occurrence would be only accidental.]

[Mergus merganser americanus Cassin. AMERICAN MERGANSER. Indian: 'Mís ti suk.'
The American Merganser breeds in the northern United States and Canada, practically across the continent from Alaska south to central California, and from Newfoundland south to Maine; it winters southward, mainly within the United States, including practically all the States.

It is, perhaps, a rare summer resident in the interior of the southern portion of Labrador. There are no records that are not open to serious question. Low (1896, 323) says, "Common throughout interior; seen May 28th; eggs June 25th," and gives essentially the same data for *Mergus serrator*. Macoun (1900, 71) says, "Mr. A. P. Low found it breeding on the shores of small lakes in Labrador; eggs were taken with the bird from under small spruces on the upper part of the Hamilton River, in the summer of 1890." Townsend and Allen (1907, 324) make the following appropriate comment on these records: "As the habit of the American Merganser is to nest in a hole in a tree or cliff it seems reasonable to suppose that *Mergus serrator* was confused with this species." Hantzsch (1928, 175) says: "Missionary Perrett does not know it on the Labrador coast farther north than the region of Maggovik [Makkovik]. The species also breeds apparently more in the interior of the country." Perrett makes no reference to this species in his notes, nor has he ever mentioned it to me. The Indians recognized its picture at once, however, and Anderson told Bent (field notes) that it "breeds up the rivers."]

Mergus serrator Linn.

RED-BREASTED MERGANSER

Local vernacular: 'Shell-bird,' 'Shell Duck.'
Eskimo: 'Pai'—probably from the voice.
Indian: 'Kah tceé nah kah teést.'

This species breeds circumpolarly in the north temperate and subarctic regions, and winters southward along both coasts of both oceans.

It is a common summer resident at the heads of the bays in Labrador, and is common along the coast in migration. Low (1896, 323) says of it, "Abundant throughout the interior; seen May 28th." Norton (1901, 149) lists a male from Lake Melville, July 26, 1891, and a female with three young from Hopedale, August 11, 1891. Bigelow says (1902, 27), "Locally common; very widely distributed." At Mary Harbor in 1906 Townsend and Allen (1907, 324) "observed several of these birds on July 12th and 13th, flying back and forth from the salt-water to the pond-like expansions of the Mary River." Hantzsch (1928, 174) calls it an "infrequent breeding bird and migrant" in the Chidley region. Cooke (1916, 163) gives the arrival date at Cartwright as May 2, 1915. Perrett records the first spring arrivals at Makkovik on May 15, 1899, and at Killinek on June 6, 1906. John Keats writes me that he "killed eight shell birds" near Davis Inlet, June 12, 1925. Wheeler found it common in the tidal estuaries in the Kiglapait region during the summer of 1928, and observed several near Nain, June 14, 1931.

I have never failed to see this species whenever I have gone a few miles up any of the rivers from the heads of the bays, and my records show them from Paradise River, Eagle River, Fraser River, and Adletok River, and on unnamed streams in Hawke Bay and Tikkoatokok Bay. My latest date is of a flock of forty I observed flying by in Table Bay, September 14, 1927.

The Red-breasted Merganser nests commonly at the heads of the bays and along the rivers in the interior. Coues (1861, 241) "found young birds apparently about a week old, on the 1st of August" at Rigolet. Turner (1885, 251) took adults and young at Davis Inlet. Low (*ibid.*) records eggs June 25 on the upper Hamilton River. Perrett describes a nest containing nine slightly incubated eggs he found June 28, 1900, on Ranger Bight Brook, which empties into the head of Makkovik Bay. It was "built in a slight depression in the ground within two feet of the water, on a small rocky island overgrown with willows, in the middle of the rapid brook, and was composed of dried grasses without down." He records another set of five eggs from English River (also near Makkovik), taken June 20, 1900, which were quite fresh. According to Bent (1923, 16), "incubation lasts from 26 to 28 days and is performed entirely by the female; the drakes are rarely seen in the neighborhood during this period." At the mouth of the Fraser River on August 3, 1928, I found a female in charge of eight ducklings that seemed only a few days old, certainly not over a week. On returning the next day to collect some of them, I found her brood had been augmented by at least twenty more, though I saw no other females in the vicinity. The difference in their sizes made it apparent that there were several broods, all being taken care of by the same female. On August 17, 1926, I encountered an adult in charge of thirty-two almost fully grown young, feeding in the tidal estuary where the river joins Nain Bay.

The Red-breasted Merganser eats mainly small fish, but a few crustaceans and water insects are added to the diet.

Astur gentilis atricapillus (Wilson)

EASTERN GOSHAWK

Local vernacular: 'Partridge Hawk.'
Eskimo: 'Kigavik' (*partim*)—a general name for all hawks.

The Goshawk breeds in the boreal and temperate portions of the Holarctic Region south of the tree line, and winters southward to the edge of the subtropics. It breaks into many races in Eurasia (see Sushkin, 1928), mainly a northern and a southern group, each containing several geographical representatives. It is Sushkin's theory that this species, at least the Palearctic forms of it, had its origin in Europe, and gradually moved eastward through Asia. He did not carry his reasoning a step farther by investigating the Nearctic forms, which are only two in number as accepted today, *A. g. striatulus*, breeding in Alaska and on the Pacific slope, and *A. g. atricapillus*, which nests from the Great Plains area eastward to Labrador and Maryland. The Goshawks are a group showing extreme individual, as well as age, differences in plumage, so that strictly comparable material is difficult to procure.

It is an uncommon summer resident in Labrador, from the tree line south, and a rare summer visitor in the north. Turner (1885, 244) obtained a specimen from Rigolet. Low (1896, 325) says: "Specimen killed . . . on lower Hamilton River. Not common." Hantzsch (1929, 16) records a specimen taken during the spring of 1901 near Ramah, and Perrett took one at Makkovik toward the end of August, 1899.

During my three summers on the coast I saw only two Goshawks, both of these September 16, 1927, at Tub Harbor.   They were both in full adult plumage, and though they did not come within gun-range, their size, manner of flight, and color made them unmistakable.

Perrett has a set of three eggs taken by Samuel Anderson near Hopedale, May 4, 1920, from a nest ten feet up in a spruce tree.   This is the only record for New-foundland Labrador.

The abundance of the Goshawk depends greatly on the presence or absence of its food, which consists in the main of hares, ptarmigan, and mice.   These are all animals which undergo an apparently cyclic fluctuation in numbers.   The years 1926, 1927, and 1928 were 'lean' periods which saw them all at a low ebb. Consequently the predatory birds and mammals dependent on them for susten-ance were forced to look elsewhere for their food, and those, like the Goshawk, that are able to fly long distances in a short time, were consequently scarce.

While they undoubtedly take a heavy toll of ptarmigan and hares during the peaks of the cycle, when such food is abundant, it is questionable that the Gos-hawks are ever numerous enough to inflict noticeable damage.   As a factor of moment, they may be practically eliminated when compared to the effect man and the ravages of disease have on these 'food species.'

Buteo lagopus s.-johannis (Gmelin)

AMERICAN ROUGH-LEGGED HAWK

Local vernacular: 'Squealing Hawk.'
Eskimo: 'Kennuajok'—meaning 'the one that begs, or implores,' from the cry.

The American Rough-leg breeds in the Subarctic, Hudsonian, and northern Canadian zones from the Aleutian Islands, northwest Alaska, and British Co-lumbia, to Ungava, northern Labrador, Newfoundland, and the St. Lawrence valley; it migrates vagrantly southward in winter to southern California, Texas, and the Carolinas.   In the homologous zones of the Palearctic Region it is replaced by related subspecies.

In Labrador it is a common summer resident along the coastal barrens, less common in the extreme north, and seldom penetrating deeply inland.   Norton (1901, 153) lists a female taken by the Bowdoin Expedition at Chateau Bay, July 14, 1891, and another specimen from Red Bay, July 13, 1891.   Bigelow (1902, 29) says: "Very common almost everywhere, nesting on cliffs some distance from the sea.   Different pairs of hawks seemed to hold definite tracts of country, from which they drove all intruders." Townsend and Allen (1907, 366) "saw one of these birds at Long Tickle on July 20th [1906], one at Pack's Harbor on July 24th, one at Great Caribou Island on July 27th, and one near Battle Island on August 1st." Hantzsch (1929, 17) says: "I only twice observed some flying birds [in the Chidley region], on the 6th and 16th of August [1906], without getting a shot at them . . . In general the species does not seem to go beyond the borders of the forest." Perrett records the earliest spring arrivals as May 1, 1899, at Makkovik, May 1, 1900, at Adlavik, and May 12, 1906, at Killinek. The bird probably starts south late in September or early in October. The latest record I have is of a specimen I took at Indian Harbor, September 14, 1927. The species prefers the open tundra country, preferably hilly and cliffy, which affords it a place both to breed and to hunt.

It breeds fairly commonly along the whole coast, building a huge coarse nest of sticks on cliff ledges. Turner (1885, 244) obtained downy young "of the black phase, July 17, 1882, at Davis Inlet." Townsend and Allen (*vide supra*) quote Dr. Storer's record for a nest and young of the Rough-legged Hawk at Red Bay. Perrett describes a nest found June 3, 1899, at Ailik as "a coarse structure of sticks lined with dry grass and a few feathers of the parent bird, set on a small sloping ledge about thirty feet from the ground in an overhanging cliff." Another he found June 29, 1900, in Ailik Bay was "on a small ledge in a cliff, the nest a rather bulky affair of sticks, some two feet long and a half inch in diameter, lined with grass and moss. The site had been used in previous years as could be seen from the sticks of the old nest thrown down from the ledge." The eggs are laid late in May or early in June. Perrett records his earliest set as of two eggs taken at Kaipokok Bay, May 28, 1900. At Ailik he collected a clutch of four eggs, June 2, 1900, and one of five eggs, June 7, 1900, and a set of three in which incubation had commenced, June 8, 1900. A set of four eggs he took June 29, 1900, had their incubation far advanced. The incubation period is about four weeks (Bendire), and it must require another four weeks or more for the young to grow enough to leave the nest and shift for themselves. Bent (field notes) found the young to have left the nest by August 1, when he visited the region in 1912.

This, the commonest hawk of Labrador, hunts its prey in the open tundra, and feeds almost entirely on the small rodents found there. The stomachs of two birds I killed, one at Gready and one at Indian Harbor, contained remains of *Peromyscus m. maniculatus* and *Microtus pennsylvanicus enixus*. It is probable that the lemming, *Dicrostonyx hudsonius*, in the northern portions where it is commoner, forms a large part of the diet. The Rough-legged Hawk has been known to take rabbits and small Ptarmigan.

Aquila chrysaëtos canadensis (Linn.)

GOLDEN EAGLE

Indian: 'Pa pis quá.' The Indians (who know the Bald Eagle well) gave this name to John Keats when he was questioning them concerning their names for the birds of prey. After discussing the Bald Eagle, they volunteered the information that there is another Eagle not uncommon in the interior. "It is a very big one, like the Bald Eagle, but never has a white head, and it preys on the caribou fawns." I assume that this must be the species to which they refer.

The Golden Eagle is a circumpolar species of the Holarctic realm, now split into several races; it is most common in the Canadian and Hudsonian zones, probably straying fairly regularly into the Subarctic, seldom going south of the Sonoran and Alleghanian or their Palearctic equivalents. It is not a common bird in any portion of its range, as each individual must have a wide territory over which to forage.

In Labrador it is a very rare permanent resident in the interior. It has been taken once in Ungava and twice on the southern coast of Labrador, but there are no specimens on record for our immediate territory. Coues (1861, 217) says: "An intelligent hunter, whom I questioned concerning this Eagle, informed me that though he knew it well, it was very rare, and very seldom obtained. His description was so exact, that I had no difficulty in determining that the present species was referred to." Low (1896, 325) claims to have found it breeding at Lake Michikamau, and to have seen it in several different places along the Upper Hamilton River. While the Indians seem to know the bird, the Eskimos do not know it at all, and Perrett has never seen it.

Probably here, as elsewhere, it usually builds its nest in ledges on high, rocky cliffs and crags, of which there are plenty in Labrador.

The Golden Eagle preys mostly on vertebrates, sometimes killing large mammals, as is borne out by the Indians' tales of the killing of young caribou. It prefers, however, rabbits, squirrels, grouse, and the like.

[**Haliaeëtus albicilla** (Linn.). GRAY SEA EAGLE. Weiz (1866) says that this species breeds at Okkak. The statement is, of course, unconfirmed by specimens, and he may have been mistaken in his identity of the bird, confusing it with the Bald Eagle. But on the other hand, the Gray Sea Eagle is known to breed in southern Greenland, and can fly far, so there is no reason why it should not during its peregrinations stray occasionally to Labrador.]

Haliaeëtus leucocephalus alascanus C. H. Townsend

NORTHERN BALD EAGLE

Eskimo: 'Nektoralik.'
Indian: 'Mit soo.'

This species inhabits North America from the tree limit south to northern Mexico. It is divided into two geographical races, a northern and a southern, the former occupying the country north of the United States, the latter within its boundaries.

It is a very rare summer resident in Labrador. Low (1896, 325) says: "A pair seen on Hamilton River below Grand Falls, April 28th. White heads distinctly seen." The Eskimo and Indian names were secured by showing pictures, and both peoples agree that, though it does occur, the bird is very rare. Cartwright has much to say about an 'eagle' on the Labrador (see Townsend and Allen, 1907, 367), and records its nesting several times, saying, "Not a rare summer resident, as I heard of about six pairs that bred at different places along the coast and always in trees." Cartwright nowhere in his journals makes any reference to the Osprey, which is a very common bird in Sandwich Bay, and which he certainly must have seen. It would seem strange that he should have overlooked it, and when one considers that he makes no reference to the very noticeable white head of the Bald Eagle, it seems more likely that he referred to the Osprey, which is an 'eagle' to the Sandwich Bay natives today.

It nests usually in tops of tall trees, rarely on cliffs.

The Bald Eagle is known to eat small mammals, but it prefers to search along the beaches for dead fish. It is well known, too, to rob the Osprey, chasing this expert fisherman until it drops its catch.

Pandion haliaëtus carolinensis (Gmelin)

OSPREY

Local vernacular: 'Eagle,' 'Fish Hawk.'
Eskimo: 'Aglakolik'—the one having marks like letters or figures.
Indian: 'Kwásh e me heé yue.'

Pandion haliaëtus is of wide distribution and breeds in both hemispheres from the tree line south to the Gulf of Mexico, northern Africa, the Sunda Islands,

Australia, and New Caledonia. There are two northern races with extensive ranges, *P. h. haliaëtus*, breeding across Eurasia, and *P. h. carolinensis*, which spreads across North America, nesting from northwestern Alaska, northwestern Mackenzie, southern Ungava, and Labrador, south to Lower California, western Mexico, and the Gulf coast of the United States, and wintering from the southern United States to South America. Three other races are recognized along the southern border of the breeding range of the species.

The Osprey is an uncommon summer resident, living along the larger rivers at the heads of the bays. In his diary for April 19, 1776, Cartwright records seeing a pair of 'eagles'[1] in Sandwich Bay. Townsend and Allen (1907, 371) "saw two hawks of this species, one on July 12th near St. Lewis Sound, the other on July 18th at Rigolet." They also record that "Dr. Grenfell noted a Fish-hawk at Nachvak in the spring of 1900." Cooke (1916, 165) says, "A pair was seen at Sandwich Bay May 28, 1915, and again the next day." Perrett shot one at Kaipokok Bay, May 5, 1900. I saw one flying over the rapids in the Eagle River, July 19, 1928. This river was named by Cartwright over one hundred and fifty years ago because he saw a pair of 'eagles' at its mouth.

Cartwright called the 'eagle' "not a rare summer resident, as I have heard of about six pairs that bred at different places along the coast and always in trees." He obtained three eggs near Cape Charles, April 30, 1775; in Sandwich Bay he records two eggs on May 30, 1776, and three more on June 11, 1773. Turner (1885, 244) says, "Mr. John Ford assured me that the Fish Hawk breeds, four or five pairs of them, about 4 miles above the station of the Hudson Bay Company on Northwest River." Cooke (*ibid.*) writes that "the species breeds on both North River and White Bear River which flow into Sandwich Bay." The Indians told Dr. Strong that it nests on the river at the head of Jem Lane's Bay. The Osprey always builds a large nest of sticks, a bulky structure in the top of a tree, which is added to yearly, and which is often visible for miles around.

This bird is supposed to eat nothing but fish, and generally only the economically valueless varieties, such as the members of the carp family. Such slow-swimming, indolent surface-feeders are naturally the easiest prey for it. It is beyond reason to expect that the mere handful of Ospreys that inhabit Labrador might catch enough trout or salmon to affect the fisheries in the slightest degree. It seldom, if ever, takes any of the economically important salt-water species.

---

[1] See discussion under preceding species.

Falco rusticolus candicans Gmelin

WHITE GYRFALCON

Eskimo 'Kigavik' (*partim*).
Indian: 'Pú na shue' (*partim*), D. I. B. and B. G. B.

The White Gyrfalcon is a sporadic visitor the year round, commoner in autumn and winter than in summer. Townsend and Allen (1907, 368) say: "At Henley Harbor on August 2d [1906], we saw a bird evidently of this species circling about some high cliffs half a mile distant . . . The bird was noticeably white, somewhat mottled with darker color, especially on the wings whose primaries appeared white at the ends." Hantzsch (1929, 18) lists a light female collected at Ramah in the fall of 1901, and adds, "I never observed the species at Killinek and only once on 22nd October [1906], a very light specimen, white on the under side, at Okkak. The falcon flew with its very characteristic flight, far more flapping than ooaring, high in the sky, and hovered at last almost directly over me." I have examined five specimens in the collection of the Museum of Comparative Zoölogy from Newfoundland Labrador that seem referable by their lighter color to the northern race. One of them purports to have been taken in the late summer at Okkak, but the rest, from Okkak, Hopedale, and Makkovik, are autumn and winter skins. On August 15, 1928, I saw a single Gyrfalcon, remarkably light in color, flapping around the top of a high cliff back of Manak Island. There is no evidence that this race ever breeds in northeastern Labrador. Weiz (1866) probably took the occurrence of individuals in summer as indicative of breeding at Okkak.

Falco rusticolus obsoletus Gmelin

BLACK GYRFALCON

Eskimo: 'Kigavik' (*partim*).
Indian: 'Pu na shue' (*partim*), D. I. B. and B. G. B.

According to Swann (1922, 207) the Gyrfalcons are all of a single circumpolar species, ranging from the high north down to the tree line as breeding birds, and migrating southward in winter to middle Europe and the United States. However, he lumps all the Greenland and Labrador birds together under one form, *F. r. candicans*, describing two phases for the same species, a dark and a light.

There are some grounds for this, but more against it. There is no good evidence showing the two 'phases' to breed within the same territory. The mere presence of a bird during the breeding season does not necessarily mean it is breeding. All the Labrador records of the White Gyrfalcon are of late summer, autumn, or winter birds, whereas all records of probably breeding birds are for the darker form. I have examined the series of Gyrfalcons from Labrador in the collection of the Museum of Comparative Zoölogy, of which three are dark and five are light in color. I can find no characters other than color by which to differentiate them successfully. They vary exceedingly in all measurements, and in no regular manner. Koelz (1920, 207-219), after examining a large series of breeding birds from western Greenland, arrived at the conclusion that they are all one species, intergrading from *F. r. candicans* in the extreme north through *F. r. islandus* in the middle section of the coast to *F. r. obsoletus* in the south. I consider the evidence strong enough to warrant the recognition of a darker bird (*obsoletus*) as breeding in Labrador and southern Greenland, and a lighter subspecies (*candicans*) as breeding in the high northern part of Greenland.

The dark form is a not uncommon summer resident in the northern portion of Newfoundland Labrador, from Port Manvers to Chidley, coming southward in the late summer along the coast, where some winter. They prefer the high mountain region, with steep cliffs in which to breed, and much open tundra in which to hunt. Baird, Brewer, and Ridgway (1874, III, 117) mention an undated specimen from Rigolet. Low (1896, 325) shot a specimen at Cape Chidley. Bigelow (1902, 29) calls it "rare. One at Port Manvers September 4 [1900]." Hantzsch (1929, 17) saw two in the middle of August, 1906, in the interior of the country south of Killinek. In 1926 I saw two of these birds flying over Pardee Island in Nain Bay, August 20, and two more four days later at Windy Tickle. In 1927 I observed two pairs of dark Gyrfalcons in Nachvak Bay, August 8, 9, 10, and 11. Each pair commanded a valley of its own, and my appearance in either valley was the signal for the resident pair to fly out from the cliffs, high over my head, uttering their piercing whistles, circling higher and higher. As long as I remained in the vicinity of the particular valley which either pair had chosen for its home, one of the pair always remained in the air high overhead, watching me, and it never returned to hunt or to resume its parental duties until I was far away and out of sight. In vain I spent several days hidden in rock crevices on the mountain-tops watching them through my glasses in the hope of locating the nest.

Perrett has never succeeded in getting any evidence of the species' breeding in the Nain or Hopedale regions. Hantzsch found no definite breeding evidence in the Chidley region, nor did I, though I am sure the birds breed in the Torngats, where there are plenty of high cliffs in which they may nest, and plenty of open tundra over which they may hunt.

The two pairs I watched at Nachvak spent much of their time scouting over the mouth of a small brook, the grassy banks of which I found to be inhabited by swarms of two species of small mammals, the northern white-footed mouse, *Peromyscus m. maniculatus*, and the larger Labrador vole, *Microtus pennsylvanicus enixus*. There was very little else in the vicinity on which they could have fed.

Falco peregrinus anatum Bonaparte

DUCK HAWK

Eskimo: 'Kigavik' (*partim*).
Indian: 'Tceȳ tce hó.'

This species is practically cosmopolitan. It is divided into many races, of which *F. p. anatum* occupies that portion of northern North America from Norton Sound, Alaska, northern Mackenzie, Boothia Peninsula, and west-central Greenland, south to central Lower California, Texas, Indiana, Pennsylvania and Connecticut. It winters to the southward, from the northern United States to the West Indies and Panama, and sometimes in South America.

The Duck Hawk is a common summer resident in Labrador. Low (1896, 325) says it is "not uncommon throughout the interior." Bigelow (1902, 29) points out that it frequented those areas "wherever the sandpipers were flocking." Hantzsch (1929, 31) states that "in the spring and fall migrations the birds still appear near Killinek most regularly, and during the month of September, 1906, single specimens were repeatedly observed." Perrett shot one at Pamiarluk in June, 1899. A female in the Museum of Comparative Zoölogy was taken by Doane at Loup Bay, June 17, 1899. The bird probably arrives on the coast late in April or early in May, as indicated by Perrett's egg records, and departs to the southward toward the end of September. I watched one attack a flock of White-rumped Sandpipers in Table Bay, September 14, 1927, which is my latest autumn record.

The Duck Hawk nests on ledges in high cliffs, sometimes making a crude nest of sticks, but often laying the eggs on the bare rock. Weiz (1866) says it breeds at Okkak. Eifrig (1905, 240) records two eggs taken at Cape Chidley. Perrett collected eggs at both Nain and Pamiarluk early in May, and found them in both cases laid on the bare rock of a cliff-ledge. One egg in his collection, undated, was found at Makkovik, "on a small tuft of grass on a projecting ledge of a cliff, no nest."

This rapacious hawk is well known as one of the most successful enemies of other birds. It attacks almost anything it can from the size of a duck down to small sparrows. It seldom eats mammals, though insects have several times been found in its stomach. Twice in Labrador have I seen this feathered thunderbolt pick its prey out of mid-air. On September 7, 1927, one swooped into a mixed flock of small beach birds almost under my nose at Indian Harbor, and sailed off with a Semipalmated Plover. Again, a week later, at North Cape in Table Bay, I stood open-mouthed and entranced, the shotgun in my hands forgotten, while a Duck Hawk suddenly materialized from nowhere out of the thin blue and smote a White-rumped Sandpiper dead in the air not thirty feet from me. Its dash and verve were magnificent, thrilling. I wanted to cheer, and, for all I know, perhaps I did. At any rate, I didn't remember that I wanted a Labrador specimen badly, until the bird and its booty were out of range.

These Hawks are too few in number to affect materially the numbers of other birds on the Labrador, or to interfere to any measurable effect with any of the colonies of breeding birds which the natives visit to replenish their larders. They might well be considered as worthy of protection for the aesthetic pleasure their ferocious, lightning-like swoop upon their prey affords the man so fortunate as to see it. Once having seen it, one no longer wonders at the fascination and popularity of falconing in days of old.

Falco columbarius columbarius Linn.

EASTERN PIGEON HAWK

Eskimo: 'Kigaviarsuk'—meaning 'the small hawk.'
Indian: 'Mas kuhtz at.'

The species is of circumpolar distribution throughout the northern portions of the northern hemisphere. The Eurasian forms are but subspecifically distinct from the four races recognized in North America. *F. c. columbarius* breeds in the forested region of Canada and the northern United States east of the Great Plains, south to southern Manitoba, northern Michigan, Ontario, northern Maine, New Brunswick, Nova Scotia, and Newfoundland. The species winters southward from the Gulf States to northern South America.

In Labrador the Pigeon Hawk is a common summer resident along the coast, from Cape Chidley to Battle Harbor. There are no records for the interior, and while this is supposedly a forest species, the only Pigeon Hawks I have seen on the Labrador have been in the coastal tundra belt, never in the bays nor among the trees. Coues (1861, 216) says: "The Pidgeon-hawk I met with on but two occasions. On the 5th of August [1860], while on a small rocky island in Groswater Bay, one was seen circling in the air at a moderate height, and constantly uttering its loud, harsh cries; but owing to its watchfulness, I could not secure it. On the 25th of the same month, at Henley Harbor, another individual was seen, foraging among the immense flocks of Curlews (*Numenius borealis*), which then covered the hills in the vicinity." Townsend and Allen (1907, 371) "saw one bird of this species near Long Tickle on July 20th." Hantzsch (1929, 31) calls it a "not rare visitor of our district and breeding on the steep cliffs near the sea or in gorges in the interior . . . I saw the swift little falcon several times myself during the month of September on the Atlantic coast . . . We were not fortunate enough to collect a specimen." Wheeler saw one at the second lake of Angutausugevik, August 17, 1928, and another at Okkak, September 18, 1931. Doane collected an adult male at Loup Bay, May 16, 1899, which is now in the Museum of Comparative Zoölogy. There is an adult female in the Field Museum, collected at Battle Harbor, August 30, 1928, by the Rawson-MacMillan Expedition. I saw one flying over Battle Harbor, July 7, 1927, and two more hunting over the small forest at Nain, August 29, 1927.

Perrett records five eggs taken at Makkovik in the spring of 1899 from a nest which he describes as "a small depression on the ground, lined with a few sticks and grasses."

The Pigeon Hawk is known to feed mostly on small birds, which it catches on the wing. Occasionally it takes small mammals, and not rarely insects. I saw a Pigeon Hawk catch a Sanderling at Indian Harbor on September 14, 1927, and I imagine that birds of the open tundra, such as Horned Larks and Pipits, must be easy prey for it.

Canachites canadensis canadensis (Linn.)

HUDSONIAN SPRUCE PARTRIDGE

Local vernacular: 'Spruce Game.'
Eskimo: 'Akkigelik'—the Ptarmigan that does not change color.
Indian: 'In yoo neé yoo,' D. I. B.; 'Neé nee yoo,' B. G. B.

This genus is endemic to northern North America, occupying the Canadian and Hudsonian zones. It consists of two recognized species, *canadensis* and *franklini*. The former is now broken into four races: *canadensis*, stretching across Canada from the tree line south through the Hudsonian zone; *canace*, occupying the Canadian zone region just to the south of it and extending into the northern United States; *osgoodi*, from the Mt. McKinley range and the Yukon region east to Great Slave and Athabasca Lakes; and *atratus*, in the coast region of southwestern Alaska. Bangs (1899, 47-48) described a race from the Labrador peninsula as *labradorius*, which Hantzsch (1929, 12) recognizes, but which Norton (1901, 151) and others, including the A. O. U. Check-List Committee, have refused to validate. Bangs compared his Labrador material solely with birds from Maine and New Brunswick, which are *canace*, so, as Norton points out, he simply renamed *canadensis*. I have compared Bangs's material, and additional Labrador specimens in my own collection with examples of *canadensis* from the Hudson Bay region in the collection of A. C. Bent, and I find no recognizable difference among them that cannot be accounted for by wear, state of moult, or age of the specimen. Hence *labradorius* may be considered a synonym of *canadensis*, the Labrador bird being the one extending from the eastern side of the Rockies eastward across northern North America in the Hudsonian zone.

The Spruce Partridge is a permanent resident in the spruce forests from the tree line south, fluctuating in abundance. Low (1896, 324) calls it "common throughout wooded [portions] and in the semi-barrens." Macoun (1900, 200) says it is "an abundant resident throughout the wooded parts of Labrador." Townsend and Allen (1907, 360) term it a "common permanent resident" and record seeing a pair in captivity at Cape Charles.

I found the species uncommon during 1926, 1927, and 1928. I saw none whatsoever during 1926 and 1927, but I collected an adult male at Caplin Bay, July 13, 1928, and found a female with a brood of young at the head of Nain Bay, August 3, 1928, and another brood at Makkovik, August 14, 1928. According to the natives, the Spruce Partridge was common in 1923, but then became very scarce until 1927, when it began slowly to increase in numbers.

Macoun (*supra*) lists "one set of eggs, taken at the Grand Falls of Hamilton River, Labrador, by Mr. A. P. Low, June 1st, 1894." Perrett records finding a nest on the ground near the trunk of a small tree at the head of Big Bight, near Makkovik, early in June, 1901, which contained two very fresh eggs. He took another set there of three fresh eggs in the middle of June, 1900, and has a set of seven eggs taken near Hopedale, June 20, 1904. Coues (1861, 226) writes: "On the 24th of July [, 1860, at Hamilton Inlet], I surprised several broods, still under the care of the parent.... A chick which I obtained at that date flew with perfect ease, though it could not have been more than two weeks old, and was as yet covered with scarcely anything but down." Bent (field notes) found a female with a brood of small downy young near Hopedale, July 18, 1912, and another with a brood of large young, strong on the wing, in Udjuktok Bay, August 3 of the same year. The young I found at the head of Nain Bay, and of which I collected four, August 3, 1928, were slightly larger than quail and flew strongly, while those I saw at Makkovik, August 14, were about three-quarters grown. Thus the eggs appear usually to be laid during the first two weeks in June, and, the incubation period being approximately three weeks, to hatch early in July. The young remain in their mother's care until the middle of August, and probably on into September.

The crops of two adults I examined were jammed with spruce needles and young tender larch buds. The digestive tracts of the four young I collected contained the remains of beetles, spiders, and dipterous insects.

They are killed by the natives for food whenever possible, and it is probable that relentless persecution by the Eskimos and liveyeres is to some extent a cause of the present scarcity of the species near the settlements.

Bonasa umbellus subsp.

RUFFED GROUSE

Local vernacular: 'Birch Partridge,' 'French Hen.'

While there is ample evidence that the Ruffed Grouse occurs in Newfoundland Labrador, there are no specimens on record, and hence it is impossible to refer this bird to its proper subspecies. There are two probabilities, *B. u. togata* (Linn.) of central and eastern Canada and the darker *B. u. thayeri* Bangs of Nova Scotia. Then there is always the possibility that a series of specimens from this northeastern edge of the range of the species might prove the resident bird to be a race hitherto undescribed, but it is very unlikely that such a series ever will be taken.

The Ruffed Grouse is a rare permanent resident in the heavy forest south of Hamilton Inlet. Turner (1885, 245) says it "occurs rarely at the head of Hamilton Inlet, but only on the south side; rather common at Paradise River, flowing into Sandwich Bay, and abundantly in the valleys to the southward where birch grows plentifully. These birds are known as 'French Hens.' " Low (1896, 325) calls it "not rare at mouth of Hamilton River. Not found on Upper Hamilton River." Anderson told Bent (field notes) that two were killed near Hopedale in 1909. I have talked with several trappers from Hamilton Inlet who described the bird to me, differentiating it beyond question from the Spruce Partridge and the Ptarmigan. They mentioned the tufts of feathers on the neck, the dark band on the tail, spoke of the drumming and the noisy flight, and added that they "could count on seeing a couple every year." I saw nothing whatsoever of the species during a week spent in Sandwich Bay in 1926, nor during three days spent on the Paradise River in 1928.

Lagopus lagopus lagopus (Linn.)

WILLOW PTARMIGAN

Local vernacular: 'Grouse,' 'Browse Partridge.'
Eskimo: 'Akkigivik,'—the large Ptarmigan.
Indian: 'Wah pi neé yoo,' D. I. B.; 'Pi neé yoo,' B. G. B.

I have carefully gone over the excellent series of Willow Ptarmigan in the Museum of Comparative Zoölogy, which includes representative individuals of all but one of the supposed North American races, and of nearly all the Eurasian. I cannot differentiate the Willow Ptarmigan of Labrador from the bird of central northern North America, nor can I either of these in turn from the bird of Europe. The species is truly circumpolar in its distribution, ranging non-plastically across northern North America and Eurasia. I have not enough material to venture an opinion on the Eurasian races, but of the North American forms the only valid ones seem to me to be *L. l. alleni* Stejneger from Newfoundland, *L. l. alexandrae* Grinnell from southwestern Alaska and the Aleutian Islands, and *L. l. leucopterus* Taverner from Baffin Island. I have not seen any material of *L. l. alascensis* Swarth, but it strikes me that he has not used any of the eastern Siberian races for comparison, and his measurements are too few in number to be a good criterion. Shades of color in breeding dress vary greatly in individuals from the same locality, and while the race may in the future prove to be perfectly good, there does not seem to me to be sufficient evidence at present to warrant its establishment. The same is true of *ungavus* and *albus*. The Newfoundland race, *alleni*, of which I have examined a splendid series, is barely differentiated from the mainland form, and intergrades with *lagopus* in the region of the Straits of Belle Isle. Its only characters are the deeper black on the rhachi of the primaries and secondaries, and a speckling of black on the tips of the primaries. Both these characters are very variable, and are nearly approached by some individuals, though not by all, from the nearby mainland.

It is a permanent resident in Labrador, fluctuating regularly and markedly in abundance (see graph). There are no accurate data on the periodicity of the Ptarmigan in Labrador, for systematic observations have not been made there over a consecutive period of years. We have to depend largely upon the fragmentary notes of the few sportsmen who have written of their occasional travels in the region and the vague and general statements of the inhabitants. The evidence tends to show, however, that the abundance of the Ptarmigan in Labrador fluctuates periodically in approximately an eight-year cycle. They reach great numbers for a short time, disappear very suddenly, and then gradually in-

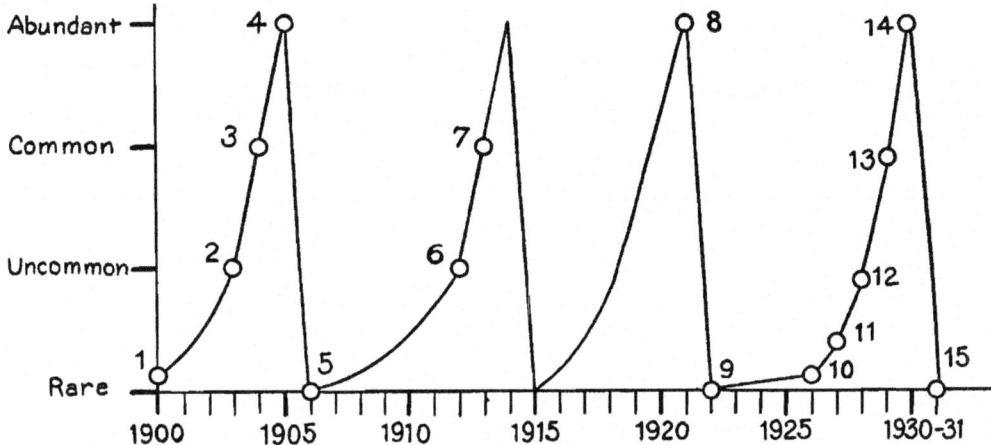

Sources of data: 1, Bigelow (1902). 2, 3, 4, 5, 7, Cabot (1920). 6, Bent (field notes). 8, 9, Hettasch and Perrett (orally). 10, 11, 12, Austin. 13, MacMillan (orally). 14, 15, Wheeler (orally).

crease up to another peak. The snowshoe rabbits and the field mice (*Microtus*) undergo similar fluctuations, synchronous with those of the Ptarmigan. Rabbit cycles elsewhere have been shown to be caused by a virus disease, tularemia, which slaughters them in wholesale fashion soon after they reach their enormous pinnacles of abundance, and it is believed by students of the phenomenon that the same disease is the cause of periodicity in the mice and the Ptarmigan. It has been shown that many rodents, and some of the gallinaceous birds (notably the Ruffed Grouse), are susceptible to tularemia, but the disease has never been reported from Newfoundland Labrador, nor has it been found in Ptarmigan. This is but negative evidence, for no one has ever searched for it in either the locality or the species.

Many theories have been advanced to explain the occurrence of the cycle, and in a country such as Labrador where the people are largely dependent on wild life for their existence, speculation runs high. The trappers are all acutely cognizant of the phenomenon, for they find that their catch of fur is small during the years of plenty. Predatory animals and birds are increasingly numerous at such times, but there is so much live food in the country that foxes and martens will not come to dead bait. The year following the peak is always their best one.

The fur-bearers have thrived and increased with the copious supply of food, and now that they are suddenly bereft of their usual prey, though not their usual appetites, they come readily to the traps. The trappers all agree that some 'wonderful sickness' ('wonderful' in the Labrador vernacular means atrocious, bad, horrible) carries the rabbits away, but they believe that the mice migrate out of the country, and that, in their absence, increased pressure from foxes, weasels, hawks, and owls, extirpates the Ptarmigan. The theory that the mice migrate out of the region probably had its origin in their superabundance during their peaks. At such times the country simply teems with them, and, according to all accounts, even the trout and cod taste 'mousey.' There are so many mice that it simply does not seem possible for them to disappear as suddenly as they do, and to those who have seen them swarming everywhere one day and gone the next, the apparently logical conclusion is that they have simply vacated the area for more suitable surroundings. That a creature so obviously unsuited for travel as a short-legged field mouse should journey hundreds of miles and cross large bodies of water, they attribute to the wonders of nature. The theory that predatory animals are responsible for the sudden drop in the Ptarmigan population is equally without foundation. Many of the birds are killed by hawks, owls, foxes, and weasels, and two or three times as many are killed by man and salted away for winter use, but the sum total of all the birds so killed can be but a small percentage of the number of Ptarmigan in existence during one of the peaks of abundance. That the rabbits, the mice, and the Ptarmigan are all subject to the same epidemic disease, is by far the most plausible theory that has yet been advanced to account for the phenomenon of the cycle.

The Willow Ptarmigan is as typically a Hudsonian bird as can be found on the Labrador. It prefers the short, low, scrub growth, and is seldom to be found either north of the tree line or in the heavier Canadian forest. According to Perrett, it seems to migrate southward and eastward to the coastal barrens in winter, but as yet nothing definite is known about the bird's movements. Bigelow (1902, 29) found it "rather common north to Nain, beyond which point we did not see it." Hantzsch (1929, 12) calls it an "occasional visitor" to the northern section of the coast. Wheeler noted "several individuals sticking to the scrub growth and willows at head of Tikkoatokok Bay," January 29, 1928, and saw "a few in the low country about Angutausugevik Brook in the willows," August 15, 1928. In the collection of the Field Museum are two adult male specimens taken by the Rawson-MacMillan Expedition at Bowdoin Harbor; one, in full summer plumage, was taken November 10, 1927, while the other, in complete white winter plumage, was collected January 10, 1928.

During the years 1926–1928 all gallinaceous birds were exceedingly rare throughout Newfoundland Labrador, and I consider myself fortunate to have encountered a male and a female Willow Ptarmigan with four young at Alleuk Bight, July 27, 1926. These are the only ones I observed on the whole coast, for though I searched for them every time ashore, I spent comparatively little time in 'ptarmigan country' during 1927 and 1928. The general consensus of native opinion during that period was that the birds were increasing slightly. I have recently been informed by Dr. Wheeler that a peak in the mouse-rabbit-ptarmigan cycle evidently was reached in 1930. Mice and lemmings were very scarce in 1931, and he saw many dead ones in the spring after the snow melted. The Ptarmigan, however, continued to be abundant until April, 1931, after which he saw none.

The Willow Ptarmigan breeds among the sheltered islands at the heads of the bays, and in the interior, in the scrubby growth where there is plenty of cover to give it protection from its enemies. It nests on the ground, according to Anderson when questioned by Bent (field notes), and usually under some sort of shelter, such as a small tree. Low (1896, 325) says: "Breeds on Upper Hamilton River. Eggs June 25th." Macoun (1900, 206) says: "Mr. A. P. Low has taken many eggs in Labrador and says that the set ranges from nine to twelve. There is nothing peculiar about the nest that would separate it from that of the Ruffed Grouse. It was always found in a sheltered place, however." A set of eight eggs in Perrett's collection was taken near Okkak in July. Cabot (1920, 60) found a mother with young, July 12-14, 1903, and during the first part of August in 1904 he reports seeing several broods of well-grown birds (1920, 145-155). Bent found a pair of old birds with young which were "about the size of quail and could fly swiftly" at Udjuktok Bay, August 3, 1912. The chicks are highly precocial, and it is a common saying along the coast that they can fly the moment they hatch, in fact while bits of the shell still adhere to their down.

It is a most important food bird in times of its abundance. During the years of plenty Willow Ptarmigan are slaughtered by the hundreds and salted down in barrels for future use.

Lagopus mutus rupestris (Gmelin)

ROCK PTARMIGAN

Local vernacular: 'Mountain Partridge,' 'Rocker.'
Eskimo: 'Niksartok,'—the one that belches.
Indian: 'Kus kán áh dgish.'

The Rock Ptarmigan is a circumpolar species of high latitudes. After a thorough comparison of the specimens in the Museum of Comparative Zoölogy, I am satisfied that the Palearctic and Nearctic forms are subspecifically distinct. But I am unable to separate the North American individuals racially with any degree of certainty. Taverner, the most recent reviser of the group, amassed the best series of Nearctic Rock Ptarmigan yet to be brought together for study. He concludes (1929) that there are in general three groups recognizable, a grayish southern race, a yellowish northern one, and a pale sand-colored form from southern Greenland. There are, however, innumerable intergrades which do not always occur in the intermediate areas where they might be expected, but (*ibid.*, pp. 29, 30) "may occur sporadically anywhere even where pure racial strains would be supposed to prevail. More disturbing still is the occurrence of typical or even ultra-typical individuals far from their centres of apparent predominance and deep in the range of other forms." He considers the bird of Labrador and Newfoundland to belong to the southern gray race, and lists as fairly typical six Newfoundland specimens in the Museum of Comparative Zoölogy and two adult males in the Carnegie Museum taken at MacLelan Strait, August 9, 1920. A young bird in the Bent Collection, however, taken at Loup Bay, September 9, 1917, he finds to be typical of the yellow northern race, and adds, "the date suggests that it might be an early migrant."

Several characteristics unite to make the Rock Ptarmigan one of the most difficult species in existence to differentiate subspecifically. In the first place, no specimens except those taken on their nests can be assigned to their proper significant locality without question. Beyond the facts that the species is highly migratory and that it wanders irregularly with a fine disregard of exact seasons and points of the compass, we know nothing of its movements. In the second place, the white winter plumage shows no recognizable characters, and it is extremely difficult to procure summer skins that are strictly comparable. While in the partially brown summer dress the species is in a perpetual state of moult, which makes it next to impossible to select specimens in approximately the same stage. In the third place, the species represents, in the avian kingdom, probably the acme of individual size-variation in both soft and hard parts. Thus it naturally follows that there have been described from both the Palearctic and Nearctic a number of races, the validity of a large proportion of which remains to be proved. No two authors of the many that have attacked the group agree on the subspecific divisions, and it is unlikely that any will for some time to come.

It is a rare breeding bird in the northern part of Labrador; an irregular migrant and winter visitor throughout the district, at times abundant, usually uncommon. It is an inhabitant of the open tundras and the bare rock barrens, and is seldom to be seen in the wooded regions. Low says (1896, 325): "Common in the valley of Hamilton River during winter. Leaves for northward about April 15th." Bigelow found it (1902, 29) "common from Hamilton Inlet northward."

Hantzsch (1929, 13) states that in the Chidley region "it is a common migrant in the spring, less abundant in the fall." Much has been written about the large flocks of Rock Ptarmigan that appear from the north in the autumn, flying high across the coast, and that return in the spring to breeding grounds farther northward in the Arctic Archipelago. Hantzsch (*ibid.*, 13-16) sums up all the evidence that had been procured up to the time of his visit, and very little has been added since. In good years the birds appear in the Chidley region, phalanx after phalanx of them, at any time from the middle of September through October, and disappear to the southward in November. Perrett records the first spring arrival at Killinek on April 7, 1906. To quote Hantzsch (*vide supra*): "Suddenly in early spring, mostly in April, seldom sooner, at times not until well into May, the wanderers appear from the south. Usually at first rather small advance posts are established. A short time after that the whole throng of birds follows . . . countless large flocks of these birds appear at times, usually passing through rather high in the air. For hours they hasten in many thousands through the sky, so that their numbers cause astonishment. Many flights of the kind are observed from the same place. The birds mostly fly directly across Hudson Strait without delaying. This is almost always covered with ice in the spring and little to be distinguished from the land." In the southern part of the district the Rock Ptarmigan occasionally fly across to Newfoundland. Frazar (1887) gives evidence of "flock after flock . . . flying in from across the water" to the Labrador side of the Straits of Belle Isle in early winter. Dr. Grenfell told Townsend and Allen (1907, 362) "that Ptarmigan sometimes alight on vessels in the Straits of Belle Isle."

For the past few years, however, Rock Ptarmigan have been very scarce. I saw none myself during my visits to the coast, nor did I hear of any being taken. Perrett told me in 1928 that the last of which he heard were four individuals killed by Hopedale Eskimos during the winter of 1924-1925. Though there is no direct evidence to prove the point, it is barely possible that the species undergoes a cyclic fluctuation in numbers like that of its larger relative, the Willow Ptarmigan.

Hantzsch (*ibid.*, p. 13) says that in the Chidley region, "according to the statement of the inhabitants, the Rock Ptarmigan is a rare breeding bird, only on the slopes of the highest mountains in our district, especially of the Kallaruselik, where eggs were occasionally found." Eifrig (1905, 239) lists five eggs taken by the Neptune Expedition at Cape Chidley in 1903. Perrett had a set of nine eggs in his collection taken at Ramah, June 27, 1895.

Hantzsch (*ibid.*, p. 14) records that the contents of crops he examined consisted entirely of vegetable matter, "bitten-off leaves and twigs of different plants, especially of willows, as well as of *Arctostaphylos alpina* Spr.; in addition a number of seeds." It is likely that this species, as do most of its relatives, lives when adult almost exclusively on a vegetable diet, with an occasional insect or two, while the young feed exclusively on insects and other animal matter until they have attained their growth.

Whenever it occurs in large enough numbers, hundreds are killed, salted down, and packed away for future use. Of recent years but very few messes of 'niksartok' have been eaten by the hungry Labrador Eskimos.

[**Rallus limicola limicola** Vieillot. VIRGINIA RAIL. Perhaps an accidental visitor. Turner (1886, 248) records that "a single specimen was taken in Hamilton Inlet a few years ago and submitted to M. Fortesque, esq. (of the Hudson Bay Company), who identified it beyond question." Bent (1926, 299) says, "there is a record of one in 1891 from Hamilton Inlet, Labrador," which probably refers to this same bird, as Bent may have taken his record from Turner's abridged notes in Packard (1891).]

Porzana carolina (Linn.)

SORA

There is but a single record of the occurrence of the Sora in Newfoundland Labrador. According to Townsend and Allen (1907, 345), "Dr. W. T. Grenfell has added this species to the list of Labrador birds, as he secured a specimen in Sandwich Bay in 1898. The skin was sent to Cambridge, England." I assume that in Cambridge it was duly identified.

Fulica atra atra Linn.

EUROPEAN COOT

The European Coot is known from Labrador by two specimens, both taken in December, 1927, one of which is now in the Field Museum of Natural History, the other in the collection of the Museum of Comparative Zoölogy (see Austin, 'Auk,' 1929b, 208). These two individuals accompanied the remarkable flight of Lapwings which presumably were blown across the Atlantic late in December, 1927. One was collected by the Rawson-MacMillan Expedition at Tangnaivik Island, Anaktalak Bay. The other was presented to me by R. L. Stevenson, the wireless operator at Gready Island. It was taken at Separation Point in Sandwich Bay.

Fulica americana americana Gmelin

AMERICAN COOT

The only specimen of the American Coot known from Labrador is one recorded by Cooke (1916, 164) as having been shot at Table Bay in October, 1913. I have examined this bird, which is now in the collection of the United States Biological Survey, and find its identity beyond question. There are two other Coots mentioned in literature as having been taken in Labrador. Turner (1886, 248) records that one was shot about 1880 on a lake near Nain. He did not see the specimen himself, but the stuffed bird was described to him so accurately by several persons that he was able to identify it "beyond possibility of doubt." Dr. Grenfell told Townsend and Allen (1907, 346) "that he took a specimen of this species at Longstretch, Sandwich Bay, in August, 1899." Neither of these specimens is now in existence, nor did anyone capable of differentiating between the American and European species examine either of them. The difference between the two, merely the presence or absence of white on the under tail-coverts, is so small that only a specialist, or someone expecting the occurrence of the European bird would notice it. Hence these birds might be either one of the two species, and must remain enigmas.

Vanellus vanellus (Linn.)

LAPWING

A specimen taken at Cartwright in January, 1917 (Bent, 1929, 149), and now in the collection of the United States Biological Survey, is the earliest record for Newfoundland Labrador of this interesting casual visitor from Europe. The remarkable flight of Lapwings that visited North America in December, 1927, (cf. Witherby, 1928, 6-13, and Austin, 1929b, 207-210) was represented in Labrador by a large number of birds. From the native accounts, the birds were spread out along the coast from Battle Harbor, Sandwich Bay, and Hamilton Inlet north to Hopedale, occurring in flocks numbering from ten to fifty individuals apiece. They arrived during a spell of exceedingly mild weather in the week before Christmas, 1927, and all perished in the cold snap that followed it, save two that were wing-tipped by a hunter at Separation Point, Sandwich Bay, and kept in captivity.   One of these died from neglect at Easter time, but the other, a male, was saved for me alive by my friend Robert Stevenson.   I tried to bring it home alive, but it died on the way back during a stormy night, off the west coast of Newfoundland.   Two skins were obtained at Hopedale by the Rawson-MacMillan Expedition and are now in the Field Museum.   One of these, a male, was shot December 24, 1927; the other, not sexed, late in December, 1927. I purchased another from an Eskimo woman at Makkovik, who had found the bird in April, after the snow had melted and partly exposed the carcass.   Such was its state of preservation in this excellent natural cold storage that she was able to make a very fair flat skin of it.   Every native I interviewed who had killed any of the Lapwings, complained that they were much too poor and thin to eat, which is quite an admission from either a liveyere or an Eskimo.

Charadrius hiaticula semipalmatus Bonaparte

SEMIPALMATED PLOVER

Local vernacular: 'Twillig,' 'Ringer.'
Eskimo: 'Kullikulliak'—from the voice.

Charadrius hiaticula is a circumpolar species divisible into three races, *hiaticula* breeding in northern Europe, *tundrae* across northern Siberia, and *semipalmatus* in northern North America.   The bird of eastern Asia has been considered subspecifically distinct by some recent authors, as has the one breeding in the Faroes, Iceland, Greenland, and Cumberland Sound (*cf.* Salomonsen, 1930.)

The breeding range of *C. h. semipalmatus* extends across northern North America, on the Pacific coast from British Columbia to Alaska, along the coasts of the Arctic Sea and in the Arctic Archipelago from the Mackenzie delta eastward to Baffin Island, and south along the Atlantic coast to New Brunswick.   It migrates southward along both coasts of North and South America to central Argentina and Chile.

It is a common summer resident in the barren coastal zone from the Straits of Belle Isle to Cape Chidley.   Coues (1861, 228) found the bird "excessively abundant during the summer months along the whole coast of Labrador."   Weiz (1866) lists it at Okkak.   Low (1896, 324) says: "Common on Upper Hamilton River.   Seen June 16th."   Bigelow (1902, 29) calls it "very common; almost as much so as the Spotted Sandpipers.   Nesting all along the coast."   Townsend and Allen (1907, 359) "found a pair at Battle Island, three pairs at Great Caribou Island, and a pair each at Long Tickle and Hopedale."   Hantzsch (1929, 11) terms it a "rather common breeding bird and migrant" in the northern section, Perrett noted the first spring arrivals at Makkovik, June 3, 1899, and at Killinek. June 4, 1906. Wheeler observed a single individual at Kikkertaksoak, June 2, 1928, and several at Naksatok, an outer island northeast of Nain, on May 29, 1931. My latest autumn date for the Semipalmated Plover is September 14, 1927, when it was still fairly common. I observed on that date at least fifty individuals mixed in with other small shore-birds scattered over Table Bay, feeding in the tide pools and on the kelp beds. Wheeler saw several at Okkak, September 16, 1931, and found one bird still lingering at Holton Harbor, October 18, 1931.

The Semipalmated Plover breeds throughout the coastal area of Labrador. Turner (1885, 246) obtained downy young with their parents at Davis Inlet. Macoun (1900, 190) lists eggs taken by Low, probably at Hamilton Inlet, though no locality is given. Hantzsch (*ibid.*) says it "breeds on flat parts of the coast near the shore and also farther in the hinterland, usually several pairs in one neighborhood." He secured eggs from the immediate vicinity of Killinek, and mentions a female in his collection that was taken with her eggs at Ramah, June 27,1907. Perrett took three sets of eggs near Makkovik, June 30, 1900. All were very fresh; one was of four, the other two of three eggs each. He collected a fourth set at Nain, June 22, 1911.

I found five nests with eggs still unhatched in the shell deposits on the south side of Indian Island, July 14, 1927. The four eggs in each case were simply laid in a shallow depression hollowed out by the parent bird in the loose crumbling shell. There was no pretense of a nest-lining at all, and so well camouflaged were the speckled eggs in their light surroundings that I had great difficulty in locating them. The nests were all more than fifty yards from the water. I found about thirty pairs of 'Ring-necks' scattered over the tundra for two miles back of Holton Harbor, June 18, 1928. The birds certainly were nesting there, for each pair evinced keen anxiety when I approached the limits of its territory, but I failed to find either nests or young. I was attended most of the afternoon by seemingly crippled adults that fluttered helplessly before me until they had lured me away from their treasures. In vain I played 'hot and cold' with them, the country was too big and too uniform, and it was next to impossible to narrow the search to any particular spot. To add to the fun, the afternoon was muggy and windless, and the mosquitoes were out in clouds. The insect pests are partly responsible for many failures in Labrador, ornithological and otherwise.

The duration of the incubation period has been found in *C. h. hiaticula* to be twenty-two or twenty-three days. I found young just hatched at Indian Island, July 20, 1926; July 18, 1927; and July 17, 1928. Wheeler found "young just cracking their egg-shell" on July 7, 1931, in the Kiglapait region. I observed young of the year on the wing for the first time at Bay of Seven Islands, August

14, 1927, and near Ford's Harbor, August 9, 1928. The juvenals are readily distinguishable from the adults by their gray, instead of black, neck ring. In each case the young birds were still in the company of their parents, and the family group easily could be recognized—the two old birds with three or four young.

The Semipalmated Plover is too small to be considered worthy of notice as food, but individuals are often included in the general messes of 'scoffs' of 'beachy birds' in which every fisherman and liveyere indulges at times. The fifteen or more pairs that breed on Indian Island must be somewhat bothered by the natives' dogs, and by their children, whom I have seen on several occasions hunting the nests. Inasmuch as the favorite nesting place of this species, on the Labrador at least, is among the shell-deposits, it will be interesting to note, in the years to come, whether or not the projected removal of the shell for commercial purposes has any effect on the number of individuals; but since the bird can nest elsewhere, as it often does, the new industry will probably do it no harm.

Pluvialis dominica dominica (P. L. S. Müller)

AMERICAN GOLDEN PLOVER

Local vernacular: 'Ground Plover.'
Eskimo: 'Ungulitik.'

This wide-ranging circumpolar species, which nests in high latitudes along the tundra-covered shores of the Arctic seas, has been divided into two subspecies. *P. d. fulva* breeds in northern Siberia and on the western fringe of Alaska, and migrates southward in winter along the western shores of the Pacific to the Hawaiian Islands, China, India, Australia, and New Zealand. *P. d. dominica* nests in northwestern North America from Point Barrow to the western side of Hudson Bay, and, swinging eastward in early autumn, travels south along the Atlantic coast to South America. It winters as far south as Argentina. On its way northward in the spring it forsakes the coast and follows up the Mississippi Valley.

In Labrador the Golden Plover is an uncommon transient visitor in the autumn. It is seldom seen along the rocky shores, but roams over the grassy open tundra in small flocks, seeking the berries of which it is so fond. The eggs are laid in the Mackenzie region during the middle of June, and the young are evidently ready to start their long journey about two months later. The vanguard reaches Labrador usually during the last week in August, and scattered flocks may be seen as late as the end of September.

Coues (1861, 228) says, "No Golden Plover were observed until a short time before we left the country; then, about the date of the departure of the Curlews, *Numenius borealis* [about September 1], they made their appearance in small numbers, in flocks of about a dozen or more." Weiz (1866) records its occurrence at Okkak. Bigelow (1902, 29) "saw several flocks after August 22 [, 1900], mostly young birds." Hantzsch (1929, 11) observed two juvenal birds at Killinek, September 2, 1906, and states that "some days later, Missionary Perrett, who had repeatedly secured the species in the south, observed a single bird. In many years they are said to occur rather abundantly." Bent (1929, 184) lists a young bird in his collection taken near Hopedale. Wheeler saw a lone individual near Nain, September 10, 1928, and encountered "some half-dozen on the sheltered side of the summit during a gale" on one of the outer islands near Okkak, September 26, 1931.

I have seen Golden Plover in Labrador but once. I encountered a flock of twelve young birds, of which I shot one, at North Cape (near Gready), September 14, 1927. They were feeding in a sheltered hollow in the tundra about a mile back from the water, and were remarkably tame and unsuspicious. The day was a bad one,—pouring rain driven by a cold northeast gale,—and the birds allowed me to approach to within fifty feet of them before flushing. The bird I killed was as fat and plump an individual as I have ever seen of any species. It had a layer of fat fully three millimeters in thickness under its skin. The entire digestive tract and the feathers of the anal region were stained a deep blue from the juice of the *Empetrum nigrum* berries with which its crop was jammed.

Squatarola squatarola (Linn.)

BLACK-BELLIED PLOVER

Local vernacular: 'Sand Plover.'

This species is circumpolar in its distribution, breeding in high latitudes on the coasts of the Arctic seas, and migrating to the southern hemisphere in winter along the shores of both the Atlantic and the Pacific Oceans. There have been three races described, one breeding in northwestern North America, one in northern Europe, and one in northern Siberia, but the differences between them are so slight that the subspecies are barely recognizable. It is still a moot question whether or not they are valid geographical forms.

In Labrador the Black-bellied Plover is a rare autumnal transient. Cartwright records killing one August 29, 1773, and four September 5, 1776. Weiz

(1866) reports it from Okkak. Cooke (1910, 79) quotes Coues for his authority in stating that "the first flocks came along the Labrador coast August 15, 1860." This is probably an error, for Coues does not mention the species in his 'Notes on the Ornithology of Labrador,' nor have I been able to find a statement to this effect in any other of Coues's published writings. It is not unlikely that the note was transposed accidentally from some other species in the compilation of Cooke's paragraphs on distribution. There are no comparatively recent records of the occurrence of the bird in the district. Perrett told me he had never seen a Black-bellied Plover on the coast, and the Eskimos do not know the species.

I have never observed it farther north than Flower's Cove, Newfoundland, where I saw a flock of twenty-seven at close range September 14, 1926. Its rarity on the Labrador may be accounted for partly by the fact that it prefers to feed on hard sandy beaches, of which there are almost none in this rock-bound region.

Arenaria interpres morinella (Linn.)

RUDDY TURNSTONE

The Turnstone is another species that nests circumpolarly in high latitudes in the northern hemisphere. Two races are recognized: *A. i. interpres* breeds from western Greenland eastward across northern Eurasia to Kamchatka, and migrates southward along the coasts of Europe and Asia and generally throughout the eastern hemisphere; *A. i. morinella* breeds in northern and northwestern North America from western and northern Alaska eastward to Southampton and western Baffin Islands, and migrates generally throughout the western hemisphere. Both races extend their winter ranges well south of the Equator.

The Ruddy Turnstone is an uncommon transient visitor in Labrador. I have always seen it on the bare, wave-washed edges of the rocky outside islands, running along at the tide line. Coues (1861, 228) saw the first ones at Henley Harbor, August 20, 1860, and notes that on the first of September "they were apparently as numerous as ever." Turner (1886, 245) collected an adult at Davis Inlet on July 25, and calls the species "not rare on the east coast." Hantzsch (1929, 12) considers it a "rather rare migrant." He collected two juvenal females south of Killinek, August 23, 1906. I observed a single individual July 26, 1926, at Puffin Island, and during the same summer saw four at the Red Islands, August 26, and six more at Puffin Island, August 28. The heaviest part of the migration seems to come through during the last week in August. An immature female in the Field Museum was collected by the Rawson-MacMillan Expedition at Battle Harbor, August 30, 1926. On September 2, 1928, Wheeler saw "a lone Turnstone near Webb's Bay, trying to get shelter from the gale behind boulders on a tide flat." My latest date for the species is September 5, 1927, when I saw four on the rocky south side of Indian Island.

The Turnstone has never been known to breed within the limits of Newfoundland Labrador, and there is no foundation for Chester A. Reed's statement (1904, 143) that "they nest commonly in northern Labrador." The individuals recorded in the region in July and early August are probably non-breeding birds, many of them young of the preceding year, that have not been north to the nesting grounds.

Hantzsch (1929, 12) records the contents of the stomachs of two birds he took near Killinek, August 23, 1907, as being "crustaceans, especially the species *Talitrus saltator* Mont., and mineral substances, namely, sand and little pebbles." Wherever I have seen the species in Labrador, it seemed to be prying open barnacles and mollusks that were exposed by the falling tide.

Capella gallinago gallinago (Linn.)

EUROPEAN COMMON SNIPE

In August, 1928, I purchased from an Eskimo woman at Makkovik the skin of a Common Snipe which she had taken near her winter house at the head of Jack Lane's Bay, December 24, 1927 (see Austin, 1929b, 209). The bird evidently had been blown across the ocean by the same storm which brought the Lapwings. It constitutes the sole record for continental North America, though the bird is known casually in Greenland.

Capella gallinago delicata (Ord)

WILSON'S SNIPE

Eskimo: 'Otototojuk'—probably from the whistling noise made by the bird in flight. Perrett is not sure of this name, for he had but one bird so identified and the Eskimo who named it seemed uncertain. I found the Eskimos did not seem to know the bird at all, though it breeds commonly at Makkovik within a few yards of their dwellings.
Indian: 'Kah mo skwa hast.'

This is another circumpolar species in the northern hemisphere, now divided into four races—*gallinago* from Europe, *raddei* from Siberia, *delicata* from North

America, and *faroensis*, a slightly differentiated form from the Faroe Islands. The American subspecies, *delicata*, reaches its northeastern limit in Labrador.

Wilson's Snipe is locally a common summer resident in suitable bogs and marshes north to Webb's Bay, just south of the tree line. Cartwright saw one near Cape Charles, September 10, 1772, and another in Sandwich Bay, September 19, 1775. Coues (1861, 229) says: "From the accounts of the natives, I should judge that the Snipe is abundant in Labrador, as it is in most parts of the United States. I met with but a single individual." Low (1896, 324) says, "Male heard and seen at Lake Petitsikapau, Hamilton River, June 28th." Bigelow (1902, 28) records "three or four near Cape St. Francis." Perrett noted its arrival in spring at Makkovik, May 14, 1899. His latest autumn date for the species is October 1, 1898, also at Makkovik. Wheeler flushed one September 1, 1928, "in a low, brackish swamp near the bottom of the first small bay east of Ugjutuarsuk [near Webb's Bay]."

I found five Wilson's Snipe in the thick tamarack swamp behind the Makkovik mission house. I discovered two little muddy clearings deep in the swamp, and surrounded by alders and larches, that were used continually by the birds, either as feeding or resting grounds or both. Their droppings and borings were numerous there, and I was almost sure at all times of finding a bird in one or the other of them. Mr. Lenz, in charge of the mission at Makkovik, told me the Snipe had formed the habit of feeding in the soft loam in the garden, whence he had flushed them on many occasions. The stomach of one bird I collected at Makkovik contained the mangled remains of one spider and several grubs.

Perrett collected a set of four eggs, incubation well advanced, near Hopedale, June 21, 1904. The nest, lined with fine grasses, was placed on the ground in the open in a swampy location. Incubation (Bent, 1927, 86) is shared by both sexes, and lasts from eighteen to twenty days. Perrett found the young were hatched at Makkovik, June 23, 1899.

Lymnocryptes minimus (Brünnich)

EUROPEAN JACK SNIPE

The only record of this species for continental North America is a skin which I purchased from the same Eskimo woman who sold me the European Common Snipe. She shot it at the same time and place—December 24, 1927, near her winter home at the head of Makkovik Bay (see Austin, 1929, 209). The bird probably accompanied the Lapwings in their memorable flight of that year.

Phaeopus hudsonicus (Latham)

HUDSONIAN CURLEW

Local vernacular: 'Jack Curlew.'
Eskimo: 'Akpingak' (*partim*).

This is distinctly a Nearctic bird, but a very similar species, *Phaeopus phaeopus*, breeds across the northern parts of the Palearctic region. *P. hudsonicus* nests on the Arctic coast of North America from Alaska through the Mackenzie delta. It migrates along both Atlantic and Pacific coasts, and winters from the Gulf States and Lower California, through Central America, to central South America. The individuals using the Atlantic route swing eastward to Labrador in the late summer before starting down the coast, but in the spring they come north along the seaboard only as far as New England before striking inland toward their breeding grounds.

The Hudsonian Curlew is an uncommon late summer and autumn transient visitor in Labrador, passing through in small flocks during the latter part of August and the first weeks of September. Coues (1861, 235) says: "Of the Hudsonian Curlew I saw but few individuals, and these were so shy that it was with difficulty that they were procured. They were most numerous at the time that the *N. [Phaeopus] borealis* were about taking their departure [September 1]." A specimen he collected at Henley Harbor, August 22, 1860, is now in the Museum of Comparative Zoölogy. According to Hantzsch (1928, 226) it is a "not common migrant in the late summer, but is said to appear annually in small flocks, and often also in rather large flocks."

The Hudsonian Curlew while in Labrador dwells in the open tundra in the barren coastal zone where there are plenty of bake-apples and crowberries for it to eat. While weather-bound at Isle of Ponds, September 4, 5, and 6, 1926, I met a flock of twelve 'Jack Curlew' daily, that were feeding on the tundra there. It was my first acquaintance with any of the Curlews in the field, and I shot one to make sure of my identification. I saw a single bird fly over Tikkerasuk, September 3, 1927, and on September 14 of the same year I found a flock of eight at Curlew Harbor. I examined one killed there by a native hunter. When the Hudsonian Curlews reach Labrador, they have plenty of fuel aboard for their southward journey. The bird I collected had a quarter-inch of fat under the skin. Its crop was jammed with *Empetrum nigrum* berries, and its entire digestive tract was stained a deep blue from their juices.

It is shot for food by the natives, whenever possible.

Phaeopus borealis (Forster)

ESKIMO CURLEW

Local vernacular: 'Dough Bird,' 'The C'lew.'
Eskimo: 'Akpingak' (*partim*).

Formerly an abundant autumn transient, the Eskimo Curlew is now believed to be extinct. Cartwright gave August 3 as the earliest arrival date, and September 18 as the latest departure date of the large flocks, recording also one arrival July 28 and one straggler October 24.

Much has been written of the fate of this once superabundant species. Townsend and Allen (1907, 354-358) give an excellent summation of all the facts of the case known up to their date of publication. Since then there have been a few straggling records for the district. Townsend (1913, 10) records seven shot near Cartwright in August and September, 1912. Cooke (1916, 165) says "a few were seen August 17, [1912] on Caribou Island; one was recorded at Cartwright in September and four at West Bay during the same month." Since then there have been no authenticated records. Word went up and down the coast in 1927 that five had been seen from the mail boat by several persons who knew the bird "in the old days." But Jack McRea, who had shot many 'C'lews' during his youth on the coast at Gready, told me he saw the flock in question go over the mail boat, and was sure they were 'Jack Curlew.' Isle of Ponds, Curlew Harbor, and Table Bay were the old favorite gunning places of the fishermen.

Actitis macularia (Linn.)

SPOTTED SANDPIPER

Eskimo: 'Sullajuk,' 'Aivigiak.'
Indian: 'Wis tim in ishué.'

Though entirely Nearctic, this is a widespread species in its breeding range, which covers North America from Alaska to Labrador, and from California to Carolina. It winters somewhat to the southward, reaching Brazil and Peru, but individuals are found throughout the southern United States all winter. It is replaced by a distinct species in Eurasia.

The Spotted Sandpiper is a fairly common summer resident at the heads of the bays and along the inland water-courses. Low (1896, 324) says: "Common along the Upper Hamilton River. Seen May 27th." Norton (1901, 150) lists two females and a male from Chateau Bay, July 14, and a young bird from Cullingham's Cove, Hamilton Inlet, July 31, 1891. Bigelow (1902, 29) found it "very abundant; breeds everywhere along the coast." Hantzsch (1928, 226) saw none in the northern part of Labrador, and came to the conclusion that it is only an occasional visitor there.

There are no arrival dates, and the earliest I have seen Spotted Sandpipers is July 12, 1928, at Petty Harbor. However, since eggs have been recorded in early June, the species must reach the region by the latter part of May. I have also observed individuals at Paradise River, Alleuk Bight, Turnavik Bay, Adletok Bay, Anaktalak Bay, and Nain Bay. I saw two pairs on the Fraser River, August 18, 1926, and two more at the same place August 4, 1928, which is as far north as I have ever met the bird. My latest entry for the species is of three adults in fall plumage I observed at Tub Harbor, September 16, 1927.

Low (l. c.) mentions eggs of this species found June 20. Macoun (1900, 181) lists a set taken by Low on the Upper Hamilton River, June 25, 1894. Bent (1929, 93) says the bird breeds at Okkak and Rigolet, and records seven Labrador sets of eggs taken from June 1 to July 16. Perrett describes a nest he found late in June at Makkovik. It contained four partly incubated eggs, and was composed of "small dry twigs, moss and leaves gathered together with a depression in the centre, six feet from high water mark." Another set of eggs is labelled "Makkovik Bay, on the beach just above high water mark, incubation fresh, June 21, 1899." I encountered a pair of Spotted Sandpipers on Egg Island, in Sandwich Bay, July 16, 1928, that were obviously nesting there in the grass. They were extremely worried by my presence, and one of them feigned a broken wing all the time I was on the islet. However, I was limited to an hour there, and the nests of a pair of Great Black-backed Gulls, several Eider Ducks, and Black Guillemots took most of my time, and I was unable, in the ten minutes I devoted to the search, to discover either nest or young of the Sandpiper.

The period of incubation in this species is about fifteen days, and most of the incubation is done by the male. There are no data as to how long the young remain in their parents' care, but they are exceedingly precocial, and probably the third week after hatching finds them well able to care for themselves.

At Battle Island on July 13, 1906, Townsend and Allen (1907, 353) "watched the manoeuvers of a pair of these birds in their efforts to drive a couple of Eskimo dogs away from the vicinity of their young which were probably hidden in the grass. The birds alternately attacked the dogs and then allowed themselves to be chased by them. In the first instance the birds flew furiously at the dogs, almost striking them and whistling loudly. In the second instance, the birds flew away slowly close to the ground so that the dogs were tempted to chase them. The incident illustrated the dangers of Eskimo dogs as destroyers of eggs and young birds."

One never sees family groups of Spotted Sandpipers in the late summer and autumn, as of other Sandpipers and Plovers. The species never flocks, and probably the young go off by themselves, and find their own way south as soon as they are able to take care of themselves.

It has a widely variegated diet, and is known to eat many species of insects, as well as small minnows and other aquatic food.

Tringa solitaria solitaria Wilson

EASTERN SOLITARY SANDPIPER

This species, endemic to North America, has been divided into two races—a far-western one, *T. s. cinnamomea*, which supposedly breeds in Alaska and British Columbia, and *T. s. solitaria*, which has been reported as nesting in Alberta, Iowa, Ohio, Pennsylvania, New Hampshire, Maine, Quebec, and Labrador. The eastern form migrates throughout the United States east of the Rockies, and winters from the Gulf States to northern South America.

The Solitary Sandpiper is an uncommon summer resident in Labrador. I have never met this bird in the region, and there are very few references to it in literature. Low (1896, 324) says: "Common throughout the interior, especially south of Latitude 54°. Breeds. Seen May 27, eggs June 19." It is possible that Low was mistaken in his identification, for the eggs of the species and its nesting habits were practically unknown until 1903. The bird prefers wooded regions, and stays pretty well in the interior, coming to the heads of the bays only occasionally. Wheeler killed one at the head of Okkak Bay, August 29, 1931.

It is now a well-established fact that this species lays its eggs in the deserted nests of passerine birds. Perrett had an authentic set of the eggs taken by H. J. Webb at Udjuktok Bay, at the end of June, 1911; the eggs were four in number, in an old bird's nest in a dead tree overhanging a pond; the parent was shot for identification, which was verified by A. C. Bent (field notes) who saw it. Perrett told me of watching one at the head of Makkovik Bay in June, 1900, which kept flying around when flushed, and showed other signs of having eggs in the vicinity, but he was unsuccessful in his attempt to find them. He also records the bird from the head of Kaipokok Bay, and from near Nain.

The Solitary Sandpiper feeds about stagnant pools, the banks of still streams, and the shores of inland lakes. Its diet is mostly animal, and runs the gamut of land and aquatic insects and other small invertebrates.

Totanus melanoleucus (Gmelin)

GREATER YELLOW-LEGS

Local vernacular: 'Nansary,' 'Aunt Sary.'
Eskimo: 'Niuluk'—the long-legged one; or 'Kanaigi'—the one with legs like tent-poles.
Indian: 'She she shué' (Strong and Keats); 'Nijwa' (Cabot, 1920, preface, p. vi.)

The Greater Yellow-legs breeds across northern North America at the edge of the barren grounds from Alaska to Labrador, and south to British Columbia, Anticosti, and Newfoundland. It migrates southward throughout the United States, and winters even to the southern tip of South America. Non-breeding individuals are to be found in the American tropics and subtropics during almost every month of the year.

It is a not uncommon summer resident in Labrador, keeping to the wet tundra and the interior during the breeding season, and appearing on the coast toward the end of July and the first of August. It wades about in the shallow, muddy pools in the tundra, and along the smaller water-courses, but comes out to suitable places along the coast to feed on the mud-flats at low tide. Cartwright shot one near Cape Charles, October 19, 1770. Coues (1861, 234) says: "This large tatler . . . is a very common bird along the coast of Labrador during the summer and early fall. During the fore part of the summer I found them very wary and difficult of approach . . . By the middle of August, however, they seemed to have laid aside their watchfulness, and numbers were procured without difficulty." Low (1896, 324) says: "Met with occasionally throughout the interior. Breeds. Seen May 31st." Bigelow (1902, 29) found it "uncommon; a few late in September at Port Manvers." Townsend and Allen (1907, 351) "heard the note of one of these birds at Battle Island on August 2d [1906]." Hantzsch (1928, 226) did not see any Yellow-legs at all on the northern part of the coast. Cooke (1916, 155) notes that "the first were seen at Battle Harbor May 14, 1913, and at Sandwich Bay June 4, 1915 . . . Several were noted September 15, 1912, at Chateau Bay and the last were seen October 12, 1912, at Ticoralak." Perrett saw the last one at Makkovik, October 15, 1898. Wheeler entered in his diary that a Greater Yellow-legs was attracted to his camp-fire after dark August 22, 1928, at Angutausugevik. He heard a single bird in Nain Bay, September 19, 1928, and saw another at the head of Okkak Bay, August 21, 1931.

I observed three adults in a tundra pool near Holton Harbor, July 18, 1928, and my notes show that individuals were seen fairly frequently from July 30 on through August and the first part of September. My latest record is September 15, 1927, when I whistled a bird at Squasho Run.

There are no definite breeding records for Newfoundland Labrador; that is to say, neither nest, eggs, nor young have ever been taken or recorded. Yet there is hardly any doubt that the species does breed here. Anderson told Bent (field notes) that the bird bred around marshy ponds inland, but did not say that he had found the nests. The species is known to breed in Newfoundland, and Bent (1927, 323) gives an excellent account of its breeding habits there. The nest is a shallow depression in the tundra, in which four eggs are laid. The female flushes very wide, so that the nests are extremely difficult to locate. The eggs are laid from June 9 to 20, but there are no data as to which sex incubates, nor is the period of incubation known.

I have never seen this bird feeding on the berries of *Empetrum nigrum*, as Turner records (1888), but have always seen it at the water's edge, where it seemed to be taking small minnows and insects.

Totanus flavipes (Gmelin)

LESSER YELLOW-LEGS

There are five specimens in the U. S. National Museum that Coues collected at Henley Harbor in 1860—three females taken August 19, 21, and 24, and two, unsexed, August 25 and 29. Strangely enough, Coues made no mention of the species in his 'Notes on the Ornithology of Labrador,' and hence his specimens have been overlooked. The only published record for Newfoundland Labrador is that of Low, who says (1896, 324), "Seen only after August 1st, on Hamilton River." The bird must be regarded in Labrador, from these data, as of only casual occurrence.

Calidris canutus rufus (Wilson)

AMERICAN KNOT

The Knot is a cosmopolitan species, breeding in the extreme high north, and migrating in winter to the southern hemisphere. It is divided into two recognizable races, *canutus* breeding in the eastern hemisphere, and *rufus* in the western.

It is a rare transient visitor in Labrador. Coues (1861, 229) writes: "This large Sandpiper I met with for the first time at Henley Harbor, on the 21st of August [1860] ... A few specimens were procured, in immature plumage, showing but slight traces of reddish on the under parts." Hantzsch (1908, 351) calls it "apparently only a rare migrant ... My information from the natives makes it appear that this species seldom occurs to their knowledge." He saw a small flock at sea, July 22, off the coast of northern Labrador, and two birds July 24 and August 1 "on ice-cakes in Ungava Bay."

A native hunter brought me four Knots he had just shot at Indian Harbor, September 5, 1927. He told me they were the first he had ever seen, and was curious to know what they were. I was able to preserve two of them.

Arquatella maritima (Brünnich)

PURPLE SANDPIPER

Local vernacular: 'Big Beachy Bird.'
Eskimo: 'Tullik'—probably from the voice.

This is a non-plastic species nesting in the high north. It breeds in the American Arctic Archipelago from Melville Island eastward to Ellesmere and Baffin Islands, in Greenland, Iceland, Spitzbergen, the Faroes, and in northern Eurasia from Norway eastward to Novaya Zemlya and the Taimyr Peninsula. It winters farther north than any other shore-bird, its range in eastern North America at this season extending from Greenland south along the Atlantic coast to Long Island, New York.

The only records of Purple Sandpipers for Labrador are those of Hantzsch (1928, 222), who says: "Rather abundant visitor and migrant ... As long as a strip of coast remains only a little open, this strongly built bird remains in the country, and appears just as early in the spring again. Whether it occasionally spends the winter also, I could not ascertain, but this is in no way improbable ... During the whole time of my stay near Killinek, I kept under observation some small companies of the Purple Sandpiper." He lists five males and seven females collected at Killinek in September. Perrett informs me that the Purple Sandpiper is a common late autumn visitor to the region about Hopedale, remaining frequently until December. The bird finds Labrador, with its kelp- and barnacle-covered rocky shores, an ideal habitat.

Hantzsch (*ibid.*) says, "Apparently breeding only in slight numbers," but the record lacks verification. I saw no Purple Sandpipers when I visited the Chidley region in August, 1927.

Hantzsch (*ibid.*) found nine stomachs to contain "fragments of mussels and snail-shells (Balanidae ? H.) in great numbers, some a feltlike, threadlike mass (Algae ? R.), of mineral substances up to 0.34g. of sand and small pebbles." In migration the bird feeds only among the weeds and barnacles on the rocks exposed at low tide.

Pisobia melanotos (Vieillot)

PECTORAL SANDPIPER

Local vernacular: 'Beachy Bird' (*partim*).
Eskimo: 'Sidjariakpak'—the big beach-runner.

The Pectoral Sandpiper breeds in high latitudes from eastern Siberia (Kolyma Delta) eastward through Alaska to northeastern Mackenzie and northeastern Manitoba. It migrates southeastward to the Atlantic coast, and winters in South America.

It is an uncommon transient visitor in Labrador. It is seldom seen on the shores, but prefers the grassy meadows by the small inland pools in the coastal belt of tundra. Coues (1861, 230) says: "I first noticed the Pectoral Sandpiper at Henley Harbor, on the 20th of August, when it had commenced its southern migration. I there found it abundant, and had ample opportunities both of observing its habits and procuring specimens." Bent (1927, 181) quotes Turner's manuscript notes, "Observed in Labrador, Rigolet, June 24 to July 8, 1882, and Davis Inlet, July 18, 1883." Macoun (1900, 159) calls the bird "a common migrant along the whole Atlantic Coast from Cape Chidleigh [Chidley] south." Bigelow (1902, 28) says: "Very common all along the coast after the middle of August. Particularly abundant about the Hopedale Mission, where they were almost as tame as English Sparrows." If his identification of the species was correct, Bigelow must have struck a very unusual flight of these birds. Townsend and Allen (1907, 349) call it a "common autumnal transient visitor ... We obtained the skin of one from the Eskimos at Hopedale." Hantzsch (1928, 223) says: "According to report of the Eskimos, not a rare migrant on the coasts and in the interior ... I met only once a flock of six individuals myself, namely on 30th August [1906] near Killinek and killed them. On the same day little flocks were observed at other places and some specimens shot from them." Cooke

(1916, 165) notes that "those individuals that were still present at Ticoralak October 12, 1912, were remaining later than usual."

I saw Pectoral Sandpipers in Labrador only once. On September 14, 1927, I encountered a flock of four individuals, of which I collected one; they were feeding in the damp meadow by the small lake behind the settlement on Gready Island.

Hantzsch (1908, 353) found the contents of four stomachs to be "fine shreds of plants, apparently algae, in one a seed grain."

Pisobia fuscicollis (Vieillot)

WHITE-RUMPED SANDPIPER

Local vernacular: 'Beachy Bird' (*partim*).
Eskimo: 'Sidjariak'—the one that runs on the shore.

This species is entirely Nearctic in its distribution, and has no Palearctic representative. It breeds on the Arctic coasts of North America from Alaska and Mackenzie eastward to Baffin Island and western Greenland. It migrates down the Atlantic coast of North America and through the Mississippi valley, wintering in extreme southern South America to Tierra del Fuego.

The White-rumped Sandpiper is an abundant transient visitor in Labrador, especially during the late summer and early autumn, occurring in immense flocks on the outer coast wherever there are small areas of sand-beach, and feeding in the bays where low tide exposes mud and rocks bearing seaweeds and barnacles. There are no spring records for the district. Coues (1861, 232) says: "I met it for the first time on the 30th of July; but on the first of September, when I left the country, they were still as numerous as ever. They are found in great abundance on the rocky shores of Labrador." Norton (1901, 150) lists an adult male taken August 6, 1891, at Webeck Harbor by the Bowdoin Expedition. Bigelow (1902, 28) found the species "very abundant at Port Manvers after August 10 [1900]." Townsend and Allen (1907, 349) "saw two flocks of these birds of twenty or thirty each at Battle Harbor on August 1st and 2d [1906]. One of the flocks was waiting quietly for the fall of tide on the weed-grown ledges." Hantzsch (1928, 223) calls it the "most abundant sandpiper species on the coasts on the migration, rarer on edges of ponds in the interior; is said to occur much more rarely in spring than in the fall." He collected thirty-two specimens at Killinek between August 16 and September 29, 1906, from the age and sex of which he deduced that the first migrants from the north are old males, and that the females and young do not appear until considerably later. Cooke (1916, 165) notes that "single birds were seen at Battle Harbor to October 29, 1912, while in August they were abundant in flocks of hundreds."

The flocks begin to appear in Labrador on their way southward late in July. My earliest record is a flock of twenty-five birds at the Red Islands, July 22, 1928. I observed a flock of thirty at Puffin Island, July 26, 1926. July 30, 1926, there were several hundred White-rumps feeding in the tide-pools at Holton Harbor. My field notes for the month of August contain almost daily records for the species. I collected a male at Nachvak, August 10, 1927, a male and a female at the same place two days later, and two females at Joksut, August 23, 1927. There were several hundred on the south side of Indian Island (always a good place for shore-birds) September 5, 1927, and I saw at least two hundred at Table Bay, September 14, 1927. Most of the birds have passed through by the end of September, but scattered individuals linger on through October. Wheeler killed one near Nain, October 28, 1927. The latest record is of a bird observed by Hantzsch (*ibid.*) at Hopedale, November 2, 1906.

Hantzsch (*ibid.*) records that thirty-eight stomachs examined showed a preponderance of small crustaceans and small black snails, while also present were fragments of mussels, remains of beetles and other insects, and fragments of fishes (scales and muscles).

As this is the commonest shore-bird in Labrador, it naturally bears the brunt of the persecution by the natives, who like to pot-hunt the 'beachy birds' when they are gathered together in compact flocks, so that the discharge of a muzzle-loading shotgun will have its maximum effect. However, the numbers do not seem to have been materially affected, mainly, I suppose, because the shooting is very sporadic.

Pisobia minutilla (Vieillot)

LEAST SANDPIPER

Local vernacular: 'Beachy Bird' (*partim*).
Eskimo: 'Sullajok,' meaning the 'busy one' (*partim*).

The Least Sandpiper is entirely Nearctic in its breeding range, though it wanders casually in migration to eastern Siberia and western Europe. Its nesting grounds extend from Alaska eastward across the northern shores of the continent from Mackenzie to Ungava, and follow the Atlantic coast south from Labrador to Nova Scotia. It migrates on both coasts of North America and in the interior, and winters from the southern United States south to Brazil and Peru.

It is a common summer resident, breeding on islands both off the coast and in the bays. Low (1896, 324) says it is "common about Upper Hamilton River." Norton (1901, 150) lists two specimens in worn nuptial plumage taken by the Bowdoin Expedition in 1901, one of which, a female, was collected at Chateau Bay, July 14. Bigelow (1902, 28) found it "abundant. Breeds commonly all along the coast." Townsend and Allen (1907, 349) say, "At Battle Harbor, where no birds were found breeding, we saw the first migrant on July 26th, a single bird feeding on the edge of a little pool." Hantzsch (1928, 225) says of it, "Apparently not particularly common migrant in our district, which may be too rocky and barren for this bird, at least in its northern part." According to Cooke (1916, 165), "This species migrates so late that the first were not seen at Battle Harbor until June 1, 1913. Migrants returned to Battle Harbor August 7, 1912, and remained for about three weeks." The northernmost point at which I found the species was Bay of Seven Islands, where I observed two and collected an adult female August 24, 1927.

When the parental duties are finished, the Least Sandpipers join the large flocks of small migrating shore-birds on the beaches and in the tide-pools. I saw ten individuals with a large flock of White-rumps at Holton Harbor, July 30, 1926. On August 28, 1926, I observed eight at close range, feeding on a narrow stretch of shell beach at Puffin Island. There were a few with the other Sandpipers at Indian Harbor, September 5, 1914, and they were still present at Table Bay, September 14, the same year.

Bent (1927, 209) records it as breeding at Ramah, Okkak, and Nain. Perrett collected at Makkovik Bay a set of four eggs laid in a "nest of small twigs, moss and leaves, about 6 feet from high water mark." Wheeler found a nest containing four eggs, "rather dirty, faint green, heavily marked with deep chocolate brown at the larger end. The nest was in a low marsh in the centre of a small island southeast of Kanauktok [near Nain], June 19, 1928." Incubation is believed to be done largely by the male, though there are cases on record of females incubating, and still others where both sexes took some interest in the care of the young. The exact duration of the incubation period is unknown, but the young hatch during the second or third week in July, and are ready to fly south by the middle of August. I found a nest of this species on top of one of the Gannet Islands, July 14, 1926. The island, about one hundred and fifty feet high, is composed of rocky cliffs in which Puffins and Razor-billed Auks breed. The place selected by the Sandpiper for its nest was under a tuft of overhanging sedge that had gained a foothold in the sparse soil on the flat top of the island. The nest contained four eggs, which seemed from crude candling in the field to be in an advanced stage of incubation. On July 26, 1926, I found a parent with a brood of four young on Puffin Island, near Indian Harbor. They were not over two days old, but were able to run about fairly actively. The old bird fluttered ahead of me, shamming a broken wing as usual, and though I stayed there photographing the young birds for fully ten minutes, the other parent did not put in an appearance. I encountered an adult attending four young, evidently just hatched, in an open, grassy meadow near a small lake on Gready Island, July 12, 1927. I had much difficulty finding the young, but the old bird told me where they were. I used it as a 'hot and cold' indicator as to their hiding-place. While I was in the vicinity, but not near the youngsters, the doting parent contented itself with flying in a large circle about my head, peeping loudly and continually. But when I approached within twenty feet or so of the spot where the brood was hidden, it came to earth immediately, and shammed a broken wing in front of me, running off in every direction, save toward the young. At times this pretended agony was horrible to behold. Its mate appeared after the first bird had entertained me for about ten minutes, and while the newcomer did little more than fly about, adding to the noise of the occasion, it once stooped to pretending it was crippled. The downy young are very deceptively colored, and twice I almost stepped on them before I saw them. The parent became quite tame after I had handled the young to band them, and ran up to within two feet of me when I held the chicks in my hand. After I had banded and photographed them, and had let them go, it did not wait for me to retreat, but immediately chuckled to the young, and took them under its breast to brood over them, though I stood not ten feet away.

Bent (1927, 205) says, "These birds appear to be feeding on small crustaceans and worms on the beaches and on insects and their larvae in the marshes." I have twice seen adult birds, while walking around the tundra within a few feet of me when I was handling the young, stop their worrying long enough to pick up, in one case a spider, and in the other an unidentifiable insect.

[Pelidna alpina sakhalina (Vieillot). RED-BACKED SANDPIPER. Weiz (1866) included it as a breeding bird from Okkak, but he was in error. Bigelow (1902, 28) records "a few at Port Manvers in early September." These are the only records for the district, and unfortunately neither is backed by a specimen.

This species, which breeds on the Arctic coasts and islands, roughly from the Boothia Peninsula westward to about the Taimyr region of Siberia, is divided into two generally recognized subspecies —alpina, breeding in northern Siberia and migrating down the Pacific, and sakhalina, breeding in North America and migrating southward on the Atlantic coast. This latter form is the one more likely to reach Labrador, for its migration route takes it along the western side of Hudson Bay.]

Limnodromus griseus griseus (Gmelin)

Eastern Dowitcher

The Dowitcher is an accidental visitor. Coues (1861, 229) "procured a single individual of this species in immature plumage on the 23rd of August" [, 1860, at Henley Harbor]. Turner (1885, 246) says, "Specimens obtained at Fort Chimo and Davis Inlet." Dr. Herbert Friedmann writes me from the National Museum as follows: "I have looked at the Dowitcher collected by Coues at Henley Harbor and have decided that it is straight *griseus*. It has an exposed culmen length of 54 mm. I can find no record or specimen of a Dowitcher from Davis Inlet collected by Turner; the only Turner bird I find is one taken at Fort Chimo, Ungava, June 10, 1883."

Ereunetes pusillus (Linn.)

Semipalmated Sandpiper

Local vernacular: 'Beachy Bird' (*partim*).
Eskimo: 'Sullajok'—meaning the busy one (*partim*).

This species breeds from northeastern Siberia eastward across northern North America, through Alaska, Mackenzie, and Ungava to Quebec, Labrador, and Newfoundland. It migrates southward down the Mississippi Valley and the Atlantic coast to southern South America, but the northward migration in the spring comes mainly up the Mississippi Valley, according to Cooke (1910, 46), with comparatively fewer birds on the Atlantic seaboard.

The Semipalmated Sandpiper is a not uncommon summer resident, and a common transient visitor, in Labrador. Bigelow (1902, 28) calls it "common, breeding locally." Townsend and Allen (1907, 350) "saw only a few migrants on July 27th at Great Caribou Island [Battle Harbor]." Hantzsch (1928, 225) says: "Not rare migrant, and according to all appearances a breeding bird now and then in our district ... I secured three young birds myself, just moulted, all males, on 18th August, 7th September, and 10th September, in different localities on Ungava Bay and on the Atlantic coast ... All three times I met three birds together, and suspect that they were siblings, which at least in the first case had been hatched at no very great distance. That the old birds desert the young which have become independent, and fly away ahead of them, one notes indeed in different species of sandpipers." In 1912 Bent (field notes) saw Semipalmated Sandpipers only at St. Peter's Bay (near Henley Harbor) on July 7, 1912, and at Hopedale on August 20, 1912, and he adds, "It is evidently not common anywhere."

I found this species to occupy the same sort of territory as does the Least Sandpiper. It nests in the swampy tundra, but after the breeding season frequents the mud-flats, tide-pools, and infrequent sand-beaches with other small Limicolae. There are no spring dates in literature, the earliest being Perrett's egg date from Ramah,—June 25, 1895,—but the species probably arrives early in June, and in the spring probably only the birds that intend to breed in Labrador touch the coast. However, migrant birds swing in from the westward usually about the third week in August, before starting down the Atlantic coast in the fall. My records show them at Turnavik, August 26, 1926, and in the Hamilton Inlet region August 28, 1926, and September 5, 1927. My latest date is September 14, 1927, at Table Bay, where several good-sized flocks were feeding.

Perrett collected a nest with four eggs June 25, 1895, at Ramah "in a swampy place, made of grass, and under overhanging grass." The period of incubation has been established by Dixon as seventeen days, and this office is shared by both parents. Bigelow found the downy young at Seal Island between July 17 and 19, 1900, which were the dates during which the Brown-Harvard expedition was weather-bound there.

Hantzsch found that the stomachs of the young birds he took contained small black snails. The diet of the species is reported by most authors to consist mostly of animal matter, including small molluscs, crustacea, and worms.

Tryngites subruficollis (Vieillot)

BUFF-BREASTED SANDPIPER

This bird is but a casual visitor to Labrador. Hantzsch (1928, 226) sums up the evidence of the occurrence of this species within our territorial limits so excellently that I feel I can do no better than to quote Anderson's translation of his statement: "Robert Bell claims to have secured this species in one specimen on 28th September, 1884, at Killinek (Port Burwell), and Townsend and Allen acknowledge this occurrence as correct (p. 360 [352]), apparently according to information about it from J. Macoun, and also the record of Coues, that on 20th August, 1860, a specimen was collected at Henley Harbor (1907, p. 352). The identity of the Bell skin does not seem to be quite without objection, since unfortunately in the same work there are also mistakes in identification in the case of the alleged occurrence of *Puffinus tenuirostris*, *Olor buccinator*, and *Heteractitis incanus*, as Townsend and Allen explain (*l. c.*). The species is more western American, and in the northeast of the continent is not known with certainty farther than up to Repulse Bay (Cat. Birds Brit. Mus., 24, 1896, p. 624). After all, an occasional occurrence in the district of these agile-winged birds, which have so often been collected in England, is not very wonderful."

Crocethia alba (Pallas)

SANDERLING

Local vernacular: 'Beachy Bird' (*partim*).

This is an almost cosmopolitan species, breeding circumpolarly, but only in the very high north, and migrating southward in both hemispheres to southern South America, Africa, and Australia.

The Sanderling is an uncommon transient visitor in Labrador, occurring regularly, though sparsely. Bigelow (1902, 28) found it "rather rare." While Townsend and Allen (1907, 350) failed to see any on the coast, they call it a "common transient visitor." Hantzsch (1928, 226) says: "Rather rare migrant in our district, entirely unknown to the natives in spite of its characteristic colouring and lack of shyness. I met only one single adult female, on 19th August [1906], on the rocky shore in northeast of Ungava Bay and killed it." Perrett records killing one at Killinek in 1906. I saw two at the Red Islands, August 2, 1926; four at Puffin Island, August 26, 1926; a single bird at Indian Island, September 5, 1927; and a flock of twenty-five at Battle Harbor, September 24, 1927, during a violent northeaster that kept us weather-bound there. The last record is quite unusual, not only for the lateness of the date, but also for the size of the flock, for although, when the species arrives on the hard sand-beaches of New England, it travels in considerable companies, in Labrador one is fortunate to pick out a single pair or so feeding among a big flock of other Sandpipers. One of the reasons for the Sanderling's apparent rarity in Labrador is doubtlessly the absence of the hard sand-beaches to which it is partial.

Hantzsch (*loc. cit.*) found the remains of small crustaceans in the stomach of one he examined.

Phalaropus fulicarius (Linn.)

RED PHALAROPE

Local vernacular: 'Gale Bird' (*partim*).
Eskimo: 'Sargak.'

The Red Phalarope breeds circumpolarly in the northern hemisphere, seldom nesting south of the Arctic Circle, and winters pelagically off the coast of Chile, south of India, and probably off the west coast of Africa.

It is an uncommon transient visitor along the coast and a rare summer resident in the north. Coues (1861, 228) shot three "at sea, off Belle-Isle, from a flock of six." Turner (1886, 248) regarded it as "abundant on the Labrador coast north of Davis Inlet." Bigelow (1902, 28) found it "rather rare. Seen several times in small flocks offshore." Townsend and Allen (1907, 346) "saw three on July 20th off Long Tickle. We also obtained the skin of a fine bird in full adult plumage at Hopedale from the Eskimos." Hantzsch (1928, 221) says that in the north it is a "rather frequent migrant, especially in the springtime, according to the statements of the inhabitants. I observed different individuals only at the end of July, and the beginning of August, on open places between the ice-cakes; later I did not see any ... In our region the birds would not settle down in large numbers on account of the steep, rocky coasts." He mentions a skin of an adult female in his collection, taken at Ramah in June, 1902. There is a specimen in the Field Museum taken at Hopedale in October, 1897. I observed a single adult female, July 13, 1928, at sea among the outer islands just north of Petty Harbor.

As to whether or not this species breeds within Newfoundland Labrador, there is still much doubt, for the nests and eggs have never been positively recorded. Eifrig (1905, 238) reports eggs collected June 2, 1904, at Southampton, which is the nearest definite record. Hantzsch found no positive evidence of its breeding, but says (*ibid.*), "The fact of their breeding now and then may be accepted with certainty." According to Bent's notes, he was assured by Anderson that it "breeds on little ponds on islands. Two sets of eggs in Perrett's collection were taken in June near Nain." I find no mention of the species in Perrett's notes. I have been told by several natives that the species breeds on the coast, but have never seen any positive evidence of the fact.

Lobipes lobatus (Linn.)

NORTHERN PHALAROPE

Local vernacular: 'Gale Bird' (*partim*).
Eskimo: 'Sargak' (*partim*).
Indian: 'Ah kume i shish.'

This is another species circumpolar in its breeding, but it nests farther south than does the Red Phalarope. It is almost cosmopolitan and winters pelagically in the tropical seas.

It is a common summer resident in the barren coastal area from Port Manvers to Battle Harbor, and a common transient off shore. Low (1896, 324) says: "Seen on Upper Hamilton River, June 13th. Not common." Turner (1886, 248) calls it "common on northern portions of the Labrador coast." Bigelow (1902, 128) found it "common. Breeding in almost all the suitable marshes; occasionally very abundant offshore." On the northern part of the coast, according to Hantzsch (1928, 221), it is "a not very abundant migrant, rarer than *Crymophilus* [*Phalaropus*]; according to report of the natives almost always observed only in spring. I merely saw a single individual once myself on 22nd July rather far from the coast. Our district seems to be too rocky for this bird. Yet it is said to resort to localities suitable for breeding here and there, namely, freshwater lakes surrounded by grass and on flat islands by the shore, in small numbers or in isolated pairs." He lists a pair of adults in breeding plumage in his collection taken at Ramah, July 1, 1907. There is an adult female in the Museum of Comparative Zoölogy taken at Loup Bay, May 26, 1899. Wheeler saw one on one of the outer islands near Nain, June 1, 1931.

I have observed Northern Phalaropes at Indian Harbor (where a pair seemed to be breeding, July 19, 1927), at Holton Harbor, at Turnavik Bay, and near Nain. I saw three at sea off Hamilton Inlet, August 29, 1926, and four off Cape Harrison, September 4, 1927, which is my latest record for the species.

It seems (*mirabile dictu*) that in finding an adult male tending three young just hatched at the Red Islands, July 21, 1928, I have proved for the first time that the Northern Phalarope breeds on the northeast coast of Labrador! There are no other definite records of either nests, eggs, or young being taken. Townsend and Allen (1907, 346) say: "The Northern Phalarope breeds along the entire Labrador coast in freshwater marshes on the borders of ponds and lakes ... We had an interesting experience with this species at Great Caribou Island, on July 27th. At the small freshwater pools only a few yards in extent, partly grown up with sphagnum and sedges we saw four of these birds and shot two, both males. It was evident from their actions that young were concealed in the sedges." Bigelow (*ibid.*) was certain they bred there, though he never found any nests, and there never has been any doubt in the mind of any ornithologist who has visited Labrador that this species breeds there. Yet Cooke (1910, 16-18) refused to credit Townsend and Allen's and Bigelow's observations at all, and when he was brought to task for it by F. H. Allen ('Auk,' 1911, 517-518), H. W. Henshaw came to his support ('Auk,' 1912, 129). Cooke's argument was solely that no definite proof of the species' nesting there had been offered to support the statement, and in a very strict scientific sense he was right. But whether eggs or young are found or not, when adult birds show great excitement and forget to be afraid of man, flying around close to one's head, scolding and twittering, and pretending to be crippled when one approaches a certain spot, one may be very certain that there are either young or a nest close by. Dr. Townsend visited Caribou Island in 1928, and had the same experience with Phalaropes that he had there in 1906, (1929, 108, 109). Though he still had no nest, eggs, nor young to prove it, this further strengthened his view that the Phalarope bred as far south as Battle Harbor.

I have no hesitation whatsoever in stating that the bird breeds between Battle Harbor and Port Manvers, though I have found it myself only on the north side of Hamilton Inlet and have seen 'positive breeding evidence' in only one case. I have twice visited a tundra area near Holton Harbor, July 30, 1926, and July 18, 1928, and on both occasions I found several pairs of Phalaropes showing unmistakable signs of having nests or young in the vicinity. A male and female adult twittered all around my head for half an hour at Black Island in Turnavik Bay while I fruitlessly searched for their young August 3, 1926, and the act was duplicated by another pair at Pigeon Island in Indian Harbor, July 19, 1927. Two females and three males I collected at Holton Harbor, July 18, 1928, showed their sex organs well developed.

My finding the young on one of the Red Islands on July 21, 1928, was very largely a matter of luck. The island is a small one, and the grass plot at its summit is hardly more than fifty yards across, which is not a large area to search thoroughly. At that I spent a fruitless hour of searching while the male scolded me and flitted nervously back and forth around me. I finally departed for half an hour, and, on approaching the place again, kept careful watch to see the exact spot where the adult flushed, intending to start searching there. I was fortunate enough to see him the moment he jumped up, about one hundred and fifty yards away from me, and on going to the exact tuft from which he sprang, I found the three young birds. They were evidently just hatched, from their size and weakness. I never found the deserted nest, though I searched for it diligently. I did not disturb the young, but returned the next day with bands and cameras. By repeating my ruse of the previous day, I shortly found them again, but this time there were only two left. Some enemy, probably a Black-backed Gull (a pair of which had a nest on the next island), had made off with the third one. After I had banded and photographed them, the male bird almost overcame his fear of us entirely. I had placed the two young birds in the crown of my hat, for safe keeping while I opened bands, and set it down about five feet from me. The youngsters started peeping, and the male ran up to the spot at once. Not being able to see into the hat, he seemed very puzzled, and ran madly round and round it probably twenty times. As I held the young in my hands to band them, he became almost delirious with anxiety and, constantly uttering his *peet-weet*, came closer and closer to me. At last he walked within six inches of my hand, so I picked him up and banded him, too. Then, putting the youngsters down and releasing the parent, I watched developments. He immediately led them both to a little pool twenty feet away. Without any hesitation they followed him, and tumbled off the tundra into the water and swam across the pool in his wake. The sides of the pool, however, were about a foot high, and there was no place where they could get out without help. The distressed parent urged them fretfully all round the rim of the pool in an unsuccessful attempt to find a place where they could climb out. They followed him energetically, jerking their downy heads in true Phalarope fashion, backing water, turning about, and manoeuvering as well as their parent. I watched them for about ten minutes, and photographed them in the water. It occurred to me that this was probably their initial introduction to water, as there was only this one pool on the island, and had they been in it before, they must certainly have stayed in it. I reached down and lifted them up onto the tundra. The old bird could hardly wait for me to put them down. The moment I did so, without waiting for me to retreat a step, he clucked to them and took them under his breast feathers to brood and warm them. It was a raw, cold, foggy day, and probably chicks only a few days old chill easily. Though I spent in all about three hours on the island in company with the male and the young, the female never put in an appearance, which is the only time that has happened to me. Whenever, elsewhere, I have found the birds obviously breeding, both parents eventually appeared, though the male was usually the first on the scene, and was always the more excited. The incubation period is supposedly about twenty-one days, and the eggs are laid anywhere from late in May to early in July. There are no egg dates for Labrador. The nest is usually on the ground at the edge of or near a small tundra pond, it is well concealed in the vegetation, and is lined with either grasses or dead leaves. Four eggs constitute the usual clutch. I saw immature birds at sea off Hamilton Inlet, August 29, 1926.

During the breeding period, while the birds are on land, the diet consists of fresh-water and land insects, grubs, etc. Townsend watched one eat several large beetles and a worm (1929, 108). Five stomachs I examined contained remains of spiders and insects, such as beetles and flies, and a small percentage of vegetable matter resembling filamentous blue-green algae. While at sea during the rest of the year, their food consists mainly of surface plankton forms of various sorts.

Stercorarius pomarinus (Temminck)

POMARINE JAEGER

Local vernacular: 'Bo's'n.'
Eskimo: 'Issungak'—the dull one, on account of its color (*partim*).

The Pomarine Jaeger breeds circumpolarly in high northern latitudes, the nearest regions to Labrador being Baffin Island and Greenland. It migrates southward in both the Atlantic and the Pacific Oceans, to winter in the northern parts of the southern hemisphere. A few straggling records from the interior of North America seem to indicate an occasionally attempted migration southward from Hudson Bay. It is a non-plastic, well defined species, and though a separate race has been described from Siberia, it has not been shown to be valid.

It is a common summer visitor. Coues (1861, 243) says, "But very few individuals of this species were observed." Kumlien (1879, 94) says "from Belle Isle to Hudson's Straits they were abundant." Townsend and Allen (1907, 310) say, "The first birds seen on our trip were off Cape Harrison on July 19, 1906, and after that we noted them almost daily until our return south to Battle Harbor at the end of July." According to Hantzsch (1928, 93), it is "not a rare visitor" in the northern section of the coast. He saw several, but collected none. He lists a specimen, however, taken at Okkak in the autumn of 1905. Townsend and Allen (*l. c.*) and Hantzsch (*ibid.*) suggest that it probably breeds in the northern part, but there are no grounds for this assumption. It is possible that the bird may breed on the Button Islands, but it assuredly does not breed anywhere else along the coast.

I observed four individuals in the Straits of Belle Isle off Red Bay, July 7, 1927; my notes contain many records for the species in July and August all along the coast; my northernmost record is of three in Gray Strait, August 20, 1927, my latest date September 14 (1926). On that day I saw thirty (of which I collected one) following a fishing-schooner which was 'dressing down' off Domino. The Pomarine Jaeger is seldom seen close to shore, though I have observed it following fishing-schooners, Kittiwakes, and Arctic Terns, well within the outer islands. It is commonest just outside the outer islands, where it levies toll upon the huge flocks of Kittiwakes. When the Kittiwakes are driven nearer shore by inclement weather, or follow their food in, the Jaegers follow along with them.

I have frequently watched the Pomarine Jaegers chasing Kittiwakes and Arctic Terns, pursuing individual birds until their victims dropped their food. I have also watched them pick up offal for themselves, and on two occasions have noted flocks of thirty or forty wheeling astern of fishing-schooners that were 'dressing down,' and feeding on the refuse cast overboard.

Stercorarius parasiticus (Linn.)

PARASITIC JAEGER

Local vernacular: 'Bo's'n.'
Eskimo: 'Issungak' (*partim*).

The Parasitic Jaeger breeds circumpolarly in high northern latitudes, as far south in eastern North America as extreme northern Labrador. It migrates southward in winter along both coasts of North America, and occasionally straggles through the interior. It also goes southward along both coasts of Eurasia, and winters generally in the equatorial regions. It is reported commonly in winter as far south as Argentina and Chile, and has been recorded from the Straits of Magellan and the Cape of Good Hope. It travels northward in spring over much the same routes.

This Jaeger is a common late summer visitor along the entire length of the coast, especially during August, and a rare summer resident in the northern part. Coues (1861, 243) "saw but a single individual of this species." Bigelow (1902, 26) says, regarding this species and the succeeding: "These two jaegers were rather common, usually two or three following each flock of Kittiwakes. They went together indiscriminately, and their habits seemed to be identical." Hantzsch (1928, 93) collected two adults at Killinek, and calls it "the most abundant of the jaegers during the period of my observation." I saw one Parasitic Jaeger, August 6, 1927, off Saglek Bay; another the same year, August 16, off Joksut; and four, September 3, chasing the Arctic Terns in the neighborhood of the Red Islands. The latest date I have for the species is September 4, 1926, at which time I saw several just south of Domino Run.

Hantzsch mentions seeing in Perrett's collection eggs that had been taken on the Metik Islands just north of Aulatsivik. Bent (field notes) saw these same eggs in 1912, and adds that the nests were "on the ground among the Eider Ducks' nests."

The Parasitic Jaeger feeds much as does the Pomarine, preying upon the large flocks of Kittiwakes among the outer islands. Literature is replete with records of the bird's catching fish for itself, and there are mentions made of its eating dead fish and other floating offal. Hantzsch examined the stomachs of two individuals he collected at Killinek, and found one to contain "fish remains, a mollusc tongue, and cephalopod remains; the other was empty." The one bird I collected was following a fishing-schooner that was dressing down, and had its stomach filled with cod offal.

Stercorarius longicaudus Vieillot

LONG-TAILED JAEGER

Like the two other Jaegers, this is a circumpolar species breeding in the high north. It nests along the Arctic coasts of both hemispheres,—in the Nearctic from Alaska to Franklin Bay, on Ellesmere and Baffin Islands, and in northern Greenland. It winters southward in both oceans to the latitude of the Mediteranean regions.

In Newfoundland Labrador it is an uncommon transient visitor. Bigelow (1902, 26) calls it "rather common." Hantzsch (1928, 94) saw a Long-tailed Jaeger in the possession of an Eskimo woman at Killinek. The Rawson-Mac-Millan Expedition collected a male at Nachvak in August, 1926. I collected a male off Domino from a mixed flock of all three species of Jaegers. I saw three small Jaegers with long tails off Cape Porcupine, September 11, 1927, but I could not be sure the birds were not of the preceding species, and I could not get close enough to shoot them.

Eifrig (1905, 235) says, "To this species probably belong two Jaeger eggs obtained at Cape Chidley on the outward trip, September, 1903, from Eskimos." On this hazy and indefinite evidence alone has rested the status of the Long-tailed Jaeger as a breeding bird in the district.

Its feeding habits are identical with those of the preceding species.

[Catharacta skua Brünnich. NORTHERN SKUA. There are no definite records of the occurrence of this species within the limits of the district, and if it occurs at all, it is as a highly accidental visitor. Turner (1885, 252) states that "a single individual was seen near the vessel, sitting in the water off the north side of the Strait of Belle Isle, June 22, 1882." Low (1906, 315) mentions having seen the bird in the eastern part of Hudson Strait. It breeds in Greenland and Iceland, wintering to the southward in the North Atlantic, wandering occasionally as far westward as the Grand Banks of Newfoundland, and there is no reason why occasional stray individuals should not wander as far west as Labrador.]

Larus hyperboreus Gunnerus

GLAUCOUS GULL

Local vernacular: 'Burgomaster,' 'Ice Gull.'
Eskimo: 'Naujavik'—the big gull.
Indian: 'Ti násk' (*partim*).

The Glaucous Gull breeds circumpolarly, largely north of the Arctic Circle, but nests as far south in North America as Hudson Bay and Labrador. It winters southward in both oceans to Japan, California, the British Isles, and New England.

It is a common summer resident. Coues (1861, 243) says, "I saw but few 'Burgomasters' that I could positively identify, on the coast of Labrador, where they appear to be rather rare." He was informed by a native that there was a colony of them on the Herring Islands, but was unable to verify the report. Low (1896, 323) found it "common throughout the interior; seen May 19th." Bigelow (1902, 26) "found Burgomasters common north of Cape Harrison, though they seldom gathered in large flocks. At Port Manvers they were particularly abundant." Townsend and Allen (1907, 313) "first met with the Glaucous Gull several miles up St. Lewis Inlet on July 12th. ... On our way north from this point we saw a dozen or more of these birds, and the same number on the return trip." In extreme northern Labrador, Hantzsch (1928, 124) says, "this stately bird is a frequent visitor, but a rather rare breeding bird."

I found that the Glaucous Gull seemed to have its centre of abundance between Hamilton Inlet and Nachvak. It is never so common as either the Herring Gull or the Great Black-back. Perrett notes its spring arrival at Rigolet, April 14, 1899. Wheeler saw the first in Tikkoatokok Bay, May 9, 1928. A single bird was swimming about in the water on top of the ice. He also noted several "hanging about the sand-bars of the fresh-water estuary at the heads of Tikkoatokok, October 26, 1927." Perrett killed four at Ailik, November 14, 1899. Wheeler observed them still present in the Nain region, December 5, 1930.

I have always found the Glaucous Gull breeding on ledges, usually in inaccessible cliffs, both on the outside islands and, less commonly, in the bays. They evidently nest occasionally farther inland, for Low (*l. c.*) found eggs June 14, presumably on the Upper Hamilton, and Dr. Duncan Strong writes me: "We saw two nests with young at opposite ends of a lake twenty miles up Hunt's River. They were also seen, apparently breeding, on lakes some twenty miles west of here." The Neptune Expedition (Low, 1906, 315) obtained eggs at Cape

Chidley. I have observed scattered colonies from Hopedale north to Bay of Seven Islands. Between Saglek Bay and Nachvak I saw many nests on inaccessible ledges in the overhanging cliffs. Frequently I could make out downy young with my binoculars. At Perkalujak Island in Nain Bay there were at least twenty pairs mixed in with the Herring Gulls. In fact it is but rarely that pure colonies of Glaucous Gulls are found. Bent (1921, 53) writes: "On August 2 [1912] we visited a breeding colony of 30 or 40 pairs of glaucous gulls on a rocky islet near Nain. It was a precipitous crag, rising abruptly from the sea to a height of 100 or 150 feet, unapproachable in rough weather, and an invulnerable castle except at one point, where we could land on a rock and climb up a steep grassy slope [this is a very accurate description of Perkalujak]. ... The upper part of the rock was occupied by the gulls, where their nests were mostly on inaccessible ledges. Near the top of the rock, which was flat and covered with grass, we found quite a number of nests that we could reach but all of these were empty. Below us we could see nests containing young of various ages and one nest still held two eggs. Some of the young were nearly ready to fly and probably some had already flown. The nests were made of soft grasses and mosses, and were not very elaborate or very bulky for such large gulls; probably they had been somewhat trampled down by the young."

Wheeler found the Glaucous Gulls starting to lay at Kikkertaksoak, June 5, 1928, and found that most of them had laid but one egg by June 8. The incubation period is supposed to be about four weeks, and it is believed that both sexes incubate. I found the young in various stages of development in late July, mostly in downy plumage, though I found one set of three young almost ready to fly at Step Hill Gull Cliff in Anaktalak Bay, August 1, 1928. By the middle of August most of the young are on the wing, and I have watched many fly from the nesting ledges during the second and third weeks of that month.

Two stomachs examined by Hantzsch (*ibid.*) contained remains of crustaceans and fish and the entrails of a small bird. I have constantly observed these birds picking at the fish entrails cast up on the beach from the fishing-stages. On the nesting ledges I have found, as indicators of the diet of the nestlings, only fish remains, mostly caplin and lance.

There is a cliff on the southwest islet of the Kidlet group on which a number of Glaucous Gulls breed. I banded seven there August 10, 1928. One of these, about three weeks old and just able to fly when I banded it, was retaken by N. Flynn at Conch, White Bay, Newfoundland, May 16, 1929.

It is shot for food by the natives whenever possible. The eggs and the young are considered delicacies.

Larus leucopterus Vieillot

Iceland Gull

This bird breeds in Franz Joseph Land, Jan Mayen Land, and Greenland, and winters southward on both coasts of the Atlantic to Great Britain and New England. A few winter in southern Greenland.

The Iceland Gull may be classed as a winter visitor. Because no one of sufficient ability to distinguish this bird from the larger, but similarly colored Glaucous Gull has ever been on the Labrador coast in the season when the bird should occur, there is but a single record for the district. Townsend and Allen (1907, 314) say: "We found on Great Caribou Island the wing feathers of a white gull, the measurements of which correspond closely to those of the Iceland Gull. The bird had evidently been killed during the previous winter (1905-6)." The nearest other records are of a bird taken May 1 at Godbout on the St. Lawrence River, and Hantzsch's records (1928, 146) of seeing the bird in Hudson Strait and Ungava Bay during the late summer. There can be but little doubt that the species does visit the coast regularly during the autumn, winter, and spring, in spite of the dearth of records.

[Larus kumlieni Brewster. KUMLIEN'S GULL. There is not a single record within the confines of Newfoundland Labrador for this interesting form, supposed by some to be a hybrid between *Larus argentatus thayeri* and *Larus leucopterus*. Inasmuch as it is supposed to breed in Baffin Island on the shores of Baffin Bay, it is not unlikely that individuals showing the characters that have given rise to the above name will eventually be found here in migration.]

Larus marinus Linn.

Great Black-backed Gull

Local vernacular: 'Saddle-back,' 'Saddler.'
Eskimo: 'Koleelik,' refers to the mark across the back.
Indian: 'Ti násk' (*partim*).

This well-marked species, the only close relatives of which are the Slaty-backed Gull (*L. schistisagus*) of the Pacific and *L. dominicanus* of the southern oceans, breeds over the coasts of the North Atlantic, from Massachusetts to northern Labrador, western Greenland, Iceland, the British Isles, Scandinavia, and northern Russia east to the Petchora River. It does not seem to breed on the east coast of Greenland, nor in the American Arctic Archipelago. It comes south in winter commonly to New England and northern Europe, and casually to Florida, the Mediterranean, and northern Africa.

It is a common summer resident along the coast as far north as Nachvak, and an uncommon summer visitor from there to Chidley. Coues, Bigelow, Bent, and Townsend and Allen, all regard it as common and breeding along the lower part of the coast. Hantzsch (1928, 146), however, found it at Killinek "only a rather rare visitor." He saw three immature birds in Gray Strait near Cape Chidley. My field notes contain almost daily references to the species north as far as Nachvak, where between August 8 and 13, 1927, I observed eighteen birds, both old and young. North of that I saw none. Cooke (1916, 163) records its arrival at Rigolet, April 9, 1915. Perrett observed seven there April 14, 1899, and saw the first ones outside Makkovik, April 30. Wheeler saw the last Great Black-backs of the season in the Nain region on October 28, 1927, but found them there as late as December 5, 1930. Cooke (l. c.) noted them as still present at Seal Islands, November 2, 1912.

The Great Black-backed Gull is not a colonial breeder, though throughout the lower two thirds of Labrador breeding pairs are thickly distributed, especially in districts where there are many small islets. I have found it nesting as frequently on large boulders in the fresh dead-waters at the heads of the bays fifty miles inland, as I have on the far outside islands, thirty miles or more off the coast proper, where every islet that is not entirely wave-washed has its pair of 'Saddlers.' Each pair shows a preference for having an island all to itself, so far as other members of its own species are concerned, though it very often breeds in proximity to the nests of other species of gulls and of other birds, such as Eider Ducks and the alcids. Perkalujak Island, for instance, boasts a large mixed colony of Herring and Glaucous Gulls along its ledged, cliffy sides, but a single pair of Great Black-backs occupies and defends against all intruders the flat top of the islet. Similarly there is usually the nest of a pair of 'Saddlers' in every alcidian rookery. When sailing along the island-dotted lower end of the coast from Battle Harbor to Sandwich Bay, one is almost never out of sight of one or two of these magnificent birds. As you draw near an island, the pair occupying it fly high at your approach, come out to meet you at a safe range, and, uttering all sorts of cries, accompany you until you are well past their home, deserting you only when the oversight is taken up by the pair from the next islet. The natives attach great importance to the fact that the Eider Ducks never nest except on an islet where there is a pair of these birds nesting. They claim the Eiders seek protection from the Raven, which the 'Saddle-back' will drive away. However, the Great Black-back nests on practically every suitable islet in the region, and its fondness for the eggs and downy young of other species suggests that the reverse may be true.

The nest itself is always a bulky hummock of grasses. I found one nest just two feet above high water, on a little glacial boulder lying in a sheltered corner of Pardee Island in Nain Bay. I rowed past this nest on August 20, 1926, not twenty feet from it, noting only the bulky grass structure perched on the rock. I decided casually to investigate it in the hope of finding the remains of food near it. It was not until I actually clambered out of the skiff on to the rock that I saw the two half-grown downy young, about ten days old, lying 'doggo' on top of the rock, out in the open in plain sight, but crouching absolutely flat, as flat, it seemed, as they might be rolled by a steam-roller. Nor did they move until I picked them up to band them, and after that I could not make them lie down again to have their pictures taken in their hiding posture. Whenever one approaches the nest of one of these Gulls, the adults circle high over head, uttering a continuous '*kowk-kowk-kowk*,' but it is an interesting commentary, noted also by Wheeler in his field notes, that the old birds stop their cries soon after the nest is found, and fly around silently far out of range, seemingly unconcerned. The eggs are laid early in June, and the incubation period is supposedly about twenty-six days. Some eggs must be laid as late as the middle of July, the delay probably being caused by robbing by eggers. Wheeler found two nests near Nain, June 11, 1928, "each containing three very fresh eggs. Nest, a depression surrounded and lined with trash on comparatively flat, undulating, rocky ground." Perrett records for June 19, 1900, "two fresh eggs in a nest on a rock in a fresh-water pond about two feet above water, nest of grass and moss, very rough affair; rock slanting, nest so built as to make the top level. Two eggs, incubation commenced, on low, flat rock in pond, about six inches above the water. Nest of grass and moss."

I found a nest with two eggs still being incubated at Egg Island, Sandwich Bay, July 16, 1928. In 1927 I banded two young about a week old, July 11, on the Bird Islands near Gready. On July 22, on the Red Islands at Turnavik, I banded two that were not five days old. In 1928 I banded a young bird about ready to fly, in other words at least three weeks old, on Gull Island, Turnavik, July 23. On the following August 9 and 10, I banded seven more on the outside islands, all about the same age. This simply goes to show the difference in time of laying of the eggs, for, other things being equal, the incubation periods and the periods of adolescence should all be about the same.

A bird I banded as a nestling, July 11, 1927, at the Bird Islands near Gready, was killed at Fox Islands, Burgeo and La Poile, Newfoundland, January 31, 1928. Another I banded, also immature, at Sandy Island, near Ford's Harbor, August 9, 1928, was found dead in a herring-net at Lennox Island, Port Hill, Prince Edward Island, May 1, 1929. One I banded August 10, 1928, at the Kidlit Islands was shot at Port aux Basques, Newfoundland, November 10, 1928.

I have never found about the nests of this species other remains than those of fish. I have found numerous cod bones, and some small minnows, besides lance and caplin. I have seen no evidence that they rob eggs or take the young of other species, but that they do so on the Labrador is without question.

The value of gulls as scavengers in Labrador is nil, for there is always more refuse when the fishing fleet is about in summer than could be cleaned up by ten million Gulls. There is so much space for the refuse to float in, and so small a human population, that offal is never a nuisance, except in harbors where the vessels are congregated in large numbers and all are getting many fish. Then the nuisance is to the stranger, and not to the natives or fishermen. They don't mind any fish smell, whether good or bad.

The Great Black-backed Gull is regarded as a fine table bird in Labrador, and receives the same treatment as the two other common species.

Larus argentatus smithsonianus Coues

HERRING GULL

Local vernacular: 'Sea Gull.'
Eskimo: 'Naujak'—the general term for any gull.
Indian: 'Ti násk' (*partim*).

Dwight (1925, 180) recognizes four races of the Herring Gull, and designates their respective ranges as follows: *argentatus* breeding over the coasts and islands of northern Europe from France northward to the Faroe Islands and eastward through the Baltic Sea to the White Sea, and wintering south to the Mediterranean and the north coast of Africa; *vegae* breeding on the northern Siberia coast from the Taimyr Peninsula eastward to Anadyr Bay, and wintering from the Aleutian Islands and the coast of Alaska to Japan and China; *smithsonianus* breeding from Alaska and British Columbia inland across southern Canada to the Atlantic Coast where colonies occur from Massachusetts to northern Labrador, and wintering southward on both coasts of the United States as far as Cuba and the west coast of Mexico; *thayeri* breeding from north of Hudson Bay to Ellesmere Island and west to Banks Land, and wintering on the Pacific coast from British Columbia to California. It is conceivable that *thayeri* might wander down to the northern end of Newfoundland Labrador, when not breeding, but its breeding there is precluded by the ancient barrier of Hudson Strait, and three specimens taken at Port Burwell by Hantzsch are definitely referred by him (1928, 147) to *smithsonianus*.

The Herring Gull is an abundant summer resident. It is by far the commonest of the Gulls known to breed in Labrador. Coues, Turner, Bigelow, Townsend and Allen, Hantzsch, and Bent, all note it, and the records extend from the Straits of Belle Isle to Cape Chidley. The earliest spring date is of a single individual seen by Perrett at Rigolet, April 14. Wheeler noted its arrival at Tikkoatokok Bay, May 9, 1928. Cooke (1916, 163) recorded the last at Battle Harbor, October 22, 1912. Perrett shot one at Ailik, November 14, 1899.

In Labrador the Herring Gull prefers the ledges of rocky cliffs on which to breed, though it has been known to nest on the tundra, or on rocks on the tops of islands. It nests most abundantly on the islands in the bays and near the mainland, but a few hardy individuals utilize the rookeries on the outside islands, where the Glaucous Gulls are common. They are frequently found breeding in mixed colonies with this latter species. The nest is most often a hummock of dried coarse grasses, in which the two or three eggs are laid. I have found nests only twenty feet above sea-level at the Red Islands at Turnavik, and eighty feet up on the Gannet Islands. I have noted it breeding most commonly between Battle Harbor and Port Manvers Run. From thence to Chidley the colonies are sparser, though in MacLelan Strait on August 19, 1927, I saw more individual Herring Gulls flocking together than I have ever observed elsewhere along the coast. Flocks of several thousand, both adult and immature, lined both sides of that terrific tide-rip as we plugged through it.

The eggs are laid late in May or early in June, but the date of laying may vary considerably, as the presence of very young birds in August testifies. Much of the delayed laying, however, is caused by the robbery of the nests for food by the natives. Perkalujak Island, where about forty pairs of Herring Gulls and twenty pairs of Glaucous Gulls breed, is a case in point. According to the Reverend Dr. Hettasch, missionary at Nain, the Eskimos get the first gulls' eggs from Perkalujak late in May. They usually rob the island only once, allowing the second clutch to hatch for posterity. However, when I visited that island August 3, 1927, I found some young not more than three or four days old, and others almost ready to fly away. I noted the same condition there August 7, 1928, and at almost every other rookery I inspected where there were more than two or three pairs of these gulls breeding together. Both sexes share in the incubation, which lasts about twenty-six days. Most of the young have left the nest by the second week in August, but birds that hatch late sometimes are unable to fly until the end of the month.

The Herring Gulls more than any others of their genus in Labrador gather astern of the fishing-boats when they are dressing down, to pick up the refuse thrown overboard. Bits of cod liver, which float better than any other part of the fish, are a favorite morsel for them, though they are not averse to picking up whatever they can find on the waters or on the beaches, in the way of dead fish. Among their regurgitations that I have found on the nesting ledges have often been cod backbones, with the meat stripped clean from them by the fledglings. These backbones are without doubt part of the offal picked up from some fishing-schooner. I have found no evidences of any other kind of food they might indulge in on the Labrador, though elsewhere they are known to eat a wide variety of animal, insect, and even vegetable food. They are prone to hang around the mouths of the fresh-water rivers at the head of the bays, where they undoubtedly pick up a certain amount of animal food brought down by the rushing torrents.

They are regarded as excellent food birds by both fishermen and natives, and are shot whenever the opportunity offers. The fishermen are especially fond of the young birds, and frequently take downy young aboard their vessels and feed them on scraps of fish until they are full grown. Aboard almost every fishing-schooner on the coast in August one sees a young gull or two in a crude crate or barrel, or else boldly promenading the deck. Just before they are able to fly away, their necks are wrung and their carcasses thrown into a 'slumgullion.' The eggs are much relished, and the bird suffers more from the eggers than does the Glaucous Gull, because it usually breeds in more accessible places.

Larus delawarensis Ord

RING-BILLED GULL

The Ring-billed Gull is a well-marked species, entirely American in its distribution. It breeds from the north shore of the Gulf of St. Lawrence westward across Canada to British Columbia and south to the northern United States from Michigan to Oregon. It winters on both coasts of the United States south to Cuba, Texas, and southern Mexico.

In Newfoundland Labrador it is a rare summer visitor. Coues (1861, 246) collected three juvenal Ring-billed Gulls at Henley Harbor, August 21, 1860. (One of these (see Dwight, 1925, 180) was sent later to Howard Saunders of London, who misidentified it as *Larus canus*). Bigelow (1902, 27) collected a young bird at Port Manvers, September 6, 1900. Hantzsch (1928, 147, note 2) says: "On Opingevik, the most northeastern tip of the mainland of Labrador, in a strong wind on the 8th of September [1906], I observed two gulls in adult plumage, which I took for *Larus delawarensis* Ord. They repeatedly came quite near, and I delayed shooting because the wind blew away from the land. Suddenly the creatures vanished again. The species breeds farther southward in Labrador." These are the only records.

There is a breeding colony of Ring-billed Gulls on the north shore of the Gulf of St. Lawrence, but the bird is not known to nest in Newfoundland Labrador. Macoun (1900, 41) says, "Breeds in the vicinity of Hamilton Inlet, east coast of Labrador. (A. P. Low)." Low, himself, never published any such statement that I can find, and the original source, if not an error of Macoun's, is likely to have been *in litteris*. However, though the record at best is an exceedingly vague and doubtful one, all the subsequent authors—Townsend and Allen (1907, 316), Cooke (1915, 43), and Bent (1921, 139)—have copied it.

[Larus canus Linn. COMMON or MEW GULL. This European species was regarded for almost fifty years as of accidental occurrence in North America, on the basis of a specimen taken by Coues at Henley Harbor, Labrador, on August 21, 1860, and sent for identification to Howard Saunders, who referred it (P. Z. S., 1877, p. 178; Cat. Birds Brit. Mus., XXV, 1896, p. 281) to this species. The identification remained unquestioned until Dr. Jonathan Dwight (1925, 180) examined the skin in the United States National Museum. He determined the bird, beyond doubt, to be an immature *Larus delawarensis* in worn plumage.]

[Larus philadelphia (Ord). BONAPARTE'S GULL. There is no definite record of this species within the confines of Newfoundland Labrador. That individuals may straggle through the interior and reach the coast in the late summer, is a possibility as yet lacking tangible proof, although Bigelow (1902, 27) reported it as "common south of Hamilton Inlet in September, particularly about the Straits of Belle Isle." The Indians of the interior know a gull with a black head to which they give a name. The Montagnais, according to Keats, have spoken of the bird to him, calling it 'Cherash.' Strong showed the Barren Ground band a picture of Bonaparte's Gull, to which they gave the name 'Mi shits nask.' It is a species that one hardly could mistake.]

Pagophila alba (Gunnerus)

IVORY GULL

Local vernacular: 'Ice Partridge,' 'Winter Gull.'
Eskimo: 'Naujarluk'—the dirty gull.
Indian: 'Shi nósk.'

The Ivory Gull breeds circumpolarly in very high latitudes, far north of the Arctic Circle. In winter it comes south to the northern coasts of Eurasia and North America, commonly to Kamchatka, the British Isles, British Columbia, and Labrador, and casually to France and New England. It represents a monotypic genus.

It is a common winter visitor. Low (1896, 323) says, "Specimen obtained at Rigolet, where it was shot during the winter; seen at Northwest River late in December after the Inlet was frozen; not common." There is one record (Dawson, 1899, p. 139A) of two birds "shot in the ice off Sandwich Bay," June 12, 1897. Townsend and Allen (1907, 311) "obtained from the Eskimos at Hopedale the skin of an immature Ivory Gull shot the previous winter at that place." According to Hantzsch (1928, 123), it is a "rather abundant migrant at the beginning of winter, until the ice blockades the coast. If the ice appears late, not until about Christmas time, the creatures often appear in great numbers. If everything is frozen up at the end of October, they occasionally stay quite far from the coast. None of the birds was seen up to the time of my departure on October 12th. In the winter they are seen occasionally on the outer edge of the belt of ice. In the spring, on the other hand, they are seen more rarely." A specimen in the Museum of Comparative Zoölogy was taken by Sornborger at Ramah in November, 1899. Perrett collected three Ivory Gulls, November 14, 1899, at Ailik. Wheeler killed one at Nain, December 1, 1927.

From all reports the bird is not finicky in either its choice of food or its table manners. Its Eskimo name is derived from the fact that its snowy plumage is continually soiled when the birds reach Labrador, from wallowing around in carrion and blood. Mr. Perrett regaled me for half an hour with a description of the way the Eskimo boys catch the birds, by concealing a fish-hook in a piece of seal meat, when they first appear in the fall at Killinek. The birds always gather, according to his report, when a seal is killed on the ice, and prove very bold in coming up to snatch tidbits from the carcass. Blood on the ice will draw them for miles. Townsend and Allen (*vide supra*) describe how the birds are baited for killing at Battle Harbor: "About a gallon of seals' blood is poured on the ice near the rocks, and as the birds hover about they are easily shot. Some of the birds in their eagerness to obtain the blood dash themselves with such force against the ice as to kill themselves."

The Ivory Gull is regarded by the liveyeres and Eskimos as fine eating, and is shot for the pot whenever possible.

Rissa tridactyla tridactyla (Linn.)

ATLANTIC KITTIWAKE

Local vernacular: 'Tickle-else.'
Eskimo: 'Nautsak'—the pretty gull.

Rissa tridactyla is a circumpolar species breeding on the coasts of northern North America and Eurasia and among the Arctic islands. Two races are recognized,—*R. t. pollicaris*, which nests in eastern Siberia, western Alaska, and the islands in Bering Sea; and *R. t. tridactyla*, which occupies the rest of the breeding range of the species, nesting as far south on the Atlantic coast as the Gulf of St. Lawrence and the British Isles. *R. t. pollicaris* winters southward in the Pacific to Lower California and Japan; *tridactyla* winters in the Atlantic along the coasts of the United States and Europe, and is casual at this season in the interior of both continents. Of greatest interest, when considering the distribution of the race *tridactyla*, are two banding records that show how widely individual birds may be dispersed. A Kittiwake banded at the Farne Islands off the coast of Northumberland, England, on June 28, 1923, was recovered at Horse Island, near St. Barbe, Newfoundland, August 12, 1924. Another, banded at the same place June 30, 1924, was picked up at Groswater Bay, Hamilton Inlet, in October, 1925.

The Kittiwake is an abundant summer resident. Coues (1861, 247) saw Kittiwakes but once, "while sailing up Esquimaux Bay several miles from its mouth. A small company hovered and circled over the boat, and a specimen was secured." Kumlien (1879, 99) says: "The Kittiwake was first noticed in the Straits of Belle Isle, on our outward passage, the 18th of August, 1877. From this point northward they were with us constantly, if we were near land or far out at sea, in storm or calm, fog or snow; no day—scarcely an hour—but some of these interesting birds were our companions; often a few individuals only, at other times flocks of many hundreds or even perhaps thousands on the islands of the north Labrador coast." Bigelow (1902, 26) calls them "by far the most abundant of all the sea fowl." Townsend and Allen (1907, 312) also found them very abundant on the coast. They record seeing ten thousand or more from the mailboat, which include two hundred near Blanc Sablon, July 10, 1906, a flock of five thousand at the mouth of Hamilton Inlet, July 18, between two thousand and three thousand between Nain and Pack's Harbor, and about twenty-five hundred in the Straits of Belle Isle, August 2. Hantzsch (1928, 123) calls it a "common migrant, especially in late summer and fall, often in flocks of many thousands, also appearing during the whole year in scattering numbers." He lists four adults he collected at Killinek between September 12 and 17, 1906.

The earliest spring record for the district is of an immature female taken by the Rawson-MacMillan Expedition at Jack Lane's Bay, June 20, 1928.   My notes teem with records for the species during July and August, whenever we spent any time among the outside islands.   My own latest record is of a flock of a hundred off Cape Porcupine, September 11, 1927, but Wheeler observed them still flying about the bays north of Nain, October 28, 1927.   Kittiwakes spend the summer in countless thousands off the coast.   They seldom venture close to the mainland except when driven in by onshore gales.   I encountered a mammoth flock among the small islets about twenty miles off Ford's Harbor, August 9, 1928.   The caplin were schooling, and the birds were swirling over them in a veritable snowstorm as the grampuses and 'jumpers' drove the fish to the surface.   All that day and the next, while we sailed in calm seas far off the mainland, we were attended by swarms of birds.   A few Jaegers, both Pomarine and Parasitic, were always present, darting hither and yon, creating havoc in the ranks.   However, the largest number of Kittiwakes I ever saw was between Port Manvers and Cape Chidley from August 20 to 26, 1927.   There I saw thousands daily and by far the greater part of them were young birds with the conspicuous black crescent on the side of the neck.   In stormy weather off Cape Chidley clouds of them flew around us in the haze and fog.   They were remarkably tame, and hovered on set wings, motionless, only a few feet over our heads.   They even coasted between the masts, and perched on the main truck as we bowled along.

Turner (1885, 251) says the Kittiwake "breeds plentifully on the northern portions of the Atlantic coast of Labrador."   Hantzsch (*loc. cit.*) is more conservative: "Breeding places, however, do not seem to be located in the neighborhood [of Killinek].   Indeed, Missionary Perrett does not know of a single place of the kind on the whole coast between Cape Harrison and Killinek . . .   Some Eskimos told me that the birds perhaps breed on the Button Islands."   The species is known to breed on Resolution Island, and south of Labrador in the Gulf of St. Lawrence, but, despite the countless thousands of Kittiwakes that summer along the entire length of the northeastern coast, there is not a single rookery known. I am positive that it does not breed between Battle Harbor and Port Manvers. I have searched for its nesting grounds fruitlessly in nearly all the important rookeries in the region.   However, about five miles north of Port Manvers there is a high rocky cliff facing the sea.   We sailed past it August 26, 1927, in a westerly gale, late in the afternoon, and could not stop to investigate it without spending an evil night at sea in a damaged vessel.   As we sailed by, half a mile off shore, I could see that the cliff was lined with Kittiwakes on every available ledge.   They were probably just roosting there out of the storm.   If they do nest there, it is exceedingly strange that the rookery has never been reported by the many ornithologists who must have sailed by it, and still stranger that Mr. Perrett does not know about it, as he would, indeed, had the Eskimos ever found the birds breeding there. He has learned nothing more of the Kittiwake's breeding on the coast than he knew in 1907, when he wrote Hantzsch that he knew of no rookeries between Harrison and Killinek. In the northern section of the coast there are abundant cliffs which the birds might find suitable for breeding purposes, but no Kittiwakes have ever been seen near them. I am sure, however, that the species breeds in considerable numbers on the Button Islands, though there are no positive evidences of it beyond the statements of the Eskimos and the Mounted Police. The officers stationed at Port Burwell told me that they had been able to get on the islands but once during the late spring, in recent years. On that one occasion they were able to get all the fresh 'Tickle-else' eggs their boat would hold. The islands are just the rugged type that the Kittiwake would select to breed on, and their very inaccessibility makes them ideal rookeries. The presence of the birds in such large numbers in that vicinity and to the southward, points to the existence of a large rookery somewhere near by, and the Buttons are the only likely localities that are unexplored.

These birds are eaten by all three classes on the Labrador,—the Newfoundland fishermen, the Eskimos, and the liveyeres,—and in large numbers, for they are easily killed when the heavy weather drives them close to shore. The fishermen have a favorite method of killing them. They fill a barrel-hoop with cod livers and let it drift on a line over the stern a good gunshot from their schooner. The Kittiwakes fight one another over the hoop to get at the tidbits, and when the doughty hunter thinks there are plenty in the tightly knotted mass of birds, he fires into the heart of it with his old six-foot muzzle-loading flintlock, which he has loaded with five fingers of black powder and a miscellaneous handful of small metal found about the ship, from stove bolts to trouser-buttons. His method is, to say the least, effective.

Xema sabini (Sabine)

SABINE'S GULL

Sabine's Gull nests circumpolarly in the very far north. It winters mainly in the subarctic regions, but strays casually south in both the Atlantic and the Pacific to northwestern Europe and the United States. The genus is monotypic, and, according to Dwight (1925, 330), the forked tail and the wing pattern, and the general form and proportion of the legs point "to a rather close relationship to the Sternidae."

In Labrador it is a rare autumn visitor. Bell (1885) records that one was shot at Port Burwell in September, 1884. There is a specimen in the Museum of Comparative Zoölogy taken at Okkak in 1894. Hantzsch (1928, 147) says: "A few individuals appear as rare autumn migrants. My companion Paksau seemed to have killed the species." Perrett collected two at Jack Lane's Bay during the autumn of 1899, which he told me he gave to Sornborger. I have been unable to trace them.

Sterna hirundo hirundo Linn.

COMMON TERN

My experience with this species and the following one in rookeries in New England where both breed together, has taught me that the Common and Arctic Terns can be differentiated in the field only by experienced and careful observers, and then only under the most favorable of conditions. Hence a sight record for either in a region where both may occur, is utterly valueless, unless elaborated so that there can be no doubt as to the identity of the species in question.

I have found Terns breeding at only one place in Labrador, and there the colony was purely of Arctics. The few Terns that I have observed elsewhere along the coast have always been under such conditions that specific determination was impossible, and I have arbitrarily recorded all of them under *Sterna paradisaea*.

The only definite record of the Common Tern for Newfoundland Labrador is a specimen, now in the United States National Museum, taken at Rigolet by Coues, August 9, 1860. Of the species Coues says (1860, 247), "During my short stay at Rigolet I saw a good many . . . but found none in any other locality." It is very probable that there may be several breeding colonies in Hamilton Inlet, but they have yet to be discovered. The Common Tern nests commonly along the north shore of the Gulf of St. Lawrence, and there is no reason why it should not breed in our territory. The species will be noted commonly in summer only in the immediate vicinity of its rookeries.

Sterna paradisaea Brünnich

ARCTIC TERN

Local vernacular: 'Paytrick'; 'Steerine.'

Eskimo: 'Immerkotaelak.' Hantzsch (1928, 147) gives the etymology of this word as meaning 'without a groin,' referring to the very short legs which are held up within the feathers in flight. Perrett, however, gave me its meaning as 'the one that hovers over or (more strictly) hinders itself from going into the water.'

Indian: 'Apih shít tcee ask wis.'

The Arctic Tern is a non-plastic species breeding circumpolarly in high latitudes. The breeding range has its centre of greatest abundance in Scotland, the islands immediately north and west of there, and the more northerly coasts of the North Sea. Thence it branches out in all directions, extending in places to within eight degrees of the pole, but never coming south of the parallel of 40° degrees north latitude. To the westward it includes Iceland, Greenland, Baffin Island, Hudson Bay, Labrador, and the coast of North America, south to Massachusetts. Eastward it reaches through Lapland, Finland, Esthonia, northern Russia, the coasts and lower river-courses of Siberia, on through the Bering Sea, south to the Anadyr and Commander Islands, and thence across to Alaska and as far east as Melville Island.

The winter range of the species is very imperfectly known, for it lies along coasts but little worked ornithologically, and in seas comparatively unfrequented by man. It is usually given as those waters lying between Brazil and Argentina and West Africa, and south to some undetermined point within the Antarctic Circle. There are no records whatsoever for the continent of South America, nor for the southern Pacific, save two accidental occurrences in the Hawaiian Islands, one on May 9, 1891 ('Auk,' 1902, 195), and the other April 30, 1902 ('Auk,' 1902, 394). There are five records for the South Atlantic, one ('Auk,' 1914, 444) taken by Murphy, November 9, 1912, northwest of South Georgia, and the other four ('Ibis,' 1907, 325-349) taken by the Scottish National Antarctic Expedition; the complete data of these four have been kindly furnished me by J. H. Stenhouse of the Royal Scottish Museum at Edinburgh as follows:

♂	64° 38″ S.	35° 13′ W.	February 25, 1904
♂	64° 38″ S.	35° 13′ W.	February 25, 1904
♀	68° 32′ S.	12° 49′ W.	March 23, 1904
♀	72° 18′ S.	17° 59′ W.	March 3, 1904

Abundant records in literature show the species to be a common visitor to Cape Colony and Natal in South Africa during November, December, January, and February, and there are a few scattering records for the west coast of Europe during migration; but it has been found nowhere commonly on the Atlantic coasts of North and South America, south of Massachusetts. There are a few accidental records between New York and Georgia. The species occurs along the Pacific coast as far south as California, where it has been taken occasionally, but there is nothing to show that a Pacific migration route to the south exists.

The bulk of the evidence indicates that the Arctic Tern migrates down the eastern side of the Atlantic Ocean, and winters about South Africa. The eastern North American birds seem to join this flight by flying directly across the North Atlantic, instead of striking it at a diagonal, and in this they appear to be acting according to the supposed natural law that species leave their breeding grounds on migration by the route their ancestors used in entering the country. The Arctic Tern, if of Palearctic origin, probably entered North America *via* Iceland and Greenland, and the descendants of that ancient stock seem atavistically to cover somewhat the same course in their yearly flights between the breeding grounds and the wintering area. That this may be the case is indicated by the returns from two nestling Arctic Terns banded in Labrador. One of these, banded at the Red Islands in Turnavik Bay, July 22, 1927, was reported October 1, 1927, from La Rochelle, France. The other, banded at the same place July 23, 1928, was picked up dead on the beach at Margate, fifteen miles southwest of Port Shepstone, Natal, South Africa, November 14, 1928. As the young birds had not left the rookery in 1928 on August 14, and as this bird probably met its death several days before it was found, it is evident that it flew nine thousand miles in ninety days or less.

In Labrador the Arctic Tern is a locally common summer resident, breeding on islands in the bays and off the coast. Eifrig (1905, 236) reports them from Cape Chidley in June, 1903. Perrett records incubated eggs from the Red Islands, July 7, 1899. Macoun (1900, 53) lists eggs of this species from Green Island, Sandwich Bay, July 15, 1895. Hantzsch (1928, 148) saw them near the Button Islands, July 25, 1906. He states the Port Burwell Eskimos "said that this bird occasionally appeared in great numbers at the beginning of autumn," which is another prop to the theory that the birds fly northeastward across the Atlantic before flying southward. Perrett killed one at Makkovik, October 4, 1899, which is the latest autumn record for the region. Thus the birds probably arrive late in May or early in June, and depart in September or early in October. I have observed individuals at various places along the coast, from Squasho Run north to Saglek Bay, in July and August and early September.

The only rookeries I have found are in Turnavik Bay, latitude 55° 13'. Between four hundred and five hundred pairs breed on the easterly island of the Red Island group, and about fifty pairs on the northwest island, a quarter of a mile

away. I found about fifty pairs more breeding on Black Island at the head of
Turnavik Bay in 1926, but I have not visited that rookery since then.   According to native reports, Arctic Terns have bred on one of the outer islands, Nanuktok, about twelve miles northeast of Turnavik, but when I visited it, July 22, 1928,
there was not a breeding bird to be seen, though several adults were hanging
about, and I found one deserted nest. The species seems to prefer the smaller,
more sheltered islands in the bays. The presence of Terns around Squasho Run
indicates a rookery somewhere in that neighborhood, as yet undiscovered. Small
rookeries have been recorded in the past in Sandwich Bay and Hamilton Inlet,
but no particulars about them are available at present.

I have spent considerable time during each of my three summers on the coast
at the Red Islands in Turnavik Bay. Island number one, the easternmost island,
which has the largest colony, is a little inverted soup-bowl in shape, about two
hundred yards in diameter, rising about thirty feet out of the sea. It is composed
mainly of quartz monzonite (according to Wheeler), the reddish color of which is
responsible for the name of the group. The sides of the islet are washed smooth
and clean by the seas, but the top boasts a covering of grasses between the out-
crops of rock, all through which the birds build their nests. Some of the nests are
on the rock itself, built in small crevices, lined crudely with pebbles and sticks, but
most of them are in the grass, where the Terns have hollowed out shallow depres-
sions, sometimes bare, more often with a scattering of other grasses, sticks, and
pebbles on the bottom. The normal clutch is three eggs, and I have found one
set of four. Two in a nest are not uncommon during normal years. When the
island has been robbed by eggers, as it was during 1926, the second laying consists mostly of clutches of one or two eggs. The incubation period is supposedly
twenty-one days.

In 1926 an Eskimo girl took about eight hundred eggs from the rookery about
a month before my visit. The birds laid again, however, and on August 2 I found
half the young out of the egg, and none of them over a week old. Many of the
eggs were just hatching, and the parents were busy trying to feed and incubate
at the same time. The island fortunately remained undisturbed by eggers in
1927 and 1928, and I found the nesting at practically this same stage on July 22,
each summer,—many eggs in the later stages of incubation and young varying in
age from a few hours to ten days. On returning to the island August 14, 1928,
I found most of the young flying about and a mere handful of birds still on the
ground unable to take wing. Many of the young, although able to fly, still spent
much time on the island, and were fed there by their parents. In 1927 I made a
late visit to the rookery, September 3, and found that the whole colony had deserted it, though a flock of about four hundred adults and young, mixed, were
roosting on, and fishing about, a nearby reef.

Both parents share the incubation and feeding duties. The process of a young bird's first few meals is a long one, each feeding taking about fifteen minutes. The only food I have seen used on the Red Islands is the lance, *Ammodytes americana*. This eel-like minnow, from three to five inches in length, is entirely too large for a day-old Tern chick to swallow all at once. The parents grasp the lance as often by the middle as by either end, so that it goes down as frequently tail first as head first. Why the backward-pointing spines and fins do not tear the tender digestive tract to bits, can only be explained by the rapidity of the action of the gastric juices. After the fish has started on its downward path, the parent stands beside the young bird, and, gulping and bowing, goes through all the motions of swallowing, which the youngster tries weakly to imitate. But there simply isn't space inside to hold the whole fish at once. The chick stands helpless, in an agony of epicurean delight, half the fish down its gullet, the other half protruding from its mouth, its head thrown back, its legs braced, for all the world like a sword-swallower in the middle of his act. Ten minutes or so must elapse while the digestive juices function and make more room, and should the young bird be deserted by its parent even momentarily at this stage of the game, it stands in grave danger of losing its meal. Time after time have I watched an adult swoop down on such a luckless chick and, grabbing the projecting lance, tear it out roughly and carry it away to one of its own hungry offspring. I even succeeded in getting a motion picture of this, including a glimpse of the rightful parent wrathfully driving off a marauder.

There is a strong sense of individual nesting territory in the Arctic Tern, just as there is in the Common Tern (see Austin, 1929c, 135). Each pair establishes a 'home area' about its nest which it guards jealously against all intruders. Straying or trespassing adults are driven away mercilessly, and wandering young are pecked to death without compunction when they venture onto the land claimed by a pair other than their own parents. The territorial sense seems to be more or less in abeyance after all the young are hatched and are running about the island. However, many still are killed by the adults for reasons as yet not understood. Young birds that stray off the island, and swim about in the water, or walk along the bare rock at the water's edge, are swooped upon and pecked continuously by a cloud of angry old birds. Dead chicks with their soft scalps badly lacerated and discolored from such treatment are a common sight.

It has been shown by banding that the Common Tern (*Sterna hirundo*) does not breed until it is two years old, or is in its third summer (Austin, 1929, 127-132). That this may also be the case with the Arctic Tern is indicated by the common occurrence of birds a year old on the wintering grounds in Cape Colony during the northern breeding season. A nestling I banded at Turnevik in 1928 was shot on the rookeries by an Eskimo in July, 1930.

These birds are seldom shot for food because they are considered too small to waste a shell on. The shots one normally gets at them are at single birds flying, and that does not appeal to the Labradorman. Though there is hardly a bird easier to shoot on the wing than a Tern, the liveyere is not a wing shot, but wants to make sure of his bird sitting. The eggs are eaten frequently, but the natives regard them as almost too small to bother with unless they can get a good load of them, when there are the larger Gull and Duck eggs to be found. As one old liveyere told me when I remonstrated with him for gathering all the eggs on the Red Islands, "Two dozen of them little eggses don't hardly fill 'un at all."

[**Plautus impennis** (Linn.). GREAT AUK. Townsend and Allen (1907, 307) sum up all the evidence concerning the possible former occurrence of this extinct species in Labrador. They say, "It is probable that the Great Auk bred in only a few chosen places, chief of which was Funk Island, lying 32 miles off the northeast coast of Newfoundland, and although the bird may have bred on the Labrador coast we have no evidence of it, either from history or from the presence of egg shells or bones, such as have been found in numbers at Funk Island. However, there is no doubt but that the bird, if not a resident, was formerly a frequent visitor to the Labrador coast. . . It is to be noted that Cartwright says that Funk Island is the only place where the 'Penguins' bred. It seems hardly probable that they would have been driven off their breeding places on the Labrador coast in his day if any such existed, and it is equally improbable that he would have failed to find any such or to record them in his valuable 'Journal.'" No new evidence has come to light since this was written.]

Alca torda Linn.

RAZOR-BILLED AUK

Local vernacular: 'Tinker.'
Eskimo: 'Akpak.'

The Razor-billed Auk is a well-defined, non-plastic species breeding along the shores of the northern Atlantic Ocean and adjacent Arctic seas north to Spitzbergen and south to the British Isles and the Bay of Fundy. It winters south to the Azores, Gibraltar, and Long Island, New York. I have compared a large series of North American breeding birds with an admirable series from Ireland in the collection of the Museum of Comparative Zoölogy, and am unable to differentiate between them.

In Labrador it is a locally common summer resident, from the southern part of the district north to the Nain region, on the cliffy outside islands. It shares with the other alcids the characteristic of staying in the immediate vicinity of its rookeries throughout the breeding season, and unless one visits the rookeries, it is seldom seen during that period. Bent (1919, 201) quotes Turner's unpublished notes: "The razorbill is very abundant along the Labrador coast; although, at the season [June 24 to July 26] I was there they appeared to be more plentiful north of Eskimo Bay or Hamilton Inlet. Off Davis Inlet and Nakvak they were very common and long streams of these birds could be distinguished flying far from land and invariably headed to the northward. While passing some of the rugged islets and points I often saw these birds sitting on the rocks or in proximity to them. They appeared to be more wary while on the wing than when sitting on the land, or water. They associate quite freely with *Fratercula* and an occasional *Larus*. They seem to be on most intimate terms with the species of *Uria*, with which it agrees so closely in habits." Bigelow (1902, 26) found the species in 1900 still "abundant all along the coast." Because subsequent authors, never having visited the rookeries, have seen but few birds, they assert that the Razor-billed Auk is now rare. While, thanks to constant persecution, it is certainly no longer so common as it once was, I found it abundant on the rookeries off Hamilton Inlet and Davis Inlet. Coues (1861, 249) says that, in 1860, "at Esquimaux Bay, the most northern point visited, they were perhaps more numerous than elsewhere, breeding plentifully among the thousands of Puffins there collected . . . Another small island on the east side of Esquimaux Bay has in a like manner been deserted, the birds apparently having retired to the Puffin islands on the opposite side of the Bay. From these facts, I could but conclude that the birds are slowly but surely retiring before the persecutions of man to more northern and inaccessible regions." I found only twenty individuals on Puffin Island in 1926, the last remnants of the hosts that once were there, but on the more inaccessible islands, such as the Gannets, in Hamilton Inlet, I found thousands.

The birds resort to the islands at some time in June, though they doubtless arrive in the region as soon as the ice breaks up. The earliest spring record is of a male in the Museum of Comparative Zoölogy, taken at Loup Bay by Ernest Doane, June 18, 1899. Another specimen, a female, was taken there July 3, the same year. Most of them migrate southward before the freeze-up in November, but individuals may stay all winter in open years. The latest autumn record is of Perrett's specimen taken at Ailik, November 14, 1899. Cartwright records in his diary for February 11, 1779, that the "Tinkers" stayed around all winter, feeding in holes in the ice.

I have found Razor-billed Auks breeding on the following islands in approximately the following numbers:

Bird Island	53°	43'	40" N.	56°	15'	30" W.	100
Wester Bird	53	44	40	56	18	15	500
Gannet Clusters	53	56		56	31		2000
Outer Gannet	54	00	15	56	31		500
Puffin Island	54	24	30	57	22		20
Tinker Island	55	53	30	60	35		200
Nunarsuk Island	56	03		60	27		2000
Kidlits	56	11		60	28		500
Negro Island	56	20	30	60	32	30	10

Their nesting sites vary considerably. Most of the nests are in crevices among the rocks, and the species is very fond of getting under the loose stones in a talus slope, much after the fashion of the Black Guillemot, when such a formation can be found high enough above the water. They like height, so as to be able to drop off into the air to gain momentum for flight. Their eggs are very often inaccessible, which, coupled with their wariness, accounts for the fact that they are now much more abundant than are the Murres. I have seen them on open ledges with Uria, and have even dragged adult birds out of Puffin burrows on Nunarsuk, to my great surprise and chagrin. The Puffin cannot inflict a hard bite, and seldom is able to break the skin on one's hand, but the Razor-bill is aptly named, and is able to chop out a sizeable bit of flesh, as I know to my sorrow.

According to Bent (1912, 203), the incubation, shared by both sexes, lasts about thirty days. I found the eggs laid at the Bird Islands by July 11, 1927, and at the Gannet Islands by July 12, 1927, and by July 14 in both 1926 and 1928. I found young just hatching August 22, 1926, on Tinker Island, which had been robbed that summer. The young averaged a week old on Negro, Kidlits, and Nunarsuk Islands, August 10, 1928, and I found them almost fully fledged at the Gannets, August 18, 1928. Coues (1861, 251) found both fresh eggs and young July 25, 1860, at Puffin Island, from which he deduced that "the species is not very exact as to the time of laying its eggs."

Some Razor-bills I banded in Labrador brought the following results:

No. 560,110, ad.,	Nunarsuk, Aug. 7, 1928.	Shot at Magdalen Islands, Aug. 5, 1929
No. 560,318, juv.,	Gannets, Aug. 19, 1928.	" " Blagard Bay, Labrador, Aug. 9, 1929
No. 560,330, juv.,	Gannets, Aug. 19, 1928.	" " French Shore, Newf., Oct. 20, 1928
No. 560,340, juv.,	Gannets, Aug. 19, 1928.	" " Forteau, Labrador, Oct. 26, 1928
No. 560,069, juv.,	Nunarsuk, Aug. 11, 1928.	" " Southampton, N. Y., March 3, 1929

Theoretically, the first bird, no. 560,110, should have been back breeding upon Nunarsuk when, instead, it was captured far away in the Gulf of St. Lawrence. I was unable to get any particulars as to its capture. It might have been breeding on the Magdalens, but it is much more likely that it suffered some injury that delayed or prevented its northward flight, such as a broken wing-tip or a dose of oil on its feathers. The second bird, no. 560,318, was summering within fifteen miles of where it had been reared the year before. The next two show the tendency to retreat southward before the ice in the autumn, no. 560,330 having travelled several hundred miles to the east coast of Newfoundland, and no. 560,340 having gone through the Straits of Belle Isle. The last bird, no. 560,069, was picked up dead on a beach on Long Island, New York, its plumage heavily covered with oil. It is the longest flight recorded for a banded Razor-bill, and shows that the birds breeding in northern Labrador may winter off the New England coast.

Uria aalge aalge (Pontoppidan)

ATLANTIC MURRE

Local vernacular: 'Turre,' 'Backaloo Bird' (*partim*).
Eskimo: 'Akpalik' (*partim*).

The Common Murre is a widely ranging species, being almost circumpolar. *U. a. aalge* breeds in the lands bordering the North Atlantic and adjacent Arctic seas from the Bay of Fundy north to Greenland, Spitzbergen, Iceland, and the Faroe, Shetland, and Orkney Islands, and northern Scandinavia. It migrates slightly southward in winter. *U. a. albionis*, breeding in the British Isles, *U. a. helgolandica* from Heligoland, and *U. a. californica* in the Bering Sea are also generally recognized.

The so-called 'Ringed Murre,' which has been dignified by a specific rank by some authors (*Uria ringvia* Brünn.), seems to be but a color phase of *aalge*. Nevertheless, there is still much conflicting evidence on the question (see Bent, 1919, 178-179), for some authors assert that they have seen it interbreeding commonly with *aalge* (which should settle the question), while others state that it always pairs with its own kind. It never occurs on the Pacific coast, but this may be no more than an additional racial character.

The Murre is an uncommon summer resident locally on the various alcid islands. I have seen a very few, mostly the ringed form (the eye-rings made them stand out from the prevalent Brünnich's Murre more sharply than the thinner-edged bill) in the colonies on both the Gannet Islands and Nunarsuk. There are two specimens in the Museum of Comparative Zoölogy, both collected by Doane at Loup Bay, a male taken June 19, 1899, and a female of the ringed variety taken July 1, 1899. Kumlien (1885, 253) says, "Plentiful on eastern and southern coasts of Labrador." (This statement certainly would not be true today, and that it was verified by Kumlien at the time is doubtful.) Low (1896, 323) called it "common in open water of Hamilton Inlet until January 20th, 1894." Macoun (1909, 24) says, "Mr. Dicks collected for me a large series of eggs of this bird at Gannet islands, coast of Labrador, July 2nd, 1895 . . . (*Raine*)." (These eggs may just as well have been *Uria lomvia*.) Norton (1901, 146) lists eight specimens—five adults and three downy young—taken by the Bowdoin Expedition at the Herring Islands, August 22, 1891. Bigelow (1902, 26) found it fairly common as far north as Hamilton Inlet in 1900, and was told of a colony near Eclipse Harbor which has never been recorded elsewhere and of which I have never been able to learn anything from either the natives or Mr. Perrett. Neither Coues nor Hantzsch saw the bird.

Uria lomvia lomvia (Linn.)

Brünnich's Murre

Local vernacular: 'Turre,' 'Backaloo Bird' (*partim*).
Eskimo: 'Akpalik' (*partim*).

This practically circumpolar species inhabits the coasts of Bering Sea, the Arctic Ocean, and the adjacent North Atlantic Ocean. It is divided into two races—*lomvia* breeding from the Gulf of St. Lawrence north along the Labrador coast, and in north Greenland, Jan Mayen Land, Spitzbergen, and Novaya Zemlya, and east to the Taimyr Peninsula; and *arra* occupying the remainder of the range in Bering Sea and the adjacent Arctic Ocean. In general this Murre is more northerly in its breeding than the preceding species, but it winters south to Japan, Massachusetts, and the British Isles.

In Labrador Brünnich's Murre is a locally common summer resident, and is the prevalent species in the few rookeries where Murres are still to be found. The birds remain in close proximity to the nesting islands during the summer, but spread all along the coast and even wander into the bays when the parental duties are completed. The Labrador birds move slightly southward in late autumn, but Murres (probably from more northern rookeries) are to be found in the region throughout the winter during open years. Wheeler records a small flock near Ford's Harbor, June 23, 1928. He observed several November 2, 1927, among the islands outside Aulatsevik. I saw three small bunches of three, eight, and two individuals, respectively, in Gray Strait, August 20, 1927.

Bent (1919, 190) says: "Mr. Lucien M. Turner found this species breeding abundantly on the Atlantic coast of Labrador in 1882, notably on the outlying islands of Hamilton Inlet, Davis Inlet, Cape Mugford, and Cape Chidley ... Since that time great changes have taken place, for in 1912 I cruised the whole length of this coast, as far north as Cape Mugford, and saw only one solitary Brünnich's Murre." It is certainly true that the Murres are no longer as common in the region as they were in Turner's day, for they have borne the brunt of the persecution by the natives and the fishermen. But there are still colonies on the coast, and I am certain that had MacMillan's launch, in which Bent was a passenger, visited the Gannet Islands and Nunarsuk, he would have seen many more birds than he did. I found four small scattered groups of Murres, totaling about two hundred and fifty individuals, on the Gannet Clusters. In the high cliff on the north side of Nunarsuk I was delighted to locate a chimney in which there were fully three hundred of them. They are strongly entrenched in the latter place, for the cliff is so precipitous that it is impossible for a man to reach the most thickly populated ledges. I was able to band only forty young birds. I have been unable to locate the colony off Cape Mugford, of which Turner speaks, but it probably is still in existence, for there are no natives living in the immediate vicinity, and fishermen almost never summer there. The Chidley colony to which Turner refers is probably also still thriving, for it is most likely to be on one of the Button Islands, which are accessible only once in a decade. Eifrig (1905, 235) found the bird abundant all through Hudson Strait, and Hantzsch (1928, 90) calls it an "occasional breeding bird on the Button Islands and in the neighborhood of Cape Chidley, from whence the Canadian Neptune expedition is said to have taken eggs (Low, 1906, p. 315)."

. This species lays its single egg only on high cliffs, where the nesting spots are often hard to reach. The birds pack themselves thickly on the narrow ledges, and are very clumsy and unheeding of their eggs. They do not flush until one is almost upon them, and then in their haste to get away knock many eggs to destruction. The incubation lasts about twenty-eight days, and is accomplished by both sexes. Bent (1919, 196) gives four egg dates as June 10, July 1, 2, and 11. I found young a few days old and many eggs just hatching at Nunarsuk, August 11, 1928. At the Gannets, a week later, all the young were hatched.

Of birds banded on August 11, 1928, at Nunarsuk, and on August 18, 1928, at the Gannets, five were shot as follows:

560,073, ad., (Nunarsuk) at Bonavista Bay, Nov. 1, 1929
560,086, juv., (Nunarsuk) at Fortune District, Feb. 12, 1929
560,153, juv., (Gannets) at Twillingate, Nov. 10, 1928
560,190, juv., (Gannets) at Conception Bay, June 14, 1929
560,308, juv., (Gannets) at Sandwich Bay, Aug. 11, 1929

The first four records indicate that the Labrador Murres tend to winter off the east coast of Newfoundland. No. 560,308 had returned, when a year old, to the immediate vicinity of the island on which it was reared. It was shot not ten miles away.

The relative scarcity of the Murres on the Labrador when compared with the other alcids shows clearly that this species, the 'Foolish Guillemot' of Europe, has borne the brunt of the persecution by eggers and hunters. It is truly a fool bird, especially on its rookeries, where the adults may be run down and captured alive with ease. Formerly abundant, it is now limited to the largest and most inaccessible of the rookeries. It will not require much more molestation to extirpate it completely from the southern part of the coast. But the more northern rookeries, because of their remoteness from habitations and their inaccessibility save during the calmest of weather, will probably flourish for some time to come.

Alle alle (Linn.)

DOVEKIE

Local vernacular: 'Bull Bird,' 'Little Bull.'
Eskimo: 'Akpaliarsuk'—a small auk.

The Dovekie breeds in the high north in Greenland, Iceland, Spitzbergen, Franz Josef Land, the Barents Islands, and Novaya Zemlya, and winters southward to the North Sea and New Jersey. A monotypic genus with no near relatives, it is most closely allied to the small Auks of the Bering Sea region, whence it probably had its origin in early Tertiary time.

The Dovekie is an abundant transient visitor. It winters on the coast during open years, and occurs casually in summer. Turner (1886, 254) says it "occurs in myriads along the eastern shore of Labrador." Low (1896, 323) found it "very common in Hamilton Inlet until January 20th, 1894. Numbers ... found frozen in bushes along the edge of the open water." Bigelow (1902, 26) observed one off Cape Harrison, September 18, 1900. Hantzsch (1928, 92) writes: "The appearance of this bird is partly controlled by the appearance of the drift ice. I observed the forerunners of the migration in the middle of October for the first time. A few days later, on the 19th of this month, we traveled on the way from Hebron to Okkak for hours through numerous individuals, which seemed to populate the whole sea at great distances from one another. Until my arrival in Newfoundland on November 16th, I could see right along at some distance from the land more or less numerous individuals of the species."

Corporal Nichols of the Canadian Mounted Police, stationed at Port Burwell, informed me that the 'Bull Birds' cross Hudson Strait in countless thousands late in September. In his notes, under the date of November 2, 1927, Wheeler writes: "The Dovekies seem to be more abundant now than the Black Guillemots among the islands just outside Aulatsivik." John Keats, the Hudson's Bay Company factor at Davis Inlet, wrote me that he shot one at the Post January 27, 1929. There is a specimen in the Museum of Comparative Zoölogy, taken by Dr. Grenfell at Nachvak in July, 1905. I collected a female in very worn plumage in Anaktalak Bay, August 1, 1928. It was exceedingly thin, and from the frayed condition of the primaries (which evidently had not been moulted) I doubt if the bird was able to fly.

The natives consider its flesh very palatable. It is seldom shot, however, unless many are found massed together, for to shoot such small birds singly is deemed a waste of ammunition.

Cepphus grylle arcticus (Brehm)

LABRADOR BLACK GUILLEMOT

Local vernacular: 'Sea Pigeon,' 'Pigeon.'
Eskimo: 'Pitsiulak'—from the whistling of the bird.
Indian: 'Kash há sti hisht,' D. I. B.; 'Ka ha sti hish,' B. G. B.

Cepphus grylle is a circumpolar species in the northern hemisphere. The distribution of the genus is interesting, for it seems obvious that the Pacific forms are more ancient than those of the Atlantic. In the Pacific and Bering Sea, *C. columba*, *C. carbo*, and *C. grylle mandti*, are all specifically distinct. In the Atlantic, however, we find only *C. grylle*, which is divisible into three races (see Austin, 1929), intergrading from *mandti* in the north, through *arcticus*, from southern Greenland to the Straits of Belle Isle, to *grylle*, from the Gulf of St. Lawrence to Maine on the one side of the Atlantic, and to the British Isles and northern Europe on the other. This distribution indicates that the genus *Cepphus* probably had its origin in the region of the north Pacific, and that the Atlantic forms invaded the territory they now occupy after the specific line had become distinct. Thus *mandti* may be assumed to be the race nearest the ancestral type of the species *Cepphus grylle*, and *grylle* the youngest of all the *Cepphus* forms.

The Black Guillemot is an abundant summer resident. It is beyond question the most universally common of the Labrador sea-birds, as all the writers on the birds of the region agree. It breeds from the Straits of Belle Isle to Cape

Chidley, and from the outermost islands far into the fiords. There is a general southward movement in winter, the Labrador breeders retreating to the Gulf of St. Lawrence and the east coast of Newfoundland. However, there are Guillemots along the coast as long as there is open water. When the shores freeze up, many remain just off the edge of the ice, fifty miles to seaward. Perrett records the fact that the birds were present at Killinek all winter long in 1905-1906, an open year. Cooke (1916, 163) says there were "several at Woody Point, December 30, 1912, and at Lewis Bay, February 15, 1913." Wheeler notes that in 1928 the ice broke up June 2. On June 4 he found Guillemots "abundant near the shores of Kikkertaksoak among the pans of ice where a brook empties in. They were chasing each other about in the water, feeding about the brook mouth, and resting on ice pans or under the overhangs of the larger cakes."

Wheeler's notes on the assumption of the winter plumage by the old birds are of interest, for very little has been written about it. He noticed that those he saw in Tikkoatokok Bay, October 2, 1926, showed the head, neck, and back strongly marked with white. By November 9, 1927, they were "quite white all over, losing the pepper-and-salt effect."

Its choice of nesting site and its preference for nesting alone or in small rather than large colonies, are all that save the Guillemot from constant persecution and permit it to be so common in a region where all birds and their eggs are eaten by man if they are large enough. The bird lays two eggs, usually far under rockpiles on the shore, or in crevices in inaccessible cliffs. To get at the nests is hard work, in fact often impossible, and the results do not appeal to the egger as worth the effort. Every cliff along the coast that is creviced, every talus rock-pile at the water's edge, has its pair or pairs of Black Guillemots. Occasionally a small islet with particularly good nesting sites will boast as many as fifty or a hundred pairs, but seldom more. While the species may be found almost anywhere and everywhere along the coast, the following localities boast rookeries of fifty pairs or more:

North cliff of Collingham Island, ten miles southwest of Gready.
Islet, uncharted, in Alleuk Bight, northwest of Indian Harbor.
Nanuktok, ten miles northeast of Turnavik.
West cliff of Achvitoaksoak, five miles north of Hopedale.
Unnamed double island, fifteen miles southeast of Ford's Harbor.
Perkalujak Island in Nain Bay.
Pitsiulak Island, off Kauk Head, four miles south of Nain.

There are doubtless several hundred more colonies that contain fifty or more pairs of breeding birds, most of them unnamed and uncharted. Every gull cliff, every island boasting rookeries of other alcids, will always be found to have its complement of Black Guillemots down near the water's edge. I found one nest fully forty-five feet straight up from the water at Step Hill Gull Cliff in Anaktalak

Bay, and another unusually lofty site on Nanuktok, probably fifty feet in altitude, back inland three hundred yards from the shore. The many Guillemots on this large island, which I investigated as being the probable site of an Arctic Tern rookery, do not nest so far under the rocks as elsewhere. Three nests I saw there July 24, 1928, were almost in the open, just barely sheltered under a protecting ledge.

The two eggs are laid either during the last week in June or early in July. Bent (1919, 161) gives seven records from July 1 to August 2, and four from July 12 to 17. He found two almost fresh eggs August 12, 1912, at Perkalujak Island, which had doubtless been robbed earlier in the summer by the Nain Eskimos. I have never been on the coast before the eggs were laid. I found twenty nests on the Bird Islands east of Gready, each containing two eggs, July 11, 1928. In a nest I watched in 1926 at the Red Islands in Turnavik Bay, one egg hatched August 1, the other the next day. The youngsters were almost ready to leave the nest when I returned to the island, August 26. They were fully fledged, and swam well when I put them in a little tide pool. I noted the first young in the water of their own accord that year on August 31, at Domino Run. In 1927 most, but not all, of the eggs on Perkalujak Island were hatched August 2. We saw the first young out of the nest of their own accord that year on September 1. In 1928 I found the first young birds at Anaktalak Bay, August 2, and these were several days old at least. The following day at Perkalujak some eggs were hatching, and others were still intact. Up to the time of our departure, August 25, no young had put in their appearance in the water.

Bent (1919, 159) gives the incubation period as about twenty-one days, and I assume that both sexes incubate and feed the young. There are always many more adults hanging about an islet than are accounted for by the nests you find. Their call-note is a distinctive sound—a soft, sibilant, sweet, low whistle, often prefaced by a little quiet chattering.

Of young birds banded in 1928, I have had these returns:

Banded, Perkalujak	August	7.	Shot at Tilt Cove, Newfoundland, no date
" Double Island	"	9.	" " Godbout, Quebec, Nov. 12, 1928
" " "	"	9.	" " Godbout, Quebec, Nov. 15, 1928
" Nunarsuk	"	10.	" " Fortune Bay, Newfoundland, spring, 1929
" "	"	11.	" " Port au Port, Newfoundland, July 21, 1929
" "	"	11.	" " Twillingate, Newfoundland, Nov. 15, 1928
" Collingham Isd.	"	20.	" " Eagle River, Labrador, Aug. 27, 1929
" " "	"	20.	" " Bonavista Bay, Newfound'd, Jan. 12, 1929
" " "	"	20.	" " Indian Harbor, Labrador, Oct. 12, 1928

These returns show that the Labrador Black Guillemots tend to winter in the Gulf of St. Lawrence and along the coasts of Newfoundland. There are two from the east, one from the west, and one from the south coast of Newfoundland,

and it is of interest to note that the only two records from the western end of the Gulf of St. Lawrence were both of birds not only shot at the same place within three days of each other but banded on the same island, from nests about twenty feet apart under the same rock ledge. The bird killed at Indian Harbor had moved northward about seventy miles across the mouth of Hamilton Inlet during the fifty-odd days between the time it probably left the nest and the day it was recaptured. The bird killed near the Eagle River had returned the following summer to within twenty miles of its 'home.'

The stomachs of the specimens I took in Labrador were all full of fish remains, mostly caplin. I have observed them carrying lance on several occasions. Hantzsch found, in addition to fish remains, crustaceans (prawns, one Gammarus), and one small snail.

The Black Guillemot is well known and appreciated as a food bird all along the coast. However, its habits of breeding singly or in small colonies, and of nesting far down in the rock-crannies, make it impossible for the eggs to be gathered in wholesale quantities. Many birds are shot for the pot, but the species is not slaughtered on its breeding grounds as are the more colonial alcids. The fishermen frequently take the downy young aboard their schooners and fatten them on fish refuse for the table. They are perky little chaps, and make excellent pets up to the time they are old enough to fly. But in captivity they are never allowed to get quite as old as that.

Fratercula arctica arctica (Linn.)

ATLANTIC PUFFIN

Local vernacular: 'Parokeet,' 'Hatchet-face,' 'Sea Parrot.'
Eskimo: 'Siggoluktok'—the ugly-billed one.
Indian: 'Tey tcúk ah téy tsue.'

This species lives in the North Atlantic and adjacent Arctic seas. Three subspecies are generally recognized—*F. a. arctica*, breeding from Iceland, southern Greenland, and Labrador south to Maine, and wintering south to Massachusetts and occasionally to New Jersey; *F. a. naumanni*, a supposedly large-billed form breeding in northern Greenland, Spitzbergen, and Jan Mayen Land; and *F. a. grabae* breeding in western Europe from Norway to Portugal. I examined the large series of Puffins from Ireland in the Museum of Comparative Zoölogy, and, on comparing them with an equally large series of American birds, found the points of difference very slight and hardly noticeable except in extreme cases.

These subspecies are very slightly differentiated, and owe their recognition mostly to their wide geographical separation.

In Labrador the Puffin is a locally abundant summer resident. It stays among the outer islands and almost never comes into the bays. The species breeds along the coast from eastern Maine through the Gulf of St. Lawrence and along the southern part of eastern Labrador as far north as the Nain region. North of that on the Labrador there are no definite records for the species, though Kumlien (1879, 103) claims to have seen them all the way to Hudson Strait. The northernmost record is of a small flock seen off the rocky islands east of Ford's Harbor by Wheeler, June 10, 1928. Incidentally, this is also the earliest spring record for the coast. The birds doubtless arrive, however, as soon as there is open water, and some probably stay all winter when the ice does not form everywhere, many of them wintering just off the edge of the sea ice. They generally stay in the vicinity, according to Perrett, until the freeze-up, which usually occurs in November. The latest definite record is of a specimen mentioned by Bent (1919, 96), taken at Davis Inlet, October 4.

Coues (1861, 251-255) and Turner (1885, 254) both found the Puffin abundant along the coast at the time of their visits. However, several recent authors have recorded the species as "rare" in eastern Labrador. Townsend and Allen (1907, 302-304) saw only fifty-six from the mail boat between Battle Harbor and Nain in 1906, though they were fortunate enough to find plenty in southern Labrador, where their boat evidently passed near some of the rookeries in the daytime. Hantzsch never saw a single bird. Bent (field notes) in 1912 "did not see a single Puffin north of the Straits of Belle Isle." From these data Townsend (in Bent, 1919, 89-96) concludes that the species had been driven out by the persecutions of the fishermen, and admits only that they might occur sparingly north to Davis Inlet. This does not indicate that the bird has been scarce and has reëstablished itself in the region between the time these observations were made and the present day. It simply means that none of these observers were ever fortunate enough to get near any of the many Puffin colonies. I am sure Townsend and Allen did not on the mail-boat, and as Bent traveled with MacMillan in a small launch I am positive he did not reach the outer islands where I have found the species so common. Hantzsch did not get far enough south; Nain was his southern limit. Unless one visits the immediate vicinity of the rookeries during the breeding season, it is very unusual to see Puffins. As Coues (1861, 251) so ably expresses it: "The habit of collecting in immense numbers at particular localities during the breeding season, so characteristic of the whole family of *Alcidae*, is a trait exhibited in the highest degree by the species now under consideration. With scarcely the exception of the Common Murre, no bird of the family shows so pre-eminently gregarious a disposition as does the Arctic Puffin. Collecting, as it does in thousands, on particular islands of small extent, it becomes a matter of astonishment that food can be procured in sufficient quantity to sustain them, or that each pair can find a place to deposit its egg. The pertinacity, too, with which they cling to the immediate vicinity of their breeding place is remarkable. But a very short distance from an island where there are thousands, it is a comparatively uncommon thing to see a Puffin." I have seen scattered individuals during the breeding season as far as ten miles away from the nearest known rookery, but never farther than that, and I have never observed the large flocks more than a mile from their breeding sites. The cold Labrador Current is rich in marine vertebrate life, and no matter how abundant the birds are in any one locality, they never have to forage far.

I have found the Puffin breeding on the following islands in approximately these numbers:

Bird Island	53°43'40" N.	56°15'30" W.	50
Wester Bird	53 44 40	56 18 15	2000
Gannet Cluster	53 56	56 31	3100
Outer Gannet	54 00 15	56 31	1000
Puffin Island	54 24 30	57 22 00	500
Tinker Island	55 53 30	60 35	20
Nunareuk	56 00	60 27 00	2500
Kidlits	56 11	60 28	1000
Negro Island	56 20 30	60 32 30	20

The birds are known to breed also on Herring Island (54° 19' N., 57° 06' W.) and Greenly Island (51° 22' N., 57° 10' W.), on which I have not had the opportunity to land. A few other small colonies probably exist on outer islands which have never been visited by naturalists, including one or two off the mouth of Hamilton Inlet and some in the Straits of Belle Isle, but there are no other sizable rookeries.

It is difficult to get an exact census of the birds in any of the larger colonies, but general impressions have shown me, especially in the case of the Gannet Islands, that the population is likely to fluctuate from year to year, depending on the depredations of the fishermen and the liveyeres. In 1927 the Puffins had a good year, for throughout the nesting season heavy gales prevented the fishermen (and ourselves, incidentally) from landing on the outer islands. In 1928, however, there was a decided falling off in the numbers of Puffins on the northern island of the Gannet Cluster. Fishermen from Gready had visited it, and I observed there not a quarter of the birds I had seen on it the previous two years. The other islands of the Cluster, however, which had evidently not been robbed, supported their usual complement of birds.

All of the Puffin rookeries I have found and visited have been on islands that appear to my ungeological eyes never to have been glaciated. On none of the alcid rookeries in our district have I ever seen any signs of ice erosion or deposition, such as striae, semilunes, or erratic boulders.   The Puffin is a relatively adaptable species, and I believe it would spread to other islands if conditions were right for it.   However, unglaciated places are the ones that best meet the nesting requirements of the species in eastern Labrador.   Since the bird prefers to lay its single egg at the back of a burrow about three feet long, dug in the tundra, it limits itself more or less to those islands which boast a certain amount of soil and low vegetation.[1]   Such islands are necessarily high ones that have not been scoured by the ice nor washed completely by the waves.   The Puffin cannot arise from a flat land surface, as it must attain considerable momentum before its wings can support it.   Hence it prefers steep slopes on which to breed, so that it may drop off into the air from the mouth of its burrow.   Occasionally, where there are too many individuals present in a particular colony for the amount of typical nesting area, pairs will substitute crannies in the rocks for the usual burrows, selecting the huge rock piles at the foot of talus slopes.   (And what geologist ever heard of high cliffs and well-developed talus slopes on a small, recently glaciated island ?)   This is the case on Puffin Island near Indian Harbor.   I have never observed Puffins utilizing the talus rock-piles where there was room to be had on the grass-covered cliffs of their rookery.

Probably the main requisite for a successful rookery today is that it be inaccessible to man and the predatory animals.   It is indeed fortunate for the Puffins that the islands offering the best nesting sites from the physico-geographical point of view, are those which lie farthest out to sea and can seldom be visited except in the calmest of weather.   Occasionally foxes are marooned in the rookeries by the break-up of ice in the spring, as happened to two on the western island of the Gannet group in 1926.   These drove the Puffins away from all parts of the island except the inaccessible cliffs.

Both sexes incubate, but the greater part of the work, according to most authorities, is supposed to fall on the females.   The exact incubation period is unknown.   Audubon gives it as from twenty-five to twenty-seven days.   Baird, Brewer, and Ridgway give it as one month.   Bent (1919, 96) lists as egg dates for this region and Newfoundland, five from June 8 to July 7, and three from July 1 to July 3.   I never have been able to reach the rookeries before the second week in July, and the laying has always been accomplished by then, and the incubation begun.   Bigelow (1902, 25) observed young fully fledged, out of the nest and in the water, August 25, 1900.   I found them just hatching on the Kidlits, August 10, 1928.   The second week in August seems to be the normal date of hatching

---

[1] The most characteristic plant found growing among the Puffin burrows is a coarse, rank sedge, *Scirpus caespitosus*, var. *callosus*, of circumpolar distribution.   I have found it in luxuriant clumps wherever Puffins dig their tunnels.

on islands that have not been disturbed. But when a rookery has been 'egged,' and a second laying accomplished, the whole breeding sequence is delayed. I found the young just emerging from the egg at the Gannet Islands, September 1, 1926, a year when that rookery was despoiled continually. Three days later we encountered a howling snowstorm.

The Puffin feeds entirely on fish, which it pursues 'flying' under water with its wings. Its main diet during the summer consists of capelin and lance. An expert diver, it is one of the cleverest fishermen among the alcids, and is able to catch and hold three fish at once in its bill. I have often watched parents coming in to feed their chicks with several lance hanging from their gaudy beaks, and I could never understand how the bird could hang on to one while catching another.

Despite its proficiency as a swimmer, the Puffin is notorious for its clumsiness when trying to rise from the water. Its first impulse on being pursued is to take refuge in diving. When this is unsuccessful, the bird tries to rise, and must patter awkwardly for many yards over the surface and through the waves before momentum enough for flight is attained.

The Puffin is one of the chief food birds of the coast, both for meat and eggs. It has no other economic value. The fishermen have a rude, but effective method of catching the adults. They go onto the breeding islands armed with a sack, a bucket, and a five-foot stick with a barbed cod-hook lashed to the end. They shove this stick into each burrow. If the mother is on her nest, they hook her out, wring her neck, and drop her carcass into the sack they carry. Then they fish out the egg, drop it in the bucket, and go on to the next burrow. I visited the outer Gannet Island in 1926 a day or so after fishermen had raided it. The destruction was shocking to see. The birds—what were left of them—were shyly hanging well off shore. The island itself was deserted, but all over it the Puffin burrows were torn open, and heads and wings were scattered over the ground. Man has been the most decisive factor in keeping their numbers down, and the only thing that is saving the birds is the failure of the cod-fishing industry.

It was of interest to me in this connection to compare the present Puffin population of Puffin Island, on the north side of Hamilton Inlet, with its condition in 1860, so enthusiastically described by Coues (1861, 252-254). This rookery lies just six miles southwest of the old fishing-station at Indian Harbor, which until fifteen years ago was one of the largest and most prosperous on the coast. There is still a store there, where a few summer shore fishermen make their headquarters. Schooners still use the port, and it is the summer site of a Grenfell hospital. Coues estimated the birds on Puffin Island as "countless thousands" when he visited the rookery in 1860. He uses such superlative terms as "they came tumbling out of their holes by hundreds, and with the thousands we disturbed from the surface of the water, soon made a perfect cloud above and around us, no longer flying in flocks, but forming one dense continuous mass." But the depredations of the fishermen from Indian Harbor have made heavy inroads on the bird population during the last seventy years. It is a wonder to me that any birds are left there at all. When I visited the island in 1926 I estimated the total population there as five hundred birds. Were the Puffins not molested, they would make a quick recovery, and, now that the fisheries have failed so as to depopulate the coast, there is a good chance for the pressure to be relieved. However, Puffin Island will be in an unfavorable location as long as members of the personnel of the Indian Harbor Hospital are permitted to kill for food there a considerable number of nesting adults at frequent intervals throughout each breeding season.

I once tried to eat the carcasses of some Puffins I skinned for specimens. I agree entirely with Coues, who terms the meat "so excessively tough as to be eatable only in cases of necessity." It is rank, oily, and fishy, and one has to start with a very small piece, for the more it is chewed, the bigger it gets.

Zenaidura macroura carolinensis (Linn.)

Eastern Mourning Dove

A casual visitor from the south. Norton (1901, 152) lists one taken by the Bowdoin Expedition at Red Bay, September 7, 1898. Townsend (1913, 10) quotes Dr. Grenfell's statement that a Mourning Dove was "found dead on the beach at Spotted Islands in August, and another seen alive at Battle Harbor on October 2, 1912." Cooke (1916, 165) adds that one was shot near Battle Harbor in September, 1912, and another one seen there October 20, the same year. There seems to have been a remarkable influx of the birds that year. Dr. Hettasch, the Moravian missionary at Nain, gave me the head, a wing, a foot, and several tail feathers of a Mourning Dove he shot June 5, 1928. He had observed the bird feeding on the ground behind the mission house, and, as it was strange to him, had killed it and kept the remains for me. This is the northernmost record for the species.

Bubo virginianus heterocnemis (Oberholser)

LABRADOR HORNED OWL

Eskimo: 'Ikketiuk'—the one that cries out, 'It is cold!'
Indian: 'Hó-hó,' D. I. B.; 'whóh', B. G. B.

Bubo virginianus is an exceedingly plastic American species, closely related to, though specifically distinct from the Eurasian *Bubo bubo*, which is just as plastic. Its range extends throughout North and South America from the tree line south to the Straits of Magellan, and it breeds throughout its range. Nineteen races are now recognized as valid. The form inhabiting Labrador, *B. v. heterocnemis*, is a large dark bird ranging from the coast of Labrador through Newfoundland and Nova Scotia. Supposedly, it intergrades with *B. v. subarcticus* to the west and with *B. v. virginianus* to the southwest.

The Horned Owl is an uncommon permanent resident in Labrador, inhabiting the wooded portions of the country. Coues (1861, 217) saw a specimen at Rigolet. Low (1896, 325) calls it "common about Northwest River during the winter." Norton (1901, 153) records a bird taken at Cullingham's Cove, Hamilton Inlet, August 1, 1891. When Oberholser described *heterocnemis* (1904, 187), he examined specimens from Okkak, Makkovik, Hopedale, and Turnavik, and made the type a male in the Museum of Comparative Zoölogy, collected by Doane at Loup Bay, April 9, 1899. Townsend and Allen (1907, 374) "obtained a very good skin from the Eskimos at Hopedale." Hantzsch (1929, 32) described two skins taken near Hopedale, one during the autumn of 1905, the other October 20, 1906.

W. Raine ('Auk,' 1896, 257) records a nest and eggs taken with the female parent at Sandwich Bay, April 17, 1895. "The nest was built in a spruce fifteen feet from the ground, and made of twigs and coarse grass." Macoun (1900, 281) credits Raine with a skin and two eggs collected at Sandwich Bay, May 1, 1896; "the nest was built in the top of a spruce, a large structure of sticks, weeds and rubbish." Bent (field notes) says, "Dr. Hettasch gave me a skin and a set of eggs taken near Hopedale."

The Great Horned Owl feeds mainly on other birds and small mammals. Rabbits are especially favored. Its exact diet in Labrador is unknown.

Nyctea nyctea (Linn.)

SNOWY OWL

Eskimo: 'Okpik.'
Indian: 'Wah púk ah noo ee,' D. I. B.; 'shá wuh tuk,' B. G. B.

The Snowy Owl is a well-defined species. It breeds circumpolarly in the barren grounds in high latitudes, and migrates slightly southward in winter when food is scarce in the north, coming commonly as far as the northern United States and sometimes farther. It may stay all winter in the north if food is plentiful.

It is a common winter visitor all through the district, and an uncommon summer resident in the northern part. The Snowy Owl hunts all through the region, both in the forested areas and on the barren grounds during the winter. Hantzsch (1929, 32) tells how a Snowy Owl attacked him at Hebron, October 16, 1906, while he was observing sandpipers on the beach, and says that "at Killinek, as a rule, the first Snowy Owls appear with the autumnal migrations of the ptarmigan." My only record is of one I observed daily at Indian Harbor while weather-bound there from the 7th to the 10th of September, 1927. It was foraging over the barren tundra, evidently hunting small rodents. I saw it most frequently perched on a prominent boulder atop a high ridge overlooking several grassy swales, but though I stalked it doggedly on several occasions, I was unable to get within shot-gun range of it.

Bendire (1892, 391) lists eggs from "Labrador" which are probably from our district. Dr. Friedmann writes me from the National Museum under the date of November 19, 1930, "The set of Snowy Owl's eggs listed by Bendire are still here, three eggs; the data slip reads 'Labrador, 1875, Moravian Missionary.' " Hantzsch (loc. cit.) says "on the east coast of Labrador the Snowy Owl goes southward at least as far as Nain as a regular breeding bird, and I saw eggs from different localities." He also mentions a set of eggs from the mainland near Port Burwell, taken by his native collector in 1907, but the specimens had not reached him, and the record is still uncertain. Townsend and Allen (1907, 374) were told by the Moravian missionary at Nain that the species breeds in that vicinity. Perrett has eggs taken at Nachvak.

Pleske (1928, 162) says: "The Snowy Owl during its breeding season inhabits the alpine zone exclusively, that is to say, those parts that are quite bare of any vegetation whatever, either the tops of the mountains . . . or the plains of the circumpolar tundra. I believe, therefore, that if these plains are quite lacking in dry hillocks or if they chiefly consist of marshy ground, the Snowy Owl does not readily breed in them and seeks more favorable situations for nesting. Evidently these hillocks are absolutely essential for the existence of this bird, because they serve it as observation-posts over its hunting grounds." The eggs, according to the same authority (1928, 168) are usually from seven to ten in number; the incubation period averages thirty-three days, and, as the eggs are laid at an average interval of forty-one hours, the period may be spread out over forty-eight days for a set of ten eggs.

According to Hantzsch (*ibid.*), ptarmigan, lemmings, and white-footed mice make up their favorite food, but "they also catch fish and other small marine animals, where water places remain open, but are otherwise satisfied with every possible animal matter, even bits of meat refuse near human dwellings."

Cooke (1916, 165) quotes Birdseye's notes: "Many of the people at Sandwich Bay set steel traps on isolated stumps for owls. These birds are usually very fat, and are good eating. The fat is not at all strong." The Eskimos, also, are very fond of them.

Surnia ulula caparoch (Müller)

American Hawk Owl

Eskimo: 'Nuilatok'—the one having a trimming around the face. The name is used for the fur trimming around the face of a 'silipak' or 'dicky.'
Indian: 'Páh pe netc tcee.'

This is another circumpolar species breeding along the tree line in the Hudsonian zone.   It is divided into three races—one in North America, the other two in Europe and Asia respectively. It migrates slightly southward in winter during hard years when food is scarce, but tends to be a permanent resident wherever found.

It is a common permanent resident in the wooded portions of Newfoundland Labrador.   Low (1896, 325) saw Hawk Owls "several times on Upper Hamilton River."   Townsend and Allen (1907, 375) "saw three or four skins of this bird in Dr. Grenfell's hospital at Battle Harbor and obtained one.   The bird had been killed at Fox Harbor.   We also saw the skin of one at Hopedale."   Doane collected two females, which he sent to Bangs,—one at Black Bay, November 19, 1898, the other at Loup Bay, April 25, 1899.   Perrett records seeing three together at Makkovik during the winter of 1898-1899.   Fred Brown, a trapper at Separation Point, who was with me when I shot one of three individuals I saw there, July 18, 1926, told me he saw them almost daily (the species is markedly diurnal) in the winter while visiting his trap-line in the interior.

The Hawk Owl usually lays its clutch of from three to eight eggs on the rotten wood in an old hollow tree or stump, and often utilizes the abandoned nests of other species which it re-lines with a few feathers. It is not known to build a nest of its own. Macoun (1900, 287) lists a set of eggs in the collection of W. Raine, taken at Hamilton Inlet, May 24, 1896. "This nest was built in a spruce tree top." Perrett related to me with much amusement his finding seven half-grown young in a hollow stub in Udjuktok Bay. He picked one up, and as he lifted it out of the nest another grasped it, to be in turn grasped by the next one, which continued until the whole brood was suspended in a chain in the air. He added that the adults were quite vicious and attacked him fearlessly. I saw young of the year on the wing at Sandwich Bay, July 14, 1926.

The stomach of the only one I killed was empty. According to Fisher (1893, 188), "the food of this Owl varies considerably at different times of the year. In summer it feeds on the smaller mammals, such as mice, lemmings, and ground squirrels as well as insects of various kinds, while in winter, when the snow is deep and its favorite food is hidden, it follows the large flocks of ptarmigans and subsists on them."

[Scotiaptex nebulosa nebulosa (Forster). GREAT GRAY OWL. There is no definite record for the occurrence of this practically circumpolar boreal species in Labrador. Townsend and Allen (1907, 372) are of the opinion that Cartwright may have referred to the Great Gray Owl in his journal for October 29, 1773, for if a large gray owl were to be found in the country, it would be more likely to be this species than the Barred Owl, which is much more southern in its distribution.

The Indians recognized the picture of this species in Reed's 'Bird Guide,' which Dr. Strong showed them, and called it 'Páh whee ut su.' This name, however, might be just as referable to Richardson's Owl, which is of the same general color and shape, for there is no way of judging size from the Reed pictures.]

Asio flammeus flammeus (Pont.)

SHORT-EARED OWL

Eskimo: 'Imaingertak.'

The Short-eared Owl is nearly cosmopolitan in its distribution, and breeds throughout its range. *A. f. flammeus* breeds circumpolarly from the tree line southward. In North America it nests from Alaska across to Labrador, and south to California and Massachusetts. In Eurasia it breeds from 70° north latitude in western Europe south to the Pyrenees and Italy, and eastward through Siberia to Kamchatka and Anadyr. There is one subspecies recognized in southeastern Russia and western Siberia, there are two in South America, one in the Falkland Islands, and one in the Hawaiian Islands. The bird is replaced by a closely allied species in the Galapagos Islands, and by another in Hispaniola and Porto Rico.

It is an uncommon summer resident in Labrador. Turner (1885, 243) obtained specimens at Davis Inlet, where he saw "a very light-colored individual," July 18, 1882. Low (1896, 325) saw it on the Upper Hamilton River. Bigelow 1902, 29) found it "rather common at Port Manvers and Nachvak, in September." Townsend and Allen (1907, 372) obtained a skin from the Eskimos at Hopedale, and were informed by Mr. Schmidt, the Moravian missionary, that the bird bred near Nain. Hantzsch (1929, 31) gives the measurements of a skin taken at Hopedale during the autumn of 1904, and says it is "an occasional breeding bird in the interior of the country, in the coast districts more common at time of migration." Bent (field notes) saw a Short-eared Owl at Hawke Harbor, July 9, 1912. Perrett collected four specimens,—two at Ailik in May, 1899, one at Pamiarluk in June, 1899, and one at Makkovik, October 7, 1899. In the Museum of Comparative Zoölogy are a female taken May 30, 1899, and two males taken June 6 and 8, 1899, respectively, at Loup Bay by Ernest Doane.

Weiz (1866) lists the Short eared Owl as a breeding bird at Okkak. Hantzsch (*loc. cit.*) says, "At Rama . . . according to the statements made to me by the inhabitants there, this owl is also said to breed and I saw and secured several clutches of eggs from localities on the coast still farther south." Perrett collected a set of nine eggs near Hopedale, June 5, 1904.

Hantzsch (*vide supra*) says the Short-eared Owls "like to feed on the frequently abundant mice of the species *Peromyscus maniculatus* (Wagner) and lemming *Dicrostenyx hudsonius* (Pallas). They are, however, content with all other possible little creatures and animal substances."

Cryptoglaux funerea richardsoni (Bonap.)

RICHARDSON'S OWL

The species breeds circumpolarly in both Canadian and Hudsonian zones across North America, and in their homologues across Eurasia. The Old World forms are subspecifically distinct, and four races have been described from Siberia.

In Labrador Richardson's Owl is a rare permanent resident. Townsend and Allen (1907, 372) mention the Bangs specimen, a female taken by Doane at Loup

Bay, March 1, 1899, and hazard the opinion that the species will probably be found breeding. Doane also obtained a male at Black Bay, December 19, 1898. Bent records in his field notes that "Dr. Hettasch gave me the skin of one taken near Hopedale. Perrett told me that a nest with young birds in it was found by some of his Eskimos, and that the old birds were very pugnacious." Perrett shot one near Makkovik in March, 1900, and another at Hopedale.

It is possible that the Indians who recognized the picture of the Great Gray Owl in Reed's 'Bird Guide,' (see p. 148) might have had this species in mind.

Chordeiles minor minor (Forster)

Eastern Nighthawk

A casual visitor. Low (1896, 326) says: "Very rare on Upper Hamilton River. Single specimen seen near the Grand Falls [Hamilton River], May 31." The only specimen on record for this species in Newfoundland Labrador is a native-made skin sent me by Mr. B. Lenz, the Moravian missionary at Makkovik. His letter accompanying the skin says, "It was shot by Alfred Winters (a half-breed Eskimo) here at the station near the houses in June, 1929, darting about after flies, and did not seem fearsome of man at all."

[Archilochus colubris (Linn.). RUBY-THROATED HUMMINGBIRD. The only record for this species for the district is the one of Turner (1885, 242), who says, "A single individual, male, was seen within 4 feet of me July 17, 1882, on a hill-top (825 feet elevation) back of the station at Davis Inlet."]

Megaceryle alcyon alcyon (Linn.)

Eastern Belted Kingfisher

Eskimo: 'Toggajovak'—the one with a big tusk.
Indian: 'Oh tceés ti mi ni soo.'

The Belted Kingfisher breeds throughout North America from the northern limits of the Canadian zone south to the southern United States, and winters south as far as northern South America. It is represented in western North America by an allied subspecies.

In Labrador it is an uncommon summer resident on the rivers at least as far north as the Makkovik region, whence Perrett reports having seen it in Island Harbor Bay during the summer of 1899. Coues (1861, 217) "ascertained the existence of this bird in Labrador, from a single skin in the possession of the natives. They considered it as a rare bird." Turner (1885, 242) says it is "a summer visitor to Northwest River, where it breeds." I have seen the bird but once on the Labrador. While we were ascending the Paradise River in Sandwich Bay, July 15, 1928, an adult female flew across the bow of our skiff just out of gun-range.

It lays its five to eight eggs at the back of a tunnel three to fifteen feet in length dug in an overhanging river-bank. The incubation, supposedly chiefly by the female, lasts about seventeen days, according to most authorities.

Perrett had a set of three eggs in his collection, which Bent (field notes) saw and verified. Dr. Strong writes me that the Bromfields and Lanes (reputable local families) and the Indians all stated separately "that the bird occurred on Hunt's River. George Lane said a pair nested in a high bank above his house, but their eggs (pure white on a bed of fish bones) were twice taken and the birds left. The accurate description of the birds and the nest by each individual leaves no doubt in my mind that this is a good record."

It is known to eat minnows of various sorts, mostly fresh-water species, and small amphibians. Its specific feeding habits in Labrador are unknown.

Colaptes auratus luteus Bangs

NORTHERN FLICKER

The Flicker is a wholly Nearctic species ranging from the tree line south to the Gulf of Mexico throughout North America east of the Rocky Mountains. Two subspecies are now recognized— C. a. luteus from the Hudsonian zone at the tree line south through the Upper Austral, and C. a. auratus in the Lower Austral. There is a perfect intergradation from north to south, the main criterion being size; the northern form is the larger, the southern the smaller.

It is a rare summer resident in the wooded portions of Labrador. Turner (1886, 342) says it is "reported to be a common summer visitor to Northwest River." Low (1896, 326) claims to have seen a Flicker near the Grand Falls of the Hamilton River on May 30. Townsend (1909, 201) reports a male collected at Sandwich Bay in August, 1908. Cooke (1916, 165) writes: "This species is probably not so rare as its few records for the eastern coast of Labrador would indicate. One was taken at Sandwich Bay in August, 1908 [see above], and one at Okpatok [Akpatok ?] Island, Hudson Strait, October, 1882. These are the only published records for eastern Labrador, but a man who lived at Sandwich Bay and had taken a specimen there the spring of 1909 said that they nested in that neighborhood. In confirmation of this two individuals were heard there June 5, 1915." Dr. Strong records in his diary for July 1, 1928, at Northwest Corner Brook, forty miles up Hunt's River from Jack Lane's Bay: "Flicker calling from snags in an old burned-over country. It flew with typical undulations, and its yellow shafts and white rump made identification a certainty."

Perrett asserts that the Flicker has bred in Kaipokok Bay, where he has seen it occasionally and has taken its eggs. A set of seven eggs in his collection was taken at Rigolet in June, 1894.

Sphyrapicus varius varius (Linn.)

Yellow-bellied Sapsucker

The Sapsucker is a casual visitor to Labrador from the south. The only record is of an adult female taken by Ernest Doane at Loup Bay, May 5, 1899, and now in the Museum of Comparative Zoölogy.

[Dryobates villosus subsp. Hairy Woodpecker. Low (1896, 325) states that he "shot [a Hairy Woodpecker] in the valley of the Hamilton River in March. Not rare." Unfortunately the specimen apparently was not preserved. There are no other records.]

[Dryobates pubescens subsp. Downy Woodpecker. Labrador specimens have never been taken. Low (1896, 325) states this species is "common on Hamilton River throughout the year." Packard says "probably does not range north of 56°." Robert Stevenson, the wireless operator at Gready, told me he took a trip into the Mealy Mountains during the winter of 1927-1928, and saw commonly in there a small woodpecker with red on the back of its head; and from my descriptions he surmised it must have been the Downy rather than the Hairy that he saw. The Davis Inlet Indians seem to know a woodpecker of this genus, but it is impossible to tell to which one, the Hairy or the Downy, to refer their name, 'Wanúh kwin ee yoo.' They told Dr. Strong that they "see the bird frequently in the interior, and consider its tapping a sign of good weather."]

Picoïdes arcticus (Swainson)

ARCTIC THREE-TOED WOODPECKER

Eskimo: 'Toggajok'—the one with a sharp bill.
Indian: 'Pas pas teé yoo' (*partim*).

Picoïdes arcticus is wholly North American and tends to be a permanent resident throughout its range. It breeds mainly within the confines of the Canadian and lower Hudsonian zones, across the continent from Labrador to Alaska and south to the northern United States. A few straggle casually in winter south to Connecticut and Pennsylvania.

It is an uncommon permanent resident in the wooded portions of the country. Low (1896, 326) considered it common throughout the lower Hamilton River region. Bangs (1900, 130) lists a specimen from Makkovik, which is now in the Museum of Comparative Zoölogy. Perrett records killing four at Makkovik in 1899, one of which is the Bangs skin. He gave the other three to Sornborger, but they are not traceable today.

Though I have searched assiduously for them, I have never seen a Woodpecker of any sort in Labrador. I quote from my own field notes, written August 4, 1928, twenty miles up the Fraser River from Nain Bay: "There is much evidence of woodpecker work. All the dead stubs, of which there are many in the spruce-larch forest, bear borings and holes. Found one boring hollowed out for a nest. The maker might be either the Ladder-backed or the Arctic. I haven't even heard one calling or drumming in the distance."

Picoïdes tridactylus bacatus Bangs

AMERICAN THREE-TOED WOODPECKER

Eskimo: 'Tooquaeuk.'
Indian: 'Pas pas teé yoo' (*partim*).

This is a circumpolar species breeding from the tree limit south into the Canadian zone in both hemispheres, and wintering slightly southward.

There are three subspecies recognizable in America: *P. t. fasciatus*, breeding from the tree limit in Alaska and Mackenzie south to British Columbia, northern Washington, and Montana; *P. t. dorsalis*, breeding in the coniferous belt of the

Rocky Mountains from northern Montana south to Arizona and New Mexico; and *P. t. bacatus*, breeding in the Hudsonian and Canadian zones from Labrador and northern Quebec, southern Mackenzie, and northern Manitoba south to northern Minnesota, New England, and Newfoundland. The species seems more variable in Eurasia, for there no less than eight races are now accepted as valid.

I cannot differentiate the bird Bangs (1900, 138) described as *labradorius*, for the characters are too slight, if they exist at all. The white in the plumage is due simply to feather wear, and I am totally unable to recognize the nuchal crest character. The measurements show no variation from those of a good series from over the rest of North America, with the exception of Alaska. The Alaskan bird is larger. But Bangs's new name for the eastern form, which I give above, holds valid, for Brehm's description of *americanus* is not only unrecognizable, but is wrong in its only discriminative word, "grosser," as our bird is definitely smaller than the European, of which it is no more than a subspecies. It certainly cannot be given specific rank. By throwing out Brehm's name, *americanus* Swainson is invalidated, for Brehm's name is not a *nomen nudum*. (See Bangs, 1930, 325.)

It is an uncommon permanent resident in the wooded portions of Labrador from the tree line south. There are no additional data on the 'Ladder-backed' Woodpecker in Labrador since Townsend and Allen (1907, 377) summed up the records. Specimens have been taken at Okkak, Nain, Hopedale, Makkovik, Northwest River, Black Bay, and Loup Bay.

Tyrannus tyrannus (Linn.)

Eastern Kingbird

The Kingbird is a casual visitor from the south. Perrett notes the bird killed at Killinek by Julius Lane, July 20, 1906, which Hantzsch (1929, 33) mentions. He claims also to have taken the species at Hopedale, but the definite record has been lost. These are the only records for the species in Labrador.

Otocoris alpestris alpestris (Linn.)

NORTHERN HORNED LARK

Local vernacular: 'Skylark,' 'Mudlark.'
Eskimo: 'Kopanoakpak'—the big little bird.

The Horned Lark is a most widely spread and plastic species, occurring circumpolarly throughout the northern hemisphere, and penetrating slightly below the Equator in Africa. It is broken up into a host of subspecies—twenty-odd in Eurasia and Africa, and twenty-two in America. The Labrador form, *O. a. alpestris*, intergrades with *O. a. hoyti*, to the north and west, and extends southward as a breeding bird to Newfoundland and the Gaspé Peninsula. It migrates south along the coast in winter to New England and the Middle Atlantic States.

It is an abundant summer resident along the coast from the Straits of Belle Isle to Cape Chidley, though less common in the extreme north. The Horned Lark is a typical bird of the treeless coastal belt, and is also found on the barrens of the interior above the tree line. It never occurs in the wooded regions. Coues (1861, 221) epitomizes it as: "Very abundant on all the barren moss-covered islands along the coast, and in every suitable situation on the mainland. Labrador, indeed, from the fact that it is the most southerly region which affords the peculiar open and exposed situations which these birds exclusively frequent, seems to be their special breeding ground." Low (1896, 326) found the Horned Lark "common on barrens of Upper Hamilton River and about Lake Michikamau." Bigelow (1902, 29) calls it "abundant everywhere on the bleakest and most exposed hillsides." Townsend and Allen (1907, 380-385) collected a series of breeding birds along the southern third of the coast. Hantzsch (1929, 33) says it is "not a rare breeding bird in our district. On the spring migration it is said to occur often in numbers and is looked upon by the Eskimos as a very welcome harbinger of spring. In the autumn, on the other hand, I observed only a few migrants." Cooke (1916, 166) writes, "The last one noted in 1912 was at Ticoralak October 12, and the first returning migrant was seen at Sandwich Bay, April 22, 1913."

I found the Horned Lark abundant all along the coast as far north as Bay of Seven Islands, where I saw fifteen, both adults and young, August 15, 1927. North of that I saw none whatsoever. Under the date of April 28, 1928, Robert Stevenson wrote me from Gready, "The Shore Larks appeared here for the first time this spring on April 15, and they are now becoming common."

Turner (1885, 241) says the Horned Lark breeds at Rigolet. Low (*ibid.*) found eggs on the Upper Hamilton, June 19. Townsend and Allen (*loc. cit.*) found a nest "composed of dried grass and a few large feathers, deeply sunk into the reindeer lichen and moss in a level piece of ground," at Frenchman's Isle, July 16, 1906. "It contained three dark-skinned young, clothed sparingly in sulphur-yellow down. Their eyes were not yet open. There was also one egg containing a large embryo." In the Nain region, on June 12, 1931, Wheeler found a "Horned Lark's nest with three eggs well up on Alagaiai, a high hill east of Naksatkok."

The Horned Lark's nest is always on the ground and in the open. I have never found one under more cover than a surrounding clump of the thin tundra grasses might give it. The usual structure is a deep cup of beautifully woven grasses, frequently lined with a few feathers of larger birds. The usual time of laying seems to be during the second or third week in June, but there is a great individual variation in the date. I found fledglings almost ready to fly at Battle Harbor, July 5, 1926, but on the Gannet Islands, July 14, the same year, there was a nest which still contained two well-incubated eggs. I have watched both parents attending and feeding the young.

Hantzsch (*vide supra*) found in the stomachs of the three Horned Larks he collected "a caterpillar skin, insect remains, seed-husks . . . apparently of *Cerastium alpinum*." He also speaks of watching one hunt spiders. The young are fed almost entirely on insects. Thrice I have watched Horned Larks approach their nests carrying what appeared to be large stone-flies in their beaks.

[Otocoris alpestris praticola Henshaw. PRAIRIE HORNED LARK. A specimen of *Otocoris alpestris alpestris* taken by the Bowdoin Expedition at Chateau Bay on July 14, 1891, was erroneously referred to this form by Norton (1901, 153) and by Oberholser (1902). The bird is a female in worn plumage with the diagnostic yellow markings on the head and throat much faded. (*Cf.* Townsend and Allen, 1907, 380-385).]

Iridoprocne bicolor (Vieillot)

TREE SWALLOW

This is a North American species, and its closest relatives are forms of the American tropics and subtropics. It breeds across North America in the Canadian, Transition, and Upper Austral zones, from Alaska to Labrador, and south from southern California to Virginia. It winters over the southern United States and south to the northern shores and islands of the Caribbean Sea.

The Tree Swallow is an uncommon summer resident locally in the southern part of our territory. Cartwright recorded the arrival of two swallows on May 18, 1778. Kumlien (1897, 74) notes that "a couple of these swallows followed the schooner for two days in succession off Belle Isle, in August, 1877." Low (1896, 327) states that it is "common throughout the interior. Seen May 25th." On July 15, 1928, I observed four Tree Swallows flying hither and yon after insects over the Paradise River. I was able to identify them beyond question, but I could not get close enough to them to secure a specimen.

[Riparia riparia riparia (Linn.) BANK SWALLOW. Probably a rare summer resident. Weiz reported that it bred at Okkak, which is doubtful. Townsend and Allen (1907, 404) say, "Mr. Goldsby, one of the Moravians, told us of finding a Sand Martin's hole with two eggs in a sand bank at Ogjuktok [Udjuktok] Inlet near Hopedale." Mr. Perrett verifies this, and tells me he has identified the bird breeding there, though he was unable to get either eggs or a specimen of the bird He says the Eskimos call the bird 'Tullugornak,' evidently another kind of 'little bird.']

Hirundo rustica erythrogaster Bodd.

BARN SWALLOW

The Barn Swallow is a casual visitor to Labrador. Turner (1885, 239) says that the bird "breeds at Northwest River," but the record is doubtful. The only definite record of the Barn Swallow for Newfoundland Labrador is a specimen taken at Hopedale in July, 1908 (see Townsend, 1909, 201).

Perisoreus canadensis nigricapillus Ridgway

LABRADOR JAY

Local vernacular: 'Whiskey Jack.'
Eskimo: 'Koppanoaksoak'—another 'big little bird.'
Indian: 'Wís kat sa.' (Note similarity to the vernacular name.)

After examining and comparing all the Canada Jay material in the Museum of Comparative Zoölogy, the American Museum of Natural History, the United States National Museum, and the collection of the U. S. Biological Survey, totalling about three hundred and fifty specimens, I find there are recognizable seven races of *Perisoreus canadensis*. All seven have been described and named, but only three are now recognized in the A. O. U. Check-List. I have likewise examined the types of all the races except that of typical *canadensis* of which no type specimen is in existence, Linnaeus having based his description on Brisson's plate. I have, however, examined topotypical material from Quebec, which Oberholser has designated as the type locality of the race.

The series I examined afforded excellent comparative material, which is very necessary when attempting to differentiate Canada Jays subspecifically. It is only rarely that such strictly comparable material can be brought together, as skins for the purpose must be approximately alike in the time of year they were taken and in their ages as specimens. There is not a little seasonal variation from feather wear, and specimens darken and turn brownish from the ravages of time, no matter how well they are preserved and protected from light and air. The skins should not be over twenty years old to appear in their true values, and, the fresher the material, the better it is for comparison.

As for criteria of the races, size is of very little value. The series of measurements I made show no regular differences except in the case of one race. In the remaining six they overlap with hopeless irregularity. Shade of coloration is the only indicator of importance that I have been able to find, and this proves easily recognizable when one has sufficiently large series of birds to contrast. I used the relative colors of the backs, bellies, foreheads, and nuchal crests as guides, and had comparatively little trouble in separating the races. In the accompanying diagram I have arranged the races I recognize with respect to the intensity

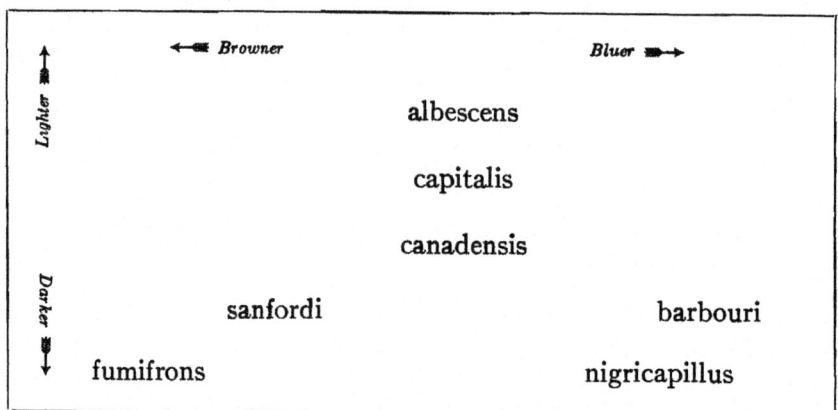

of their coloring and its shade. The differences range from dark to light in intensity, and from brownish to bluish in shade. For a starting point let us use *canadensis*, the most widely spread, and the best known, of the races, as a standard of comparison. *Capitalis* is a slightly lighter bird with a wider white forehead and a less expanded black nuchal crest. It is larger in general than any of the other races, and this one characteristic sets it off from them distinctively. Its closest affinity, however, is with *canadensis*. The lightest in intensity of all the races is *albescens*, which is even lighter than *capitalis*, though smaller and of about the same shade. Going the other way from our starting point, the next darker are *sanfordi* and *barbouri*, two birds about equal in intensity of color, but the former is slightly browner, and the latter much bluer than *canadensis*. Of the two, *sanfordi* has the darker belly and forehead, while *barbouri* has the darker back and nuchal crest. By its distinct lavender-bluishness, *barbouri* approaches in shade *nigricapillus* only, and is very distinct, while *sanfordi* shows more direct shade affinity to *canadensis*. The remaining two subspecies are the darkest of all, and are of approximately the same general intensity, the nuchal crest being wider and the white forehead duskier and less extended than in any of the other races; but while *fumifrons* is slightly browner and smokier, *nigricapillus* is a shade bluer.

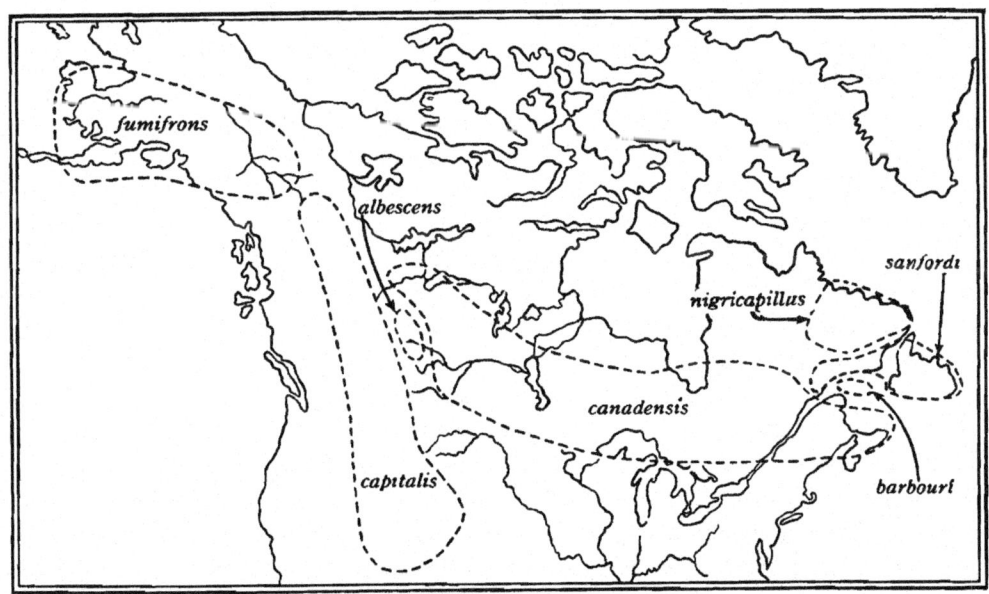

The accompanying map shows the approximate ranges of these seven races. It is noteworthy that the species is practically confined to the Canadian and Hudsonian zones, and is a confirmed dweller in the evergreen forests. Thus we have *fumifrons* from Alaska, *capitalis* from the Rockies, *albescens* from the Red Deer River region of Alberta, *canadensis* with a type locality at Quebec and spreading over most of the Canadian Zone territory from Manitoba to Nova Scotia, *bar-*

bouri limited to Anticosti Island in the Gulf of St. Lawrence, *sanfordi* extending from Newfoundland across the Straits of Belle Isle and along the coast of southern Labrador, and *nigricapillus* finding whatever cover it can along and inland from the east coast of Labrador.

How can we relate this peculiar distribution to the obvious color affinities of the races in the light of our present knowledge of past geological history? To know the origin of a form is to know most of the reasons for its present distribution, but to discuss the origin of any of the transitory stages in the natural scheme of things that we call species or subspecies is a precarious thing at best, for we are working by hypothesis with artificial and made-to-order definitions. That the different color values of the various races are to some extent a result of environmental conditions, there can be no doubt. It certainly is significant that here in the Jays, as with the races of so many other species, we find the largest form in the mountain regions, the lightest in comparatively arid country, and the darkest in the damp northern forests. But environment cannot tell the whole story, for those races that border on the Gulf of St. Lawrence dwell in approximately the same type of country, and we have the two obviously related forms, *barbouri* and *nigricapillus*, separated by the intervention of a third form, *sanfordi*, totally unlike either of them. And while it is not at all impossible, it does seem strange to me that three forms as closely alike as are *barbouri*, *nigricapillus*, and *fumifrons* should evolve in parallel fashion in regions so widely separated as are their ranges. The rest of the explanation of the existence of these subspecies lies in their past history. Let us review it briefly, keeping in mind that even today Perisoreus nests in the cold weather of early spring while the snow is on the ground, and that while it tends to be a permanent resident in most parts of its range, and migrates hardly at all, it does not necessarily follow that the species in times past was not much more aggressive in matters of territory than it is today.

That Perisoreus is a comparatively plastic and hence youthful genus, is evidenced by the tendency of its three species to break into geographical races all over its territory. It appears to be still evolving, still segregating. It is a circumpolar genus, represented in Eurasia by one species, *infaustus*, of which some European ornithologists recognize fifteen subspecies, and in North America by *canadensis*, as we have seen, with seven and by *obscurus* with two. This present distribution points to a common ancestor for all three species, that extended its range throughout the circumpolar regions in Cenozoic time, probably as late as the Miocene, when the entire area probably was still united by the Bering Land Bridge (and, if one subscribes to the Wegener hypothesis, before the continents drifted apart), and uniform temperature, climate, and forest conditions probably prevailed over the entire northern hemisphere. The Pliocene saw the submergence of much of the northern land mass, the breaking up of this overworked land bridge, the start, according to Wegener, of the drifting of the northern continents, and a change in climate. It was probably soon thereafter that the species of Perisoreus as we know them today came into being. In this connection it is noteworthy that, while the *infaustus* races of Eurasia are all brownish birds with red tails, the grayest of them lives in the easternmost part of Siberia. Of the *canadensis* races, the brownest is *fumifrons*, lying geographically closest to Siberia, so that although the specific line between the two is sharp and well marked, there is some evidence of an old intergradation. Shortly thereafter *obscurus* may have separated out from *canadensis* stock on the western side of the Rocky Mountains, for that barrier must have been as effective then as today. At any rate, it is more than likely that by the start of the Pleistocene the bird with which we are most concerned, *canadensis*, was already well established as a species.

It has come to be generally held that during the Pleistocene the temperature varied more than once between a cold and a warm climate. However, as to the number of the alternations there is as yet no unanimity among geologists, because of the great difficulties in correlating the separated masses of glacial material, all of which are so much alike. Some geologists recognize three, others as many as six glacial stages, with from two to five interglacial warmer times. The lesser number of warmer times seems to be the more probable, and I am assuming two for my hypothesis. It is also now widely accepted that the interglacial times were markedly variable in duration, and that all of them were not only warmer than the present, but lasted longer, and sometimes much longer, than the glacial stages themselves. As each successive glacial stage advanced, the ice-sheet drove the fauna and flora out from the country it covered. With each retreat of the ice, the flora and fauna pushed back in again, driven not only by the normal tendencies in all species to expand and acquire new territory, but also by the active competition in the southern regions where so many forms may have been crowded together. Those species that followed the ice back would most naturally be the ones that in the past were accustomed to more rigorous climates, so that the country would be repopulated, with minor exceptions, by essentially the same flora and fauna that had previously been driven out of it. In the light of this extermination and reclamation by the ice advances and retreats, some otherwise seeming incongruities may be explained.

Thus at the start of the Pleistocene we have an ancestor of our present races of Canada Jays ranging widely over northern North America. I believe this ancestor to have been more like *fumifrons* than any of the other races, and that it resembled the present Alaskan bird very much indeed. Inasmuch as *fumifrons* is the only one of the races whose present range has not been glaciated, and as there are no evidences showing that it has not been able to live in its present area ever since the breakdown of the Bering Land Bridge, it probably has undergone few, if any, environmental changes, and without these there is no reason for any change in the race.   The first glacier swept most of the rest of the country, however, and drove everything before it, wiping out the central and eastern birds, or driving them southward and eastward.   We must not forget the probable existence during each of the ice advances of a land area outside the ice on the now submerged coastal plain, on which a flora and fauna may have persisted.   There is some evidence that a few may have persisted on the eastern unglaciated areas, but as two of these, the Shickshock Mountains and the western range of Newfoundland, are high mountain ranges where the necessary forest cover hardly could have existed, especially during a glacial period, it is highly improbable that they persisted there.   Thus the end of the first glacial advance apparently saw the Canada Jays in three separated areas—Alaska, the region south of the glaciers, and the outlying coastal plain.   At this time I believe the southern bird started to differentiate along the lines which have produced typical *canadensis* and its nearest allies.

When the first glacier retreated, the invasion of the Jays into the evacuated territory must have come from all three areas.   The southern birds were forced on by stiff competition, and it is not unreasonable to suppose the Alaskan and coastal-plain birds had not yet been isolated long enough to lose their aggressiveness in acquiring new territory.   I believe the Alaskan bird swept eastward at once, the coastal-plain bird went westward and northward, and the southern bird penetrated northward, all three so mingling that the end of the first interglacial period saw the Nearctic regions covered with two races of *Perisoreus canadensis*, a darker one to the north, that was essentially *fumifrons*, intergrading with a lighter one to the southward which has since totally disappeared; also that a branch of the pure southern stock at this time invaded the Rocky Mountains, and, persisting through the remaining glacial advances in some place or other, eventually evolved into *capitalis*.

The second glaciation was not as severe as the first in many places.   The evidences along the northeast Labrador coast show that the area as a whole received but one thorough scouring—and that probably by the first glaciation. The remaining glacial periods were represented in that region only by local valley glaciers.   This fact is shown by the existence of fresh striae, boulders, semilunes, and other evidences of glaciation only in the valley mouths.   These features elsewhere on the northeast coast are all marked by signs of great weathering and erosion, signifying their antiquity.   So, during this glaciation there were areas in the region where a flora and fauna Hudsonian in type might have persisted through it, and the evidences from the zoölogical and botanical sides are all in favor of just such a thing having happened.   Newfoundland and southern Labrador were covered with ice at this time, with the exception of the western range of Newfoundland, but that the Jays persisted on this throughout the glacial time is very improbable, though possible. The coastal plain was probably re-submerged during the interglacial period, as the ice melted, more water flowed into the sea, and isostatic balance reasserted itself. But with the second advance of the ice it probably emerged again and was populated with a jay southern in type, so that here the ancestors of *sanfordi* may have persisted. At the same time, some part of Anticosti in all probability remained unglaciated. Geologists have been almost unanimous in agreeing that Anticosti was entirely glaciated, but the interior of the island, small as it is, has never been explored or studied intensively by either geologist or zoölogist. Frère Marie Victorin, who has made a special study of the plant life of the island, has produced almost incontrovertible botanical evidence to the effect that some part of the island rose above the ice sufficiently to allow certain endemic plants to persist. If this was the case, there is no reason for not supposing that an accompanying avifauna persisted with the flora. Hence, during this second glacial advance, we may suppose that, while *fumifrons* was again isolated in the northwest from the birds driven southward before the ice, there were several other islands of survival, with the ancestors of *barbouri* remaining on Anticosti, the progenitors of *nigricapillus* somewhere in northeastern Labrador, and part of the southern stock perhaps persisting on an eastern coastal plain outside the ice limits.

During this advance isolation would have begun to tell on the races that were cooped in small areas with but scant competition, as were these forebears of *fumifrons*, *nigricapillus*, and *barbouri*. They must have lost to some extent their powers of aggression, so that when the ice receded a second time, they stayed right in their respective areas, and made no attempt to follow the ice back, while at the same time the areas in the St. Lawrence region, as well as in the rest of the Canadian and Hudsonian regions that had been ice-covered, were repopulated during the second interglacial stage by a southern intrusion of relatively unspecialized birds. The bird that came into Newfoundland and southern Labrador, which at that time were connected by land where now exist the Straits of Belle Isle, probably intruded from the southeast off the coastal plain, though it may possibly have immigrated either from the south or southwest. Undergoing the same sort of environmental conditions that kept the other races there so dark, this ancestor of *sanfordi* soon began to feel the influences and to break away from its parent stock. It was likewise probably somewhere about this time that *albescens* started to break away from the *capitalis* stock in the Alberta region. That it could have persisted through the last glaciation is still a moot question, for all its present range was to the best of our knowledge heavily glaciated. There is some evidence, however, that during the last advance the edge of the Keewatin sheet barely touched that area, and further geological studies may show some region in or near the present range of *albescens* where the bird may have persisted. That it could have differentiated from its parent stock so distinctively since the retreat of the last ice-sheet, or in other words about forty thousand years at the outside, seems highly improbable.

The last advance but lightly touched the extreme northeastern part of the continent. It, again, left islands of survival in the ranges of *nigricapillus* and *barbouri*, but according to the best authorities this last sheet swept downward from the height of land in central Labrador southward over the coast of southern Labrador into the Gulf of St. Lawrence, and it is hard to imagine any locality here where *sanfordi* may have survived. That it was able to persist in Newfoundland or on the adjacent coastal plain, there is no doubt geologically, and that it was able to do so also on the north shore of the Gulf seems to be an established fact, for at this time the land bridge between Newfoundland and the mainland broke down, and the Straits of Belle Isle came into existence. If *barbouri* had become too ultra-specialized to cross the twenty miles of water between Anticosti and the mainland, it hardly seems likely that *sanfordi* should cross the fifteen-mile stretch at the Straits. The region today is one of emergence, and the past may have seen these bodies of water even larger than they are today.

The Labrador Jay is a common permanent resident throughout the wooded portions of the country. Coues (1861, 226) found it abundant at Rigolet. Weiz (1866) lists it as a breeding bird at Okkak. Low (1896, 326) calls it "very common throughout the interior." Norton (1901, 155) records four specimens taken by the Bowdoin Expedition at Northwest River in 1891. Bigelow (1902, 29) says of it, "Locally common, even abundant as far north as Port Manvers." Townsend and Allen (1907, 387) "saw the Labrador Jay only at Rigolet on July 18th, about six individuals in all."

My notes contain abundant references to the species from July through the first part of September. The bird is always to be seen the moment one starts hunting in the forested areas in the bays. I observed it most commonly between Sandwich Bay and Nain. North of that I never visited country favorable for it. Sornborger got one at Okkak, which is now in the Museum of Comparative Zoölogy. Doane took two at Loup Bay, March 12 and 22, 1899. Wheeler notes Canada Jays as "abundant at the head of Tikkoatokok Bay January 29, 1928, where they were sticking pretty closely to the scrub growth of evergreens and willows." All the natives I have questioned inform me that the bird is as common in the winter as in the summer, and none have ever noticed any apparently migrating flocks.

Macoun (1903, 381) quotes Raine as follows: "I have a nest and four eggs of this bird that were taken at Hamilton Inlet, Labrador, March 20th, 1894. The nest was built in a larch tree and is a beautiful structure of interlaced twigs, the nest proper being a compact woven feltlike structure of fur, hair and feathers." He goes on to say: "A nest taken by Mr. A. P. Low at Rigolet, Hamilton Inlet, Labrador, 25th March, 1894, is quite a bulky affair. The outside is chiefly made up of dead twigs chiefly of tamarac [larch] with a few of white spruce. The inside is of down, feathers, hair, fur and strips of the inner bark of willow felted together." He also lists two sets of eggs taken by Low at Rigolet, March 25, 1894, one of three, and the other of four eggs. Perrett records "4 eggs, fresh, April 16, 1900, Makkovik: nest of juniper twigs, wood moss, rotten wood, grass, and lined with partridge feathers; 4 feet from the ground in a white spruce, no other tree within ten yards." He lists another set of "2 eggs, fresh, April 23, 1901, Kaipokok Bay; in a tree about ten feet high; nest, outside of twigs, then twigs and tree moss, lined with moss and feathers." Nothing is known of the incubation period of the Labrador subspecies, but it is probably the same as that of *canadensis*, which is supposed to last about seventeen days. Low (*loc. cit.*) notes, "Young able to fly from nest on May 18th, at Grand Falls, Hamilton River." After leaving the nest the young seem to remain with their parents frequently, in what seem to be family groups, throughout the summer.

There are almost no data on the feeding habits of the Labrador form. Of six stomachs I examined four were empty, the other two contained remains of spiders and dipterous and coleopterous insects matted with unidentifiable vegetable matter, probably spruce or balsam buds. The Labrador Jay is largely a scavenger, as is its more southerly cousin. It comes at once to a camp-fire and snatches bits of refuse right from under one's nose. On the Eagle River, July 16, 1926, two young birds and two old ones investigated our smoke, and spent most of their time carrying away bits of bread that we tossed to them. They usually appear in the vicinity soon after a gun is fired, for, as Turner's manuscript notes, transcribed by Bendire (1895, 393), say, "Experience has taught [them] that food may be procured at such times."

The Jay is much disliked by the trappers because of its trap-robbing propensities. Turner (*loc. cit.*) says, "It is one of the greatest nuisances the trappers have to contend against, and one of these assured me that he had taken fifteen of these birds from a line of less than forty traps in a single day, and with good reason he called this bird a 'wolverine with feathers on.'" This observation has been verified by all the trappers with whom I have talked. Fred Brown, at Separation Point, was particularly bitter against them, and told me that in very severe weather he had difficulties in catching fur solely because most of his traps were sprung by Jays before fur-bearers had an opportunity to get into them.

Corvus corax principalis Ridgway

Northern Raven

Local vernacular: 'Crow.'
Eskimo: 'Tullugak'—probably from the voice.
Indian: 'Kah kah tcew.'

Corvus corax is widely distributed in the northern hemisphere. Two races are recognized in North America — *C. c. principalis*, breeding across the continent in high latitudes from Alaska to Greenland, and south through the Hudsonian zone from British Columbia to Maine, New Jersey, and the southern Alleghanies, and *C. c. sinuatus*, breeding in the western United States and Central America, from Oregon, Montana, and South Dakota south to Honduras. Ravens tend to be permanent residents wherever found.

The Raven is a common permanent resident. It is the most universally distributed of all the Labrador birds. I have observed it from the Straits of Belle Isle to Cape Chidley, and almost as frequently on the outside islands as in the inland forests and barrens. The natives all regard it as the commonest of the winter birds. Coues (1861, 225) "saw them frequently." Low (1896, 326) found it "common throughout the interior." Bigelow (1902, 29) calls it "locally common, especially so at Port Manvers." Townsend and Allen (1907, 388) saw "one at Henley Harbor, one at Snug Harbor, three at Great Caribou Island, and two or three at Cape Charles." Hantzsch (1929, 34) says, "This large form of the Raven is not rare, in certain localities is even a rather frequent breeding bird of our district." He lists in his collection skins of two males and four females taken from September 4, 1906, to October 26, 1906, at Killinek and Ramah. Doane obtained a female at Loup Bay, May 26, 1899.

Townsend and Allen describe a nest on Great Caribou Island which they found July 27, 1906, "in an inaccessible recess about 80 feet above the base of the cliff and 20 or 30 feet from the top. It was as large as a great clothes-basket and made of twisted and weather-bleached branches of fir and spruce. The rocks about were painted white with excrements. A full-fledged young was clinging to the rocks." The incubation, performed by both sexes, is supposed to last twenty days. Perrett has records of two clutches—one of six eggs, fresh, taken May 15, 1900, on a cliff on an island in Stag Bay; the other, also of six eggs, incubation advanced, taken May 24, 1900, on a cliff in Makkovik Bay. Wheeler notes that at a nest he saw in Kikkertaksoak Bay, June 8, 1928, "the young are hatched and are now pretty big."

According to Hantzsch (1929, 34), "they feed upon anything which is to some extent palatable. In the autumn they like berries and even mushrooms, in the summertime mostly animals caught alive, or carrion, of which the sharp-sighted birds always find enough on the beach. They also pick up mussels and other marine animals which remain behind at low tide." He took berries (*Arctostaphylos alpina* Spr.) and fish bones from one stomach. The digestive tract of the only Raven I killed was empty, but I have seen the ebon robbers frequently skulking around the sea-bird rookeries, doubtless awaiting a chance to sneak in for a meal of eggs or young. In 1926, in the Arctic Tern colony at Red Islands, the Terns suddenly left the island in a body, and temporarily suspended all their other activities, to unite in driving away a Raven which evidently in their opinion had approached too near the rookery.

[**Penthestes atricapillus** (Linn.). BLACK-CAPPED CHICKADEE. Turner (1885, 236) says of this species, "I am informed by credible persons long resident in the country that two species of Chickadee occur at Northwest River." Turner must have been misinformed.]

Penthestes hudsonicus littoralis (Bryant)

ACADIAN CHICKADEE

Eskimo: 'At-ser-ta-ta-jok'—the one that says, 'At ser ta ta.'

Penthestes hudsonicus is entirely a North American species, though its ancestry is doubtlessly Eurasian, since the greatest development of the genus occurs in the Old World. It breeds across northern North America in the Hudsonian zone from the Canadian Rockies to Labrador and Nova Scotia, and migrates southward irregularly in winter to New Jersey and Pennsylvania. It is divisible into three races—the type race *hudsonicus*, in central Canada around Hudson Bay; *columbianus*, a darker subspecies, in the western Rockies; and *littoralis*, a smaller, browner form, extending through the eastern section of the species' range, from northern New England, New Brunswick, and Nova Scotia north to parts of eastern Quebec and the east coast of Labrador.

The Hudsonian Chickadee is not as plastic as the Canada Jay. While both species doubtlessly existed contemporaneously in the same areas throughout glacial time, the Chickadee did not react so positively to its environment. The eastern subspecies probably had its origin early in the Pleistocene in the southeastern part of its range, and has persisted through to the present with little change. The eastern coast of Labrador was evidently populated by this stock, rather than by an invasion of *hudsonicus* from Hudson Bay over the height of land. Dr. Townsend's supposed Labrador race, *nigricans* (see Townsend, 1916, 74), is based on immature birds. My series of breeding birds from Labrador shows no recognizable differences from typical *littoralis* of Nova Scotia.

It is an abundant summer resident in the spruce and tamarack forests from the tree line south; a few winter. Coues (1861, 220) says: "This species I met with on several occasions, always finding them associating in small restless companies. . . . Those procured were all young birds, exhibiting the marking of the adults very indistinctly." Low, (1896, 327) regards the bird as "abundant on Hamilton River from April 1st." Bigelow (1902, 30) listed *Parus [Penthestes] atricapillus* as "locally common in timbered regions." In this he was in error. The species he meant was *hudsonicus*, as he himself recognized in his second paper (1902a). Townsend and Allen (1907, 414) "saw only three Hudsonian Chickadees in Labrador and these were in the woods near Rigolet." Doane collected two males and a female at Loup Bay, May 5 and 6, 1899. My latest autumn date is for two individuals I shot at Tub Harbor, September 16, 1927. Wheeler observed Chickadees in abundance north as far as Angutausugevik, August 17, 1928, and found several individuals at the head of Tikkoatokok Bay, January 29, 1928.

Macoun (1904, 693) quotes Raine: "I have several sets of eggs that were taken at Hamilton Inlet, Labrador, in June, 1896. The bird lays six to eight eggs in a hole in a decayed stub." Turner (1885, 236) obtained young of the year at Davis Inlet on July 19, 1882. There are no details known about the incubation period. While the Chickadees are occupied with their nesting duties, they are very quiet and unobtrusive. They keep out of sight and are seldom noticed, even by one looking for them. I had to hunt, and hunt persistently, to get three specimens at Sandwich Bay, July 16, 1928. But the moment the young leave the nest, usually during the last two weeks in July, the Chickadees alter their demeanor, and the woods suddenly seem overrun with them. Small bands of young and old together, probably parents with their broods, meander inquisitively through the spruce and larch forests amid the clouds of mosquitoes and black flies. Their tameness, in contrast to their previous reticence, is surprising. Their buzzing statements of facts greet you on all sides. They seem to follow you about. Hunting industriously for aphids, they explore every nook and cranny of the larch branch within two feet of your face. Perched upside down, rightside up, in all manner of conceivable and inconceivable attitudes, they regard you perkily with their bright beady eyes, burst suddenly into their commonplace *atser-day-day-day*, and flutter past your ear to the next promising branch. At this season you could almost catch them with a butterfly-net.

The Acadian Chickadee is mostly insectivorous in summer, but probably partakes of considerable vegetable matter, such as seeds and buds, in the winter. Three stomachs I examined contained nothing but the unidentifiable remains of small insects.

[Sitta canadensis canadensis Linn. RED-BREASTED NUTHATCH. Perhaps a casual visitor from the south in the southern part of the district. Townsend and Allen (1907, 413) "heard one in a small grove of spruces near Indian Cove at Cape Charles on July 30th." There are no other records.]

Turdus migratorius migratorius Linn.

EASTERN ROBIN

Eskimo: 'Ikkagilik.'
Indian: 'Pee bee tceý oh.'

The Robin is a wide-ranging bird, breeding across North America from northwestern Alaska to Labrador, and south to the Gulf States and the Mexican tableland. Four subspecies are recognized—*T. m. migratorius*, breeding from Alaska to Labrador along the tree line, and south to New Jersey, Pennsylvania, Illinois, Kansas, and Wyoming; *T. m. achrusterus*, in the southeastern United States; *T. m. caurinus*, in the Pacific coastal region, from Glacier Bay, Alaska, south to Washington; and *T. m. propinquus*, in western North America. The Robin of Labrador, at the northern extreme of its range, is certainly larger and darker than more southern birds, but I am unable to differentiate between a series of ten breeding specimens from Labrador and a much larger series from New England sharply enough to warrant further separation.

It is a common summer resident north to the tree line, occasionally straying farther north shortly after the breeding season. Perrett records seeing a Robin at Cape Chidley in August, and Mr. Lenz told me one stayed about the mission station at Killinek all through the summer of 1920; but both agree that the bird is very rare there, and is seldom seen north of Nain, where it breeds commonly about the settlement. It is usually to be found in the small-tree growth, but comes out into the barren coastal zone to build its nest in abandoned dwellings and under the cod-flakes. To one accustomed to the tameness of Robins farther south it is always surprising to find how wild the bird is in Labrador. It keeps its distance and flushes wide, and is as hard to approach and observe as the wariest of game-birds.

Coues (1861, 218) found the bird abundant on the coast in 1860, and as every author since his time has written similarly of it, it would be pointless to quote all the records. Cooke (1916, 167) says, "The last was seen at Forteau, September 11, 1912, and the first at Sandwich Bay, May 1, 1915." Perrett notes the first ones at Makkovik, April 30, 1899, and at Adlavik, May 8, 1900. Wheeler found them common at Tikkoatokok Bay, May 10, 1928, and on September 10, 1927, and observed "a few" at Okkak, September 23, 1931.

Townsend and Allen (1907, 419) "found a nest containing three eggs at Rigolet on July 18th. It was placed about seven feet up in a spruce, near the houses of the Hudson's Bay Company's Post, and was constructed of twigs, lichens, and mud, lined with finer material." Macoun (1904, 721) mentions a set of four eggs taken by Low on the Upper Hamilton River, July 5, 1894. I found my earliest nest June 8, 1927, under the cod-flake at Battle Harbor. It contained two eggs, just hatching, and as the incubation period of the Robin is about fourteen days, the eggs must have been laid during the latter part of May. The Robins nest persistently under the Battle Harbor flake. I have found nests there on numerous occasions, but the birds are seldom successful with their broods, for the combination of small boys and husky dogs is deadly. The nest I found June 8 was destroyed by the dogs the next day. I found a pair of Robins occupying a deserted fisherman's shanty at Gready, with young about a week old, July 12, 1927. I banded the four youngsters in this nest; one of them was taken from a domestic cat on the island August 7. Bent (field notes) observed young of the year on the wing, July 14, 1912, at Ailik.

The ten Robins I collected in Labrador had all been feeding on the berries of *Empetrum nigrum*.

Hylocichla guttata faxoni Bangs and Penard

EASTERN HERMIT THRUSH

The Hermit Thrush breeds across northern North America in the Canadian and Transition zones from the Mackenzie region to southern Labrador. Six other subspecies are recognized, breeding in western North America from Alaska south to the mountains of New Mexico and Arizona and Lower California.

It is a rare summer resident in the extreme southern part of our district. Norton (1901, 156) lists a male taken by the Bowdoin Expedition at Chateau Bay, July 14, 1891. Townsend and Allen (1907, 418) mention the Bangs specimen taken by Ernest Doane at Loup Bay, June 1, 1899, and add: "We found the Hermit Thrush only at Mary Harbor, St. Lewis Inlet. Here we heard two or three singing in the afternoon and evening of July 12th and the morning of July 13th." There are no other records.

Hylocichla ustulata swainsoni (Tschudi)

OLIVE-BACKED THRUSH

Hylocichla ustulata is typically a breeding bird of the Canadian zone, but pushes into both the Transition and the Hudsonian, and hence ranges rather widely over much of northern North America. *H. u. ustulata* breeds in the Pacific coast district, from Alaska to California, while *swainsoni* occupies the rest of the range.

It is a not uncommon summer resident in the wooded areas in the more southern parts of the district. Low (1896, 327) records it from the upper Hamilton River, where he saw it May 16. I observed the species at Petty Harbor, July 12, 1928, and saw two at Caplin Bay, July 13, 1928. I took one, July 15, 1928, at Paradise River, where the species was very common, occurring in about equal numbers with the Gray-cheeked Thrush. It stays well in the spruce forests, and its habits are much like those of the Hermit Thrush. It is exceedingly shy, and difficult to observe.

Low (*loc. cit.*) says the eggs were laid on the upper Hamilton River by June 30. Macoun (1904, 713) lists a set of four eggs taken by Low on the upper Hamilton River, July 3, 1894. Incubation lasts supposedly about twelve days, and is performed chiefly by the female.

Hylocichla minima aliciae (Baird)

GRAY-CHEEKED THRUSH

Eskimo: 'Ittipornipippiok' or 'Viu.' The former name is of uncertain origin, the latter doubtlessly from the call note.

This species is the only member of its otherwise exclusively North American genus to occur in Eurasia. It breeds from northeastern Siberia across northern North America to Labrador and Newfoundland in the Hudsonian and upper Canadian zones, and winters south to northern South America. A closely allied subspecies, *minima*, occurs in Nova Scotia and in the mountains of New England and New York. There is much intergradation between them.

It is a common summer resident north to the tree line. Bigelow (1902, 30) found Thrushes "common as far north as Aillik." Townsend and Allen (1907, 417) found the Gray-cheeked Thrush plentiful between Forteau and Mary Harbor in July, 1906.

In Labrador the Gray-cheeked Thrush is very shy, and is seen but seldom. It frequents the thickest woods, and does not show itself. Nevertheless, it is one of the most typical and noticeable inhabitants of the spruce forests, to which it adheres closely. In the heavy evergreens at Paradise River I found its lovely fluted arpeggios at evening to be the outstanding bird song. I observed it only as far north as Nain Bay, and I have never encountered it in a pure stand of larch. I collected specimens at Sandwich Bay, Manak Island, Makkovik, and Nain. Perrett noted that the latest one was seen at Makkovik, September 28, 1898.

Perrett records three sets of eggs. The first, taken June 27, 1899, at Makkovik, was of four eggs in a "nest of twigs, grass, lined with rootlets and fine grasses, on the ground under a small juniper." Another, taken two days later in the same vicinity, contained also four eggs, incubation fresh, "nest of small twigs, covered with a layer of moss, lined with fine rootlets and grass, on the ground under a very small juniper." The third, of three eggs, was taken at Okkak, July 10, 1896. Coues (1861, 218) says: "On the 24th of July I came upon a family of these birds in a deep thickly wooded ravine. The young were apparently just commencing to fly. Both parents uttered constantly a rather melancholy *pheugh*, in a low whistling tone. The female evinced the greatest anxiety for the safety of her brood, and endeavored to lead me from their vicinity by fluttering from bush to bush." I found young of the year on the wing for the first time at Nain, August 8, 1928.

Five stomachs I examined contained the mangled chitinous remains of spiders and beetles.

Oenanthe oenanthe leucorhoa (Gmelin)

GREENLAND WHEATEAR

Eskimo: 'Erkogolik' or 'Okalajok'—meaning the preacher.

This is essentially a Palearctic species, breaking into several races across Eurasia, the east and west extremes of which have extended their ranges across to the North American continent. Thus we have *oenanthe* in Alaska, and the larger *leucorhoa* in Labrador. Each apparently migrates out in autumn by the route its ancestors used when they first entered the country probably in late Pilocene or early Pleistocene times, the Alaskan bird crossing over to Siberia, and the Labrador form going back via Greenland, Iceland, and the British Isles on its journey to Africa.

The Wheatear is a rare summer resident, mostly in the northern section beyond the tree line. It evidently strays farther south along the coast after the breeding season. Coues (1861, 218) "had the good fortune to procure a specimen of this interesting bird, at Henley Harbor, on the 25th of August. The sailor who brought it to me stated that it was in company with two others, but could give no intelligible account of its voice or manners. It was in immature plumage, very different from that of the adult, and was excessively fat." Baird, Brewer, and Ridgway (1874, 61) note that the specimen described and figured by Cassin "was secured late in the summer near Cape Harrison, Labrador, where it had evidently just reared its brood." Hantzsch (1929, 58) secured five specimens from Okkak. He says, "The bird leads, however, a shy, uneventful summer life, arrives late in the spring and seems to leave its breeding districts again as soon as the young are ready to fly, on which account it is easily overlooked." A male and a female in the Museum of Comparative Zoölogy were taken at Ramah, June 1, 1899, and May 29, 1899.

Bigelow (1902, 31), though he did not see the bird, says it "nests near Nachvak, for the Hudson Bay Company factor there had nests which he had taken." Hantzsch (loc. cit.) says: "Near the Killinek mission station, Wheatears are said to come annually for breeding, and Mr. J. Lane repeatedly found their eggs. Missionary Perrett confirmed this for 1906, but the birds were disturbed in this year and disappeared." Perrett has a set of two eggs from Okkak.

Hantzsch (loc. cit.) found click-beetles (Elateridae) and the remains of other beetles in the stomachs he collected.

[Regulus regulus satrapa Licht. GOLDEN-CROWNED KINGLET. The Kinglets are seemingly of Palearctic origin. Regulus regulus is of Holarctic distribution, but has its centre of greatest development in Eurasia, where about twenty subspecies are recognized.

This Kinglet may be a rare summer resident, but specimens to substantiate its occurrence are lacking. Low (1896, 327) calls it "common on Hamilton River between Grand Falls and Sandy Lake; rare to northward; seen May 19th." Bigelow (1902, 30) calls it "fairly common in patches of spruce timber, as far as Aillik," but it is possible that the statement may refer to the more common Ruby-crowned Kinglet, which he does not mention at all.

Macoun (1904, 697) records a set of seven eggs from Cartwright in the collection of W. Raine, taken June 15, 1895, and says the "nest was suspended to a branch of a spruce tree, 15 feet from the ground." The identity of these eggs seems very doubtful.]

Corthylio calendula calendula (Linn.)

EASTERN RUBY-CROWNED KINGLET

Indian: 'Kah mee whist shagatee vist.'

The Ruby-crowned Kinglet is entirely North American in its distribution. Its nearest relatives are Eurasian, but it shows several generic differences from them which indicate that it probably separated from that stock long before Pleistocene time. Four subspecies are recognized— *C. c. calendula*, breeding in boreal zones from the tree limit in northwestern Alaska, northwestern Mackenzie, northern Manitoba, central Quebec, and Labrador, south to Arizona, New Mexico, northern Michigan, Maine, New Brunswick, and Nova Scotia; *C. c. cineraceus*, breeding in the Canadian zone of the Sierra Nevada Mountains from southern Oregon south to Tulare County, California; *C. c. grinnelli*, breeding from Prince William Sound and Skagway, Alaska, south to British Columbia; and *C. c. obscurus* on Guadelupe Island.

This bird is a fairly common summer resident in Labrador. Coues (1861, 219) obtained "a bird of the year . . . at Rigolet, on the 6th of August [1860], shot in a very densely wooded ravine." Low (1896, 327) calls it "very common along Hamilton River between Grand Falls and Sandy Lake. Seen May 29th." Cooke (1916, 167) gives a sight record for Sandwich Bay, May 26, 1915. Perrett took two specimens at Makkovik in 1900. I secured a female at Petty Harbor, July 12, 1928, and a pair at Paradise River, July 16, 1928, all three in heavy spruce forest. It is possible that some of the records for the preceding species may refer to this one.

Anthus spinoletta rubescens (Tunstall)

AMERICAN PIPIT

Local vernacular: 'Mudlark,' 'Titlark.'
Eskimo: 'Aviortok'—refers to the note, the one that raps.

The genus Anthus has its centre of greatest development in the Old World, whence undoubtedly the American forms have sprung. It is an ancient genus, and the antiquity of its entrance into this continent is indicated by the existence here of two distinct species, *A. spinoletta* and *A. spraguei*. *A. spraguei* is a comparatively sedentary, non-plastic form. As it has no obviously close relatives, and occupies a localized range on the interior plains of North America, it seems not improbable that its ancestors entered this continent in Tertiary time. *A. s. rubescens*, on the other hand, is the most widely spread of all the *spinoletta* races. Its breeding range extends over the Hudsonian and Subarctic regions of North America from eastern Siberia to Labrador and southwestern Greenland. It winters southward from southern California and the Ohio and lower Delaware valleys to Guatemala and the Gulf Coast. It probably pushed into the region it now occupies from the north or west after the first glacial retreat. Closely related races occur in Eurasia and in northern Africa.

The Pipit is an abundant summer resident. Coues, Weiz, Turner, Bigelow, Townsend and Allen, and Hantzsch, all note it as abundant and breeding along the east coast. I found it perhaps the most abundant of all the land birds in Labrador. While it is especially common in the treeless coastal zone from the Straits of Belle Isle to Cape Chidley, it also is found inland on the barrens above the tree line. Wheeler writes in his notes for August 23, 1928: "Pipits abundant on the higher hills above the timber line at the head of Webb's Brook. They seem to replace the Horned Larks in the barren country of the interior, the Horned Larks being in apparently identical surroundings on the outer islands." Cooke (1916, 167) gives the arrival of the Pipit at Battle Harbor as May 16 (1913) and records the last one seen at Tikoralak, October 11 (1912). Wheeler found the bird "common" on the outer islands near Nain, May 26, 1931, and observed many individuals still present at Okkak, September 13, 1931.

Numerous nests of this species that I have found have always been practically identical in situation and construction—a deep cup neatly woven of fine grasses, set down underneath the vegetation in the open tundra. Macoun (1904, 655) quotes W. Raine as writing, "I have sets . . . taken at Hamilton Inlet, Labrador, June 30th, 1895, by Lambert Dicks, as well as sets taken at Nachvak, Labrador, June 15, 1897." Perrett records two sets of eggs taken at Long Tickle on June 20, 1901, one of five eggs, one of four, incubation fresh. The incubation is performed by both sexes. Its duration is unknown, but is probably not over fourteen or fifteen days. There may be a discrepancy of two or three weeks in the date of laying. On July 8, 1927, I found two nests within a hundred yards of each other at Battle Harbor. One contained five fairly fresh eggs, the other four young at least a week old. Townsend and Allen (1907, 412) "found a fully fledged young at Battle Harbor on July 15th [1906]." Wheeler encountered in the Kiglapaits "young able to fly short distances when pressed, June 16, 1928." The young stay with their parents after leaving the nest, and family groups are commonly seen. Toward the end of August and early in September they begin to gather in larger flocks, evidently preparatory to migrating. I observed fourteen in one such flock at Battle Harbor, September 18, 1927.

Hantzsch (1929, 57) examined ten stomachs and found that the contents showed the species to be almost entirely insectivorous. I have watched parents feeding their young with spiders and small beetles. The bird is fond of foraging on the mud- and sand-flats and in the seaweed around the tide-pools at ebb tide.

Lanius borealis borealis Vieillot

NORTHERN SHRIKE

Local vernacular: 'Butcher Bird.'
Eskimo: 'Kopanoarniut'—the hunter of little birds.
Indian: 'Mas kat au.'

The genus Lanius is most widely developed in the Old World. In the western hemisphere there are but two species— the one under consideration, spreading as a breeding bird throughout the Hudsonian and Canadian regions from Alaska to Labrador, and wintering irregularly to the southward, and *ludovicianus*, a bird of more southern distribution, which splits into several races. *Lanius borealis*, however, is a comparatively non-plastic species (but one, slightly differentiated, subspecies is recognized— *invictus*, from Alaska and western Canada) which seems more closely related to some of the Palearctic forms than to its Nearctic brother. This seems to indicate that, whereas *ludovicianus* probably split off from the hypothetical ancestral Holarctic stock back in the mid-Tertiary, *borealis*, on the other hand, became separated later, and was probably in close connection with the Eurasian forms as late as the start of the Quaternary.

The Shrike is an uncommon summer resident from the tree line southward. Low (1896, 327) gives it as "common on Hamilton River; seen April 16th." Norton (1901, 156) lists a female in faded juvenal plumage taken by the Bowdoin Expedition at Lake Melville, July 29, 1891. Bent (field notes) took specimens during July and August, 1912, at Udjuktok Bay, Nain, and Okkak. On July 30, 1926, I saw two young birds at Makkovik that had been taken from a nest in the vicinity some time previously, and were being reared in captivity. I shot a male at the head of Nain Bay, August 18, 1926, and saw two more at the head of Tikkoatokok Bay the following day. Wheeler observed Shrikes in the Kiglapaits, July 2, 1931, and near Okkak, September 23, 1931.

Under the date of May 14, 1779, Cartwright records that at Sandwich Bay he took "an egg out of a butcher bird's nest, which is in the top of a spruce tree." He took six more eggs on May 20th, and shot and stuffed the adult birds. Perrett robbed one pair of Shrikes of three sets of eggs at Rigolet during the spring of 1899. The first two sets were of six eggs each, the last of only five.

The specimen I took had the remains of an adult *Peromyscus maniculatus* in its stomach.

[Mniotilta varia (Linn.). BLACK AND WHITE WARBLER. The only record is Birdseye's, given by Cooke (1916, 167) as, "one seen at Sandwich Bay June 2-4, 1915. It was undoubtedly a straggler for the species had not previously been known northeast of Anticosti Island." It is difficult to accept an unelaborated sight record for this species in a district where the Blackpoll is the most abundant Warbler.]

Vermivora peregrina (Wilson)

TENNESSEE WARBLER

The Tennessee Warbler breeds in the Canadian and Hudsonian zones in northern North America, chiefly east of the Rockies, but also in the upper Yukon valley and in southwestern Mackenzie. It winters southward to northern South America.

It is an uncommon summer resident south of the tree line. Townsend and Allen (1907, 406) heard a warbler song at St. Lewis Inlet, at Rigolet, and at Cape Charles, which they attributed to this species, but they were unable to see the bird to identify it or to secure it. I took an adult male in the larch-spruce swamp behind the mission station at Makkovik, August 15, 1928, which appears to be the only definite record for Newfoundland Labrador.

Dendroica aestiva aestiva (Gmelin)

EASTERN YELLOW WARBLER

The Eastern Yellow Warbler breeds from the Hudsonian through the Upper Austral zones in northern North America east of Alaska and the Pacific slope. In the western and southwestern United States it is replaced by closely allied races.

The bird is a locally common summer resident in the alder thickets that line the streams in the southern part of the district. Low (1896, 327) says, "Seen near Grand Falls, Hamilton River, May 31st." Townsend (1909, 201) records a skin sent him from Northwest River by Dr. Grenfell, taken September 1, 1905. Cooke (1916, 167) gives Birdseye's note of a pair seen at Sandwich Bay, June 6, 1915. Perrett shot one at Kaipokok Bay.

I found them common about the first rapids on the Eagle River while salmon-fishing there July 19, 20, and 21, 1926, and I saw two a fortnight later at Holton Harbor, which is my northernmost record for the species.   On July 15 of 1928 I found them common in the alder scrub along the Paradise River, but I failed to secure any, owing, I confess, to repeated faulty shooting.   I was surprised, during the first week in August, 1928, not to find the Yellow Warbler in apparently simi-lar cover at the lower end of the Fraser River in Nain Bay.   In alder thickets along fast-moving northern streams one half expects to hear the song of this bird, and when it is lacking entirely, one misses it.   I searched for the bird in vain along the northern streams, which leads me to believe that in Labrador it ventures barely into the Hudsonian zone at its edges, dwelling almost entirely in the Cana-dian.

Dendroica coronata (Linn.)

MYRTLE WARBLER

Eskimo: 'Erkotikut.'

The Myrtle Warbler breeds in the Hudsonian and Canadian zones across northern North America.   It winters southward to Central America.

It is a common summer resident in the forested region north to the tree limit.   Low (1896, 327) records a "specimen from Grand Falls, Hamilton River, May 31st."   Bigelow (1902, 30) found it "rather common on the southern half of the coast."   Cooke (1916, 167) says, "The earliest warblers to appear at Sand-wich Bay the spring of 1915 were about a dozen Myrtle Warblers that arrived May 24."   The latest autumn record is a flock seen by Wheeler at the head of Tikkoatokok Bay, September 10, 1928.

I found this bird slightly commoner in the Hudsonian than in the Canadian zone, and particularly abundant in the spruce-larch forests.   I collected two males at the head of Nain Bay, August 4, 1928, and a male, female, and juvenal in the tamaracks at the head of Tikkoatokok Bay, August 7, 1928.   I have found Myrtle Warblers in the little evergreen wood back of Nain every time I have visited it.

This Warbler's nesting has never been recorded for Labrador.   The young are usually on the wing by the last week in July.   I saw an adult female with three young of the year on the wing at Separation Point, Sandwich Bay, July 23, 1926. Wheeler noted a large flock of mixed adults and young at the second lake of An-gutausugevik, August 17, 1928.

Five stomachs I examined all contained a few chitinous remains of insects.

[**Dendroica virens virens** (Gmelin). BLACK-THROATED GREEN WARBLER. The only record for the district is by Cooke (1916, 167): "The list of the known birds of the east coast of Labrador has been increased by the addition of the Black-throated Green Warbler, a specimen of which was seen at Battle Harbor June 6, 1913. The most eastern previous record was that of one at Eskimo Point." In view of the discussion following the publication of his 'Distribution and Migration of North American Shore Birds' (see 'Auk,' 1911, pp. 517, 518; and 'Auk,' 1912, pp. 128, 129, 130) I wonder if Professor Cooke really expected to have this sight record accepted as valid.]

[**Dendroica castanea** (Wilson). BAY-BREASTED WARBLER. The only record for the species within the district is that of Turner (1885, 237), who says: "Three individuals were seen at Black Island, Hamilton Inlet, by me, July 9, 1882. Two were shot but lost in the thick undergrowth; one of the birds was actually in my hand, but escaped." This species breeds most commonly in the Canadian zone farther south, and must occur but rarely in Newfoundland Labrador.]

Dendroica striata (Forster)

BLACKPOLL WARBLER

Eskimo: 'Missaktak'—the one that smacks his lips (from the call note).
Indian: 'Pas ah kwa bu tee tsish.'

The Blackpoll breeds across northern North America in the Hudsonian and Canadian zones, from the tree line south to central British Columbia, Manitoba, Michigan, and the mountains of New York and northern New England, and winters south from Guiana and Venezuela to Brazil.

It is an abundant summer resident from the tree line south. I found it most typically a bird of the Hudsonian zone. It is the commonest of all the Warblers in Labrador, but in the southern part of the district, which shows more Canadian characteristics, the Blackpoll is usually to be found not in the lowlands, but up near the edge of the altitudinal tree line.

Low (1894, 327) says: "Common on the Upper Hamilton River. Seen May 31st." Bigelow (1902, 30) found the Blackpoll abundant "as far north as the limit of timber near Cape Aillik." Townsend and Allen (1907, 408) noted it as common from St. Lewis Inlet to Rigolet "wherever we came in contact with the Hudsonian fauna." Cooke (1916, 167) writes, "The first were noted at Battle Harbor June 6, 1913, and at Sandwich Bay May 27, 1915." Wheeler found Blackpolls at Port Manvers, June 15, 1931.

When you can hear anything above the distracting buzzing of the mosquito that has mysteriously found its way inside your head-net, the thin lisping call note of the Blackpoll Warbler is the most prevalent bird note in the spruce-larch forests. I collected a breeding series covering Petty Harbor, Caplin Bay, Manak Island, and Nain. My latest date is one seen at Davis Inlet, September 1, 1927.

Macoun (1904, 618) lists a set of three eggs taken by Low on the Upper Hamilton River in 1894. Perrett records two sets of five eggs each from Makkovik, June 27, 1899, both of which were taken from nests "of rootlets, grasses and wood-moss, lined with feathers, two feet off the ground in a small spruce." Coues (1861, 220) took a young Blackpoll "apparently just able to fly," August 1, 1860, at Groswater Bay (see further, under *Dendroica pinus*).

[**Dendroica pinus** (Wilson). PINE WARBLER. Coues (1861, 220) lists a young Warbler collected August 1, 1860, at Groswater Bay as *Dendroica pinus*. However, in 1877 ('Birds of the North-west,' p. 69) he writes: "The quotation 'Labrador' originated in an error of mine some years since. On a reëxamination lately of the specimen I thought was *pinus*, I find that it is a newly-fledged Blackpoll Warbler, in the spotted plumage common to very young birds of many species of Warblers." A letter from Dr. Herbert Friedmann on December 1, 1930, regarding this specimen, informs me that it "is a young blackpoll warbler. The skin is in very poor shape, being much flattened against itself, but is perfectly identifiable."]

Seiurus noveboracensis noveboracensis (Gmelin)

NORTHERN WATER-THRUSH

The Northern Water-Thrush breeds mainly in the Canadian zone, occasionally in the Hudsonian, in North America east of Ontario and the Hudson Bay region, and winters southward to northern South America. It is replaced in the West by *S. n. notabilis*, which intergrades with it where their ranges meet.

It is a not uncommon summer resident from the tree line south. Kumlien (1879, 74) caught one "on board the Florence in Straits of Belle Isle, August 18 [1877]." Turner (1885, 238) says, "Several individuals, young of the year among them, were procured by me at Davis Inlet in August, 1884." Low (1896, 327) says it is "common about Grand Falls, Hamilton River. Seen May 31st." Bigelow found it "locally common as far north as Aillik."

I saw a pair near Separation Point, Sandwich Bay, July 23, 1926, and obtained a female at Makkovik, August 15, 1928. Wheeler saw the bird in heavy woods near Angutausugevik, August 15, 1928, which is the northernmost record for the species in Newfoundland Labrador.

Wilsonia pusilla pusilla (Wilson)

WILSON'S WARBLER

Wilson's Warbler breeds in northeastern North America east of the Great Plains, from the tree line south through a part of the Canadian zone, and winters southward to Central America. It is replaced by two allied races in western North America.

It is not uncommon as a summer resident in the wooded regions from Hamilton Inlet south. In Labrador, Wilson's Warbler is typically a Canadian zone species, and has never been recorded north of Hamilton Inlet. Low (1896, 327) gives it as "seen near Grand Falls, Hamilton River, May 31st." Townsend and Allen (1907, 410) "saw two Wilson's Warblers among the alder and fir thickets at Mary Harbor, St. Lewis Inlet, on July 12th, and three at Cape Charles on July 29th and 30th. They were in song at this time." I shot an adult male in low, scrubby alder growth at the Deer Pass in Squasho Run, July 12, 1926, the only one I have ever encountered in the region.

Setophaga ruticilla (Linn.)

AMERICAN REDSTART

The Redstart is an accidental visitor to Labrador. Eifrig (1905, 241) says, "A poor skin of one was shown to Mr. Halkett at Port Burwell by the factor of the station, showing that this species occasionally reaches the north of Labrador."

Dolichonyx oryzivorus (Linn.)

BOBOLINK

I am able to add this species to the list of Labrador birds, though merely as a casual visitor. I took a female in fall plumage at Gready, September 12, 1927. The bird was fat and in good condition. It was feeding near a swamp immediately behind the small fishermen's settlement on the larger island.

Euphagus carolinus (Müller)

RUSTY BLACKBIRD

Eskimo: 'Tullugarsuk'—the little Raven.
Indian: 'Suk i tee yoo.'

The Rusty Blackbird is entirely American in both distribution and origin. It breeds across northern North America from Alaska to Labrador in the Hudsonian and Upper Canadian zones, and winters southward to the Gulf States.

It is a common summer resident locally, north to the tree line. Low (1896, 326) says, "Common throughout the interior." Townsend and Allen (1907, 390) saw none, "but obtained the skin of a bird from the Eskimos at Hopedale." Perrett took a specimen at Makkovik during the summer of 1899. Wheeler found a large flock "among low spruces and alders at the head of Webb's Bay, on the hillside on the south side," August 28, 1928.

I have seen Rusty Blackbirds in Labrador only at the head of Nain Bay. In the tamarack swamp near the mouth of the Fraser River I saw three, August 17, 1926. At the same place, August 3, 1928, I saw a flock of thirty, from which I obtained a pair.

Stearns (1886, 35) lists the Rusty Blackbird as a summer resident at Loup Bay, where he was informed by an inhabitant that the bird built its nest in his woodpile. Perrett has a set of eggs taken near Nain in June, 1912. Coues (1861, 225) says, "On the 24th of July I came upon a family of these birds, in a densely wooded, marshy spot. The young were at that time just fully fledged and were fluttering around the vicinity of the nest."

Pinicola enucleator leucura (Müller)

CANADIAN PINE GROSBEAK

Local vernacular: 'Mope,' 'Spruce Bird.'
Eskimo: 'Isaluk' or 'Issavok'—meaning, 'it is moulting.'
Indian: 'Mees wee,' D. I. B.; 'mee tsoon', B. G. B.

The Pine Grosbeak is a circumpolar species, breeding across North America and Eurasia from the tree line south to the middle of the Canadian zone and its Palearctic homologue, residing mainly in spruce forests. After examining and comparing all the specimens in the Museum of Comparative Zoölogy and in the U. S. National Museum, I find that the bird of eastern North America, *leucura*, which ranges west to the Rocky Mountains, and in the western part of the continent is replaced by several other races, is barely separable from the European form, *enucleator*. I can find no grounds for separating a Labrador subspecies, nor can I recognize *eschatosus*, which Oberholser described (1914, 51) from Newfoundland. My Pine Grosbeaks from Labrador seem at first glance to be a trifle larger and darker than birds taken farther south, but the differences do not stand careful scrutiny. The measurements of the whole series overlap so that there is no possibility of correlating size with locality. The color of the plumage varies somewhat, but it does not vary regularly with distribution, and the differences can in all cases be accounted for by the differences in the age of the specimens, the ages of the birds when killed, or the time of year they were taken.

It is a common summer resident in the forested regions, from the tree line south. Pine Grosbeaks may remain all winter in certain localities, provided there is plenty of food to be had, but probably most of them retire somewhat to the southward during the cold season. Cartwright took one March 20, 1776, and records another early arrival March 30, 1778. Low (1896, 326) says: "Common on the Upper Hamilton River. Male seen May 1st." Norton (1901, 155) lists two adults, male and female, and an immature female from Cullingham's Cove, Hamilton Inlet, July 31 and August 1, 1891. Bigelow (1902, 29) found it "common in the spruce woods north of Aillik, beyond which the spruces dwindled into low bushes." Townsend and Allen (1907, 390) "saw the skin of a Pine Grosbeak taken near Hopedale by an Eskimo." Doane got an adult male at Loup Bay, April 7, 1899. Wheeler noted the species at Tikkoatokok Bay, September 10 and October 3, 1927. I took an adult male at Nain Bay, August 3, 1928, an immature bird at the same place the following day, and an adult female in Tikkoatokok Bay, August 7, 1928.

Perrett has a set of four eggs taken at Stag Bay.

Cartwright found a 'mope' full of partridge-berries March 20, 1776. The birds subsist mostly on seeds and buds, both of evergreens and of deciduous trees and bushes.

Acanthis hornemanni hornemanni (Holboell)

HORNEMANN'S REDPOLL

The series of breeding Redpolls I have examined in the Museum of Comparative Zoölogy has led me to the conclusion that the Hornemann's and Hoary

Redpolls are subspecies of each other, and that both are specifically distinct from the *A. linaria* forms.   In the first place, there is evidence showing that *A. h. hornemanni* and *A. l. rostrata* breed in the same territory in Greenland.   Hence they must be specifically distinct.   In the second place, there is no intergradation between the *hornemanni* and *linaria* races such as Salomonsen (1928) and Koelz (1929) claim.   True, occasional hybrids may come to light now and then, but this is not to be wondered at in species of a genus which is believed to have hybridized with another genus (Brewster's Linnet *Acanthis brewsteri* Ridgway, is considered a hybrid between *A. linaria* and *Spinus pinus*).   The occurrence of infrequent hybrids between two otherwise apparently specific forms is certainly no indication that a racial intergradation exists.

Townsend and Allen (1907, 391) state that this race is an "abundant winter visitor in the northern portions" of the Labrador peninsula.   The only evidence, however, that the bird has ever occurred in Newfoundland Labrador is a specimen in the Museum of Comparative Zoölogy taken by Perrett at Hopedale, November 1, 1897.   It strays through the region occasionally in its wandering migrations, and at best it can be considered as little more than a casual visitor.

[**Acanthis hornemanni exilipes** (Coues).   HOARY REDPOLL.   There is no record for the occurrence of the Hoary Redpoll in Newfoundland Labrador that is not open to serious question. Macoun (1904, 437) lists "a large series of eggs taken at Nachvak, Labrador, in 1895," and "one set of five eggs and nest taken at Nachvak by G. Ford in 1897."   I hunted Redpolls industriously at Nachvak for a week while fog-bound there from August 7 to 14, 1927, and found only *A. l. linaria*, which, moreover, was rather common there.   *A. h. exilipes* apparently breeds farther northwestward, in the Ungava district, and it is not improbable that individuals stray into the region during the winter.]

Acanthis linaria linaria (Linn.)

COMMON REDPOLL

Eskimo: 'Saksariak'—the homeless one, or the one that wanders about aimlessly.
Indian: 'Nuht su gów i hish.'

In 1861 (pp. 222-223) Coues described *Aegiothus fuscescens* as a new species of Redpoll from Labrador.   The form has been denied recognition in the A. O. U. Check-List, but has been recognized by Hantzsch (1929, 53) and stoutly defended by Salomonsen (1928).   I have examined, measured, and compared twenty-eight specimens from Labrador in summer plumage, including Coues's type and co-types, twenty-four breeding birds from elsewhere in the United States, Alaska, Northwest Territories, Saskatchewan, and Alberta, and eleven breeding birds from northern Europe, including several from Norway. The Labrador bird has in general a darker appearance, which in itself might warrant separation, were the character valid. In the males the breast is a deep blood-red instead of pink, and the gray of the females is darker. However, all the Labrador specimens are taken in July and August,—no collector has ever been there to get April or May birds,—and hence each individual either is moulting, or else has exceedingly worn feathers. The difference in coloration I find to be due solely to feather wear. The red coloring matter in the breast feathers lies solely in the barbs. In fresh feathers the presence of the grayish white barbules diffuses the red, and makes it seem lighter and pinkish. As the feathers become worn away, the barbules disappear and leave the barbs standing forth naked in their deep, dark red. I have seen one specimen taken during the summer in Alaska which is inseparable in color from the Labrador individuals, and I am certain the same phenomenon will hold for the Eurasian breeding birds. I am unable to perceive as a valid character the bill differences claimed by Salomonsen. The only subspecies of *linaria* that I can recognize, besides the type race, are *cabaret* from the British Isles and western Europe, and *rostrata* from southern Greenland.

The Redpoll is an abundant summer resident all along the coast, and a common, though irregular, winter resident in the wooded portions. One sees Redpolls most frequently during the summer in the small larch forests of the Hudsonian zone, but the birds are almost as numerous out over the coastal strip of bare tundra, where they come to feed. Low (1896, 326) found the Redpoll "abundant about the Hamilton River," while Bigelow (1902, 29) says it is "very common everywhere." Townsend and Allen (1907, 392) "noted 57 Redpolls on our trip north and 77 on our return, most of them at Great Caribou Island, Cape Charles, St. Lewis Inlet, and Rigolet. They were seen singly or in pairs, and occasionally in small loose flocks up to 8 or 10."

I have observed Redpolls all along the coast, from Caplin Bay, where my notes show it as fairly common, July 13, 1928, to Port Burwell, where I saw two adults August 19, 1927. I have a large series of July and August specimens taken at Holton Harbor, Manak Island, Hopedale, Anaktalak, Nain, Saglek, and Nachvak. My earliest record is a pair at Gready, July 12, 1927, and my latest a young bird seen at the same place, September 14 of the same year. Wheeler, however, noted several flocks at Nain, January 29, 1928, which is the only winter record, and found them singing, April 20, 1931, while he was traveling by dog team some fifty miles inland from the head of Nain Bay.

The Redpoll is a bird that the ornithological visitor to Labrador cannot help noting, though one seldom sees it at close range. Throughout the early part of

July the birds flit hither and yon over the tundra in mated pairs, singing their goldfinch-like 'chicker-ee' as they go, stopping momentarily here and there to feed on the edge of a persistent snow-bank. After the young leave the nest, during the latter part of July, the Redpolls band together in small flocks and visit the weed patches together, much as they do when they drift to New England in the winter. There is a pair of birds at Nain that evidently hatch their young in the spruce forest near by. They spend the month of August feeding in the open fields and the Moravians' gardens near the mission station. At Windy Tickle on July 27, 1928, I found the tamaracks fairly alive with Redpolls. The greater part of them were fully fledged young, which were singing a song that was new to me. My field notes record it as "something like the *chee-chee-chee* of the old birds' song, but delivered with a sore throat, and not unlike in quality the *mew* of the Catbird."

Macoun (1904, 440) quotes Raine as having "several sets that were taken at Cartwright, Labrador, by the late Lambert Dicks during June, 1899." Macoun's record for eggs of *Acanthis hornemanni exilipes* from Nachvak is probably also referable to *linaria*. Perrett records a nest in the small larch-spruce forest at Nain which contained four fresh eggs, April 28, 1910. Nothing is known of the incubation.

Six stomachs I examined contained vegetable matter exclusively, mostly weed seeds that I could not identify.

Acanthis linaria rostrata (Coues)

GREATER REDPOLL

Common transient visitor in the northern portion of Labrador and probably a winter resident. Eifrig (1905, 240) says, "A specimen of what seems to be this species was taken on the vessel off the Labrador coast, September 4, 1903." Hantzsch (1929, 53) collected twenty-eight specimens of the Greater Redpoll in the Chidley region between September 10 and 20, 1906. Concerning the bird he says: "I met this subspecies as a common migrant in northeastern Labrador . . . Up to September 6th I observed no Redpolls, although they were said to have been seen some days before; from then on, scattered individuals appeared almost daily. I was lingering at that time on the islands on the Atlantic side of Labrador. The birds came in little bands . . . The first arrivals flew so high, that one frequently could only hear them but not see them, and they were exceedingly restless, wild, and shy . . . After 13th September the birds gradually appeared in greater numbers, behaved more quietly . . . we then at times met scattered bands of 50 to 100 members which were busily hunting food and had crop and stomach stuffed full of little grains." Perrett took one at Hopedale, November 1, 1887.

Macoun's note (1904, 441) of the breeding of the Greater Redpoll in northern Labrador is obviously in error, and his record of eggs is a case of mistaken identity. The race breeds in southern Greenland, and doubtless wanders south along the Labrador coast about as irregularly as *linaria* wanders into New England during the winter.

[Spinus pinus pinus (Wilson). NORTHERN PINE SISKIN. The Northern Pine Siskin breeds across northern North America, mainly in the Canadian zone, and winters casually southward throughout the United States. There is a closely allied subspecies in the mountains of Mexico. Its Eurasian homologue, *S. spinus*, is specifically distinct.

The Pine Siskin may be a rare summer resident in the southern part of the district. Bigelow (1902, 29) says, "Occasionally I noticed a few with the Redpolls before we passed the tree-line." There is a possibility that Bigelow may have confused this species with juvenal Redpolls. Townsend and Allen (1907, 394) "saw only one Pine Siskin in Labrador, a single bird that flew over Battle Island on July 15th." I have never met the species anywhere on the coast.

Macoun (1904, 447) quotes Raine: "I have several nests with sets of eggs that were taken at Hamilton Inlet, Labrador, during the summers of 1895 to 1898. One nest before me is a pretty specimen of bird architecture, and made externally of fine twigs and roots held together by moss with the inside lined with feathers. It was found June 17th, 1898, in a spruce tree 10 feet from the ground and contained five greenish white eggs spotted with brown."]

Spinus tristis tristis (Linn.)

EASTERN GOLDFINCH

An accidental visitor. The only record is by Kumlien (1879, 76), who reports that an adult male was caught aboard his vessel off Cape Mugford on August 22, 1877.

[Loxia curvirostra Linn. RED CROSSBILL. *Loxia curvirostra* is a plastic circumpolar species of very wide distribution. It has its greatest development in the Palearctic regions, where several subspecies are recognized. It is not only boreal in its range, but penetrates southern regions in both hemispheres, living at high altitude among the coniferous trees. *L. c. pusilla*, the most widespread American form, breeds across northern North America in the Canadian zone and winters irregularly southward. Four other subspecies, rather weakly characterized, are generally recognized from North America— *L. c. bendirei*, breeding in the western United States; *L. c. stricklandi*, from the southwestern States southward into Central America; *L. c. sitkensis*, of the coastal district of southeastern Alaska; and *L. c. percna*, a larger bird, in Newfoundland.

It is perhaps a rare summer resident in the southern part of the district. The only record is a somewhat doubtful one. Macoun (1904, 428) quotes Raine as follows: "I have a set of 4 eggs collected by L. Dicks at Cartwright, Labrador, April 20th, 1895. The nest was built in the top of a cedar, and was composed externally of twigs and roots and the interior lined with animal fur and feathers. The eggs are greenish white, spotted chiefly at the larger end with dark brown and grey and average in size .75 by .58."]

Loxia leucoptera Gmelin

WHITE-WINGED CROSSBILL

Eskimo: 'Erkungatuk'—meaning, having the bill crossed.
Indian: 'A stun gi tish,' D. I. B.; A stun ki tuh,' B. G. B.

The White-winged Crossbills are circumpolar, but the Nearctic and Palearctic forms are specifically distinct. The much larger Eurasian *L. bifasciata* is divided into two races—one in Europe, the other in Asia. The American species breeds across the northern part of the continent in the coniferous forest belt of the Hudsonian and Canadian zones. It winters irregularly southward, but tends to be a permanent resident in most parts of its range.

It is not an uncommon summer resident; a few winter. Cartwright notes the 'crossbeak linnets' in full song March 12, 1776, and March 29, 1778. Low (1896, 326) says it is "common on the Hamilton River in March and April." I first had the pleasure of listening to the White-winged Crossbill's delightful song at Makkovik, where I collected a male, female, and three fully fledged young, August 15, 1928. The birds were living in typically Hudsonian spruce-larch forest, and the male's favorite singing-perch was the thick clump of cones at the top of a tall spruce.

Weiz (1866, 267) lists it as a breeding bird at Okkak. Macoun (1904, 432) quotes Raine: "I have a set of 4 eggs taken at Sandwich Bay, Labrador, April 9th, 1894, by L. Dicks. The nest is made of fine roots and twigs, lined with moss and animals' fur, and the 4 eggs are pale bluish white, spotted at the larger ends with brown of various shades, black and lilac grey. The eggs of the two species of Crossbill are seldom obtained, for like the Canada Jay they have eggs while the snow is on the ground very early in the spring and at a time when it is difficult to get into the woods on account of the snow." Perrett has a set of three eggs taken near the end of June, 1912, near Hopedale, "nest a few feet up in a small spruce."

Passerculus sandwichensis labradorius Howe

Labrador Savannah Sparrow

Local vernacular: 'Chip-bird,' 'Little Hound.'
Eskimo: 'Atserikiterak.'

I have examined Howe's type of this well-marked form, and a series of eighteen adult birds from Labrador, taken mostly in July and September, and have compared them with a much larger series of breeding birds from New England in the collection of the Museum of Comparative Zoölogy. I have been careful to use for comparison only specimens taken at the same time of year and of the same sex. A series of eight birds taken in July on the northeast coast of Labrador between Loup Bay and Okkak, when compared with a series of thirteen birds taken in July at Shelburne, New Hampshire, show the following subspecific characters by which they may be recognized: the yellow of the eye-line is much deeper, brighter, and more extensive; the spots of the breast are fewer in number, but larger, heavier, and darker in color; the feathers of the upper parts have the dark centres larger and blacker. The breeding plumage of the Labrador birds seems not quite so worn as that of the New Hampshire birds taken at the same time. A series of eight birds from Gready and Indian Harbor taken September 5, 7, and 14, when compared with seven adults taken during the first two weeks of September in Massachusetts and New York, show the following differences: the spots on the breast, flanks, and sides are fewer in number, but are larger, much darker in color (almost black) and more sharply defined; the top of the head and the back are more heavily streaked with black, and the margins of the feathers are of a darker brown, there being almost no grayish edgings to these feathers, such as usually occur in the southern bird. The Labrador bird looks considerably larger, and a series of weights might show it to be so, but my measurements show the bills to be almost identical, and the wing and tail of the northern form to average only slightly longer.

Passerculus sandwichensis breeds across North America, from Alaska to Labrador, and south to California and to New Jersey and Pennsylvania. It is a rather plastic species, broken into six races, of which four are western. *P. s. alaudinus* breeds easterly as far as the Great Plains, and probably intergrades with both our eastern forms. *P. s. labradorius* breeds as far south as the Gulf of St. Lawrence and Cabot Strait. I have seen four birds from western Newfoundland and one from the Mingan Islands which belong to this race. Birds from Nova Scotia and New Brunswick are *savanna*. A specimen from the old Bryant collection, now in the Museum of Comparative Zoölogy, labelled solely "Hudson Bay Territories," is a very light individual, nearer *alaudinus*, and certainly not referable definitely to either *savanna* or *labradorius*.

The Savannah Sparrows in general migrate southward in winter as far as Mexico and the Bahamas and Cuba, but the actual travels of the various races have yet to be worked out accurately. Transient individuals referable to the northern race may be picked out of the excellent series of Massachusetts specimens in the Museum of Comparative Zoölogy by their larger and darker breast spots. The preponderance of these individuals occurs in late September and October, and in May.

The Savannah Sparrow is a common summer resident along the barren coastal zone well into the northern third of the coast. Low (1896, 326) says it is "very common on Upper Hamilton River." Norton (1901, 155) lists two adults in worn nuptial plumage from Chateau Bay, July 14, 1891. Bigelow (1902, 30) found it "fairly common at Port Manvers (Lat. 57°) during the last half of August and the first week in September." Cooke (1916, 166) says: "The last record made of a Savannah Sparrow at Battle Harbor was on September 12, 1912, when the species was still common. The first arrived the next spring on May 15." Townsend and Allen (1907, 395) found it common all along the eastern coast, and saw two pairs with their young at Battle Island, and "four or five pairs" on Great Caribou Island. Bent (field notes) saw one at Okkak, August 7, 1912. Hantzsch (1929, 56) lists two specimens, a male and a female, in breeding plumage, from Ramah, June 8 and 30, 1907. Howe's type was collected at Loup Bay, May 17, 1899, by Doane, who also collected an adult male there May 4, 1900.

I have found the Savannah Sparrow common all along the coast, my northernmost record being of an adult female taken at Ryan's Bay, just south of Cape Chidley, August 15, 1927. It seems commonest, however, in the region between Battle Harbor and Port Manvers. Its constant little *chip* is a familiar sound in the damper parts of the tundra. I have never seen the bird in the wooded regions.

Turner (1895, 240) says it "breeds . . . at Davis Inlet." Low (1896, 326) found eggs June 24 on the Upper Hamilton River. Hantzsch (*loc. cit.*) lists two clutches of eggs from Ramah. On July 5, 1926, I found a nest at Battle Harbor, containing two young about a week old. The nest, composed of fine grasses and lined with rootlets, was level with the ground in a little cup under an overhanging tuft of *Empetrum nigrum*. I saw fully fledged young of the year on the wing at Holton Harbor, July 18, 1928.

Five stomachs I examined contained weed seeds and a few insect remains.

Junco hyemalis hyemalis (Linn.)

SLATE-COLORED JUNCO

Local vernacular: 'Black Snowbird.'
Indian: 'Pi ney shish.'

The genus Junco is a most plastic one, wholly North American in its distribution. No two authorities agree on the status of its recognizable forms, of which some eighteen have been described, nor is it necessary for our purposes to go further into the matter. Suffice it to say that the genus has its maximum development in the western and southwestern portions of the continent, where at some time during the Cenozoic probably it had its origin. The subspecies inhabiting Labrador, *J. h. hyemalis*, is the most widespread form in the genus. It breeds across northern North America in the Canadian and Hudsonian zones from Alaska to Labrador and New England, and winters mainly in the eastern United States. It is doubtful if breeding stock could have persisted throughout the Pleistocene in Labrador; hence it is most likely that the bird has entered the region since the retreat of the ice.

The Junco is a fairly common summer resident in the wooded regions from the tree line south. Coues (1861, 224) found it "not so abundant as might be expected in Labrador.... From the fact that I was not in a suitable locality, I did not observe it until the latter part of July, at which time it was in small companies, the old and young associating together. They kept entirely in the thick woods, and were rather timid." Kumlien (1879, 78) secured one on shipboard off Belle Isle in October, 1878. Low (1896, 327) says: "Common at ... Upper Hamilton River. Seen May 29th." Norton (1901, 156) lists two adult specimens taken by the Bowdoin Expedition in 1891, "a male and a female. The latter is labelled Northwest River, July 28." Bigelow (1902, 30) found it "locally common as far as the tree line, particularly at Aillik." Townsend and Allen (1907, 400) saw Juncos only at Cartwright and Rigolet, July 17 and 18, 1906. They saw two at Cartwright and about eight at Rigolet, of which they collected an adult male. Cooke (1916, 166) records one at Lewis Bay, August 13, 1912, and one at Rigolet, September 30, 1912, and says: "The following spring a single bird appeared at Battle Harbor on the unusual date of April 16, and a few were seen for ten days; then they disappeared and were not noted again until their usual time of arrival the middle of May. In 1915 the first appeared at Sandwich Bay on May 12." Doane obtained a male at Loup Bay, May 11, 1899. Perrett saw the first one at Makkovik, May 15, 1899. Wheeler observed a flock near the head of Tikkoatokok Bay, September 10, 1928. I have never seen Juncos farther north than Nain, where, however, I found them common on several occasions, especially in the gardens and the woods near the mission station.

Turner (1885, 240) says it "breeds at Davis Inlet and Rigolet," Low (*vide supra*) records eggs from the Upper Hamilton River, June 27. Townsend and Allen (*loc. cit.*) were told by the missionary at Nain that a few bred there at the end of June. I took a female at Petty Harbor, July 12, 1928, which had an egg in its oviduct ready to lay. Bent (field notes) found a nest containing half-fledged young in the bay behind Hopedale, July 18, 1912. I observed two adults and two fully fledged young at the Eagle River, July 23, 1926. There are no details known as to the nesting in Labrador. The nest of the species, made of grasses and rootlets, is usually on the ground, and the incubation period lasts about twelve days.

Spizella arborea arborea (Wilson)

EASTERN TREE SPARROW

Eskimo: 'Kutsertarusek'—meaning a small 'kutsertak,' or sparrow.

This species is a distinctly American one, and probably had its origin farther south on this continent. It ranges across North America from coast to coast in the Hudsonian zone during the breeding season, and winters southward through the northern United States. It is divided into only two, not very strongly differentiated races—*S. a. ochracea*, breeding from the coast of the Bering Sea to central Mackenzie, and *S. a. arborea*, thence eastward to Labrador and Newfoundland.

The Tree Sparrow is a common summer resident in the Hudsonian forests as far north as there is any scrubby growth. It is seldom found in the barren coastal zone, in the tundra region of the northern third of the district, or in the Canadian forests in the southern part. It makes its home throughout the middle third of the coast, from Port Manvers to Hamilton Inlet, and comes south of that in a narrow strip where there is scrub country to its liking between the barren coastal zone and the wooded interior. Coues (1861, 224) says: "This little Sparrow is quite common in all wooded districts in Labrador. It is there a very tame and unsuspicious bird, showing no fear even when very closely approached." Low (1896, 327) calls it "common everywhere in Labrador. . . . Seen May 31st [on Upper Hamilton River]." Bigelow (1902, 30) "observed a good many at Port Manvers." Townsend and Allen (1907, 399) found three pairs July 27, 1906, at Great Caribou Island, "in small thickets of balsam fir and black spruce which in sheltered localities managed to reach a height of three or four feet." They saw several more at Cape Charles from July 28 to 31, 1906.   Cooke (1916, 166) gives the time of arrival at Battle Harbor as May 15, 1913.   Doane collected two males and a female at Loup Bay, May 10, 1899, and a pair, May 16, 1899.   Perrett noted the first spring arrivals at Makkovik, May 9, 1899.

I found the Tree Sparrow most common from the region of Holton Harbor, where it was abundant July 18, 1928, about the dwarf spruces and copses of juniper, to Nain, where it was common at the mouth of the Fraser River, August 3, 1928.   I have found it as far north as Saglek Bay, where I obtained an immature bird August 7, 1927.

Low (*vide supra*) says, "Breeds in great numbers on Upper Hamilton River.... Eggs June 21st."   Cooke (*ibid.*) says, "It seldom nests on the coast, but is a common breeder in the wooded country inland, nesting for the most part on the ground and occasionally in the trees."   Perrett lists a set of eggs brought him by an Eskimo from Kaipokok Bay in June, 1900, and a set of four eggs taken at Okkak, June 22, 1893.   Bent shot a young bird at Udjuktok, August 3, 1912 (field notes).

Four stomachs I examined contained unidentifiable vegetable matter, and another a few chitinous insect remains.

Zonotrichia leucophrys leucophrys (Forster)

WHITE-CROWNED SPARROW

Eskimo: 'Kutsertak.'

The genus Zonotrichia is entirely North American in its distribution.   As Boulton (1926) has shown, it probably had its origin in the table-lands of Mexico during Cenozoic time, and has spread northward from there to occupy its present range.   The birds inhabiting Labrador have undoubtedly entered the region from the southwestward since the retreat of the Pleistocene ice.   Though *Z. leucophrys* is not a very plastic species, it is nevertheless a strong and aggressive one.   Four races are recognized—*Z. l. gambeli*, breeding in the Hudsonian and Canadian zones of northwestern North America; *Z. l. pugetensis*, breeding on the Pacific Coast from Vancouver Island to Mendocino Co., California; *Z. l. nuttalli*, breeding in the Humid Transition zone of the California coast; and *Z. l. leucophrys*, breeding in two separated groups, one in the Hudsonian and Upper Canadian zones of central and northeastern North America, the other in the conifer belts of the high mountain regions from southern Oregon to central California and east to Wyoming and New Mexico.   *Z. l. leucophrys* winters from the southern United States through northern Mexico.

The White-crowned Sparrow is a summer resident, and is one of the most abundant and universally distributed of the Labrador land birds. It occupies the barren coastal strip as a common breeding bird as far north as Hebron, and inhabits likewise the forested Hudsonian and Canadian zone areas back from the coast. Coues, Weiz, Turner, Bigelow, and Townsend and Allen, all refer to its abundance along the coast. Low (1896, 326) found it "very common on Upper Hamilton River. Seen May 16th." I observed it commonly in the alder and willow scrub at Paradise River, as well as thirty miles inland up the Fraser River, from Nain Bay. The average date of arrival in spring seems to be in the middle of May. Townsend and Allen (1907, 398) were told by Mr. Schmitt at Nain that "this species arrived there on May 18th." Cooke (1916, 166) records the first at Battle Harbor on May 22, 1913, and at Sandwich Bay, May 28, 1915. Perrett noted its arrival at Makkovik, May 9, 1899. Wheeler saw the first 'Kutsertak' of spring at Nain on May 23, 1931. There are no departure dates in the literature. I saw a few at Gready, September 12, 1927, but when I reached Battle Harbor, September 17, 1927, there was not a single White-crown to be seen on the island.

The bird is rare in the more typically arctic barrens on the northern part of the coast. I have seen it only as far north as Saglek Bay, where on August 7, 1927, I observed it to be fairly common on the hillsides, but was surprised to find no young in evidence. There is a breeding record, however, for Nachvak, which is still farther north. Hantzsch (1929, 56), while he lists a specimen from Hopedale, taken in May, 1905, and another from Ramah, June 8, 1907, says, "During my stay at Killinek I never caught sight of a specimen." Perrett took one at Killinek, June 1, 1906. Mr. Lenz informed me the Eskimos all regarded a single White-crown that summered in the vicinity of the Killinek mission station in 1920 as a strange bird. None of them was able to name it. The Eskimos farther south know the bird well.

Low (loc. cit.) found eggs June 25 on the Upper Hamilton River. Macoun (1904, 480) lists a set of four eggs taken at Nachvak by J. Geer in June, 1896. Perrett collected nests and eggs as follows: four eggs at Makkovik, incubation commenced, June, 1899, nest about three feet from the ground in bushes thrown over a boat to protect it from the sun; four eggs at Makkovik, incubation just commenced, June 28, 1901, nest on the ground under the upturned root of a willow; five eggs from a nest on the ground at Makkovik, June 29, 1901; four eggs, incubation commenced, July 1, 1901, at Makkovik, on the ground under the low branches of a spruce. Wheeler found the young hatched in the Kiglapaits on July 7, 1931, but observed eggs still being incubated at Okkak, July 30, 1931. Coues (1861, 224) saw many young birds at Rigolet, August 1, 1860. I found three nests at Battle Harbor, July 5, 1926, all of them grass-lined cups set in the ground among the crowberry vines. One of them contained one incubated egg, another three young just hatched, and the third two young about a week old. I found another nest at Gready, which contained five well-incubated eggs, July 14, 1928. I saw fully fledged young of the year on the wing at Cartwright, July 16, 1928. They do not usually make their appearance until toward the latter part of the month.

I have watched the White-crowned Sparrow catching spiders frequently. Six stomachs I examined contained insect remains, as well as weed seeds and other vegetable matter. Wheeler in his field diary for August 4, 1928, in the Kiglapaits, notes: "The young flying and catching flies. They seem to eat mosquitoes!"

Zonotrichia albicollis (Gmelin)

WHITE-THROATED SPARROW

Zonotrichia albicollis breeds in the Canadian zone across North America from Mackenzie and Montana eastward to the Atlantic coast, and winters south to the Southern States.

It is a rare summer resident in the extreme southern part of the district. The northernmost record is Low's (1896, 326), "Heard at Grand Falls, Hamilton River." The only specimens recorded are a male and a female taken by the Bowdoin Expedition at Chateau Bay, July 14, 1891, and listed by Norton (1901, 156). Townsend and Allen (1907, 398) "found four of these birds in the shelter of the woods at and near Mary Harbor, St. Lewis Inlet, on July 12th [1906], and three in the woods near White Bear Bay, Cape Charles." Cooke (1916, 166) says: "It is rare [at Battle Harbor] and the first arrived May 19, 1913, and several were heard May 22. The last was heard in 1912 at Forteau on September 11."

On July 12, 1928, while ashore collecting at Petty Harbor, I heard the distinctive song of this species coming from a thick spruce copse halfway up a hillside. I at once investigated it, and though I searched for two hours, until darkness made me stop, I was unable to see the bird. It sang only intermittently, but I was delighted to hear the second half of the Zonotrichia melody finished off as *Peabody-Peabody-Peabody* again. It was refreshing, and even a little startling, after becoming accustomed to the heterogeneous jumble with which the White-crown endows this part of the song.

Passerella iliaca iliaca (Merrem)

EASTERN FOX SPARROW

Local vernacular: 'Partridge Bird.'

Passerella is endemic to North America. It is a monotypic genus, but its single species is extremely plastic. Sixteen subspecies are now generally recognized as valid, most of them in western North America. (*Cf.* Swarth (1920) and Linsdale (1928)). The subspecies inhabiting Labrador, *P. i. iliaca*, is the most widespread of the group. It breeds across northern North America in the Hudsonian and Canadian zones, and migrates southward in winter to the southern United States. Of all the Fox Sparrow races it is the one farthest removed geographically from the southwestern section of the continent, where, at some time in the Cenozoic, the species probably had its origin. It is interesting to note that the territory it now occupies is the 'youngest' on the continent. The bird has acquired its present breeding range since the retreat of the last ice-sheet.

The Fox Sparrow is a common summer resident in the wooded portions of Newfoundland Labrador from the tree line south. Bigelow says (1902, 30): "Common along the southern part of the coast. We found a few as far north as Aillik." Townsend and Allen (1907, 402) "found the Fox Sparrow common at Forteau, Cartwright, Rigolet, and Cape Charles. At Forteau we found them directly on the coast." Cooke (1916, 167) "heard the first arrival at Sandwich Bay on May 5, 1915." Perrett gives the arrival date at Makkovik as May 15, 1899. Wheeler saw several "in the scrub growth at the outlet of the first lake on Angutausugevik, August 15, 1928." There is a specimen in the Field Museum taken by the Rawson-MacMillan Expedition at Bowdoin Harbor, Anaktalak Bay, June 12, 1928.

I have found the Fox Sparrow in Labrador ever a shy and retiring bird. It sticks closely to heavy cover, preferring the heavy copses of thick, stunted spruce. I found the bird in full song at Paradise River, July 16, 1928, and took two specimens the next day at Cartwright. My northernmost record for the species is an adult female I shot at the head of Tikkoatokok Bay, August 7, 1928.

Turner (1885, 241) obtained young at Rigolet late in June and early in July, 1882. Macoun (1904, 520) records a "set of five eggs taken at Nachvak, Labrador, by Mr. R. Guay [Gray ?], in June, 1897." I took a young bird, fully fledged and on the wing, at Manak Island, July 21, 1928. Nothing is known about the nesting habits in Labrador. Elsewhere it usually lays four or five eggs in a rather large nest of grasses, moss, and leaves on the ground under the shelter of a bush or low branch, or in a bush or small tree a few feet from the ground. The incubation of about thirteen days is performed chiefly or entirely by the female.

Four stomachs I examined contained unidentifiable vegetable remains and a few insects.

Melospiza lincolnii lincolnii (Audubon)

LINCOLN'S SPARROW

This most northern representative of the genus breeds across northern North America in the Hudsonian and Canadian zones from Alaska to Labrador, and south in the West through the mountains to southern California and New Mexico. It is divided into two subspecies: *M. l. lincolnii* breeds over the entire range except the northwest coast region from Prince William Sound to the Sitka District, Alaska, which is occupied by *M. l. gracilis*. It winters southward through the Southern States and into northern Central America.

It is a fairly common summer resident south of Hamilton Inlet. Bigelow (1902, 30) says it is "common. A characteristic bird of the wooded parts of the coast, as far north as Hamilton Inlet." Townsend and Allen (1907, 401) "found Lincoln's Sparrow only at Mary Harbor on July 12th [1906] where we saw four; and at Cape Charles where on the 28th, 29th, and 30th of July we saw 4, 10, and 4 respectively." The northernmost record is a single individual collected by Perrett at Hopedale in 1898.

I searched in vain for Lincoln's Sparrow during 1926 and 1927, but in 1928 I learned the secret and was able to collect three specimens. I saw three at Caplin Bay, of which I obtained one, July 13, and I took two at Cartwright, July 16. The bird is very unobtrusive and shy, and keeps to the shelter of thick cover. The three I encountered at Caplin Bay were in an alder copse on a stream through open tundra. I was attracted to the cover by the alarm note of the bird, which is an unostentatious *chip*. I had to still-hunt them to get a specimen. When I had ascertained that the birds were in the vicinity, I sat down on a convenient rock and waited for one to show itself. It was hopeless to try to flush them into the open, as I tried fruitlessly to do at first.

Calcarius lapponicus lapponicus (Linn.)

Lapland Longspur

Eskimo: 'Nessaúligak'—the one with a cap or hood.

The genus Calcarius has its best development in North America, where it would seem that it probably had its origin. *C. l. lapponicus*, the most widespread form of the genus, breeds from the eastern boundary of Alaska, across northern North America in the tundra belt, through Greenland, Iceland, and Spitzbergen to northern Scandinavia and on to central Siberia, and winters irregularly southward to the snow line. Two other subspecies—*C. l. alascensis* in Alaska and the islands of the Bering Sea, and *C. l. coloratus* in eastern Siberia—make the species completely circumpolar. The existence of three other species in North America indicates that the ancestral stock probably had one or more periods of rapid development at some time in the middle of the Cenozoic, during which it gave rise to these offshoots, but their subsequent history is difficult to trace.

The Lapland Longspur is a not uncommon summer resident in the tundra region of the northern third of Labrador, and an abundant spring and autumn transient all along the coast. Low (1896, 326) gives it as "common on Hamilton River in early spring." Bigelow (1902, 30) says: "Common after August 3 [1900]. ... South of Nachvak they occur only as migrants." Townsend and Allen (1907, 395) "saw a pair of these birds evidently breeding at Holton, just north of Hamilton Inlet, on July 19th [1906]." Hantzsch (1929, 55-56) says: "Not until 27th August [1906] did I meet some Lapland Longspurs at Killinek; from this time on, numerous individuals daily. The birds kept loosely together in flocks of 15 to 20 individuals at the most. At the beginning they were rather shy, later often quite tame.... In October I still met single birds, apparently old males; the last met upon my visit to the Labrador coast on 18th October at Hebron." Cooke (1916, 166) notes the first Longspurs at Battle Harbor, on May 13, 1913. Bent (field notes) saw one at Okkak, August 7, 1912. Perrett observed its arrival at Killinek from the south, May 20, 1906, and shot one at Seal Cove, near Makkovik, in April, 1899. Wheeler writes, "In 1931 occasional Longspurs were present around Nain throughout the early part of May, and they began to come through abundantly in flocks on May 17."

I first met the species at the Bay of Seven Islands, where on August 14 and 15, 1927, I encountered several small flocks that seemed to be families of old birds with their young of the year. I collected six of them there. I saw a few more that summer at the far northern end of the coast, and met them again at Indian

Harbor, where, on September 6, I shot two early migrants on their way south. I saw a few at Gready, September 12, 1927, and two days later, during a terrific northeast storm, I found four large flocks, numbering over a hundred individuals each, feeding among the crowberries on the sheltered barren hillsides near Table Bay. On July 18, 1928, I took a pair in breeding plumage on the tundra at Holton Harbor. They were the only individuals I saw all that summer. Whether or not they were breeding there, is doubtful. I found no signs of it other than the mere presence of the birds, but it is interesting to note that Townsend and Allen observed a pair at this same place July 19, 1906.

Bigelow (*loc. cit.*) says the Lapland Longspurs "breed about Nachvak and northward to Hudson Strait." Macoun (1904, 453) lists three sets of eggs taken at Nachvak Bay by R. Buy [= Gray?] in 1897. Perrett has a set of four eggs taken at Okkak in 1896. Hantzsch had a set from Ramah.

Hantzsch (*vide supra*) examined eighteen stomachs, which he found to contain about equal parts of insect remains and seeds.

Plectrophenax nivalis nivalis (Linn.)

EASTERN SNOW BUNTING

Local vernacular: 'White Snowbird' (in contradistinction to the Junco).
Eskimo: 'Amauligak'—the one with a white hood.
Indian: 'Wóp uh shoosh,' D. I. B.; 'Wóp i nee i whi zish,' B. G. B.

The Snow Bunting is a circumpolar species, breeding in the barren grounds of high latitudes, and wintering generally to the southward on both continents, seldom, however, coming below the snow line. On the islands of Bering Sea and the Aleutian chain we find *P. n. townsendi*, a slightly differentiated race, characterized by its larger bill, and on Hall and St. Matthew Islands, *P. n. hyperboreus*, which is recognized in the A. O. U. Check-List as a distinct species. Salomonsen (1931) recognizes also, as subspecifically distinct from *P. n. nivalis*, the Snow Buntings breeding, respectively, in Greenland and in Iceland.

The Snow Bunting is a common summer resident in the north, an abundant spring and autumn transient throughout the region, and an irregular winter visitor in the south. Low (1896, 326) found it "plentiful on Hamilton River in early spring." Bigelow (1902, 30) says, "Snow Buntings appeared at Port Manvers about the 10th of August [1900], after which they were abundant." Hantzsch (1929, 54-55) noted only the resident birds in the vicinity of Port Burwell during August. He says these individuals gathered into small bands toward the end of that month and disappeared to the southward, after which the species was rare until the end of September, when large flocks appeared, to remain "by far the most abundant small bird through all of October." He adds that while migrating they are shy and restless, but that when they are resting between flights, because of inclement weather, they are often quite tame. Cooke (1916, 166) writes: "This species is an abundant migrant at Battle Harbor, but does not breed there and is rare through the winter. ... After Nov. 6, 1912, the only ones seen were on Dec. 29, 1912, and one on February 15, 1913. The first song was heard May 1, 1913, when the species was abundant, but most left the latter part of that month, the last seen being three on May 31, and one the next day."

Perrett notes in his diary: "First ones going south at Makkovik October 11, 1898; all passed south by November 3, 1928. Seen at Cape Harrison, April 6, 1899. First going north Killinek March 29, 1906." Keats wrote me that "the first Snowbirds arrived on April 6," 1928, at Davis Inlet. Wheeler found them abundant on Bart Island in Nain Bay, April 18, 1928; and on July 27, 1928, he makes this entry in his field notes: "A large flock running and feeding in the rocks by a lake in the pass of the Kiglapaits south of Perry's Gulch. The birds were largely black and white with large white patches on the wings." He found them "very abundant, still black and white, among the hills behind Nain, September 10, 1928." On March 22, 1931, he writes, "Two Snow Buntings and two seals sunning on the ice at the head of Tikkoatokok Bay."

I saw my first Snow Buntings, August 17 and 18, 1927, at Joksut, just south of Cape Chidley. There was a small flock of about twenty individuals there, both old and young, which led me a merry chase up and down the cliffs and over the rocky talus slopes. They were very shy and very wild, but I managed to collect four badly moulting adults and two young birds in juvenal plumage. I saw twenty-eight at Port Burwell the next day. While banding Black Guillemots, August 9, 1928, on a little bare, low, unnamed island about thirty miles to sea off Nain, I was surprised to see a single juvenal Snow Bunting dart out of the rocks ahead of me. I did not have a gun with me, but I wigwagged at once to the schooner to have one sent ashore. I followed the bird over the island and was able several times to observe it closely through my glasses. It left the island and disappeared before the gun arrived. It is possible that Snow Buntings may breed south to the latitude of Nain on the bare islands off the coast, but it is more likely that they do not stray down so far until after the breeding season.

Macoun (1904, 451) lists "a large series of eggs from Nachvak, Labrador, taken by Mr. R. Gray in 1897." Eifrig (1905, 241) says, "From Cape Chidley come two [sets] of seven eggs collected by the Eskimos in July, 1903." Perrett has a set of five eggs from Killinek, and one of four eggs taken at Okkak, July 7, 1893. He tells me he has always found the nests in crevices in the cliffs, or under large boulders, and never in the open. Eifrig (*loc. cit.*) gives a good description of the nests as follows: "All the nests found were not placed in the open, as stated in most books, but below rocks and boulders. In a typical nest the material consists of grasses, old feathers and plant pappus, lined with the last and feathers of larger birds. Some have a lining of caribou hair and the outside rim of moss and lichens." The incubation is supposedly about fourteen days, and chiefly by the female.

Six stomachs I examined contained fine gravel, seeds, unidentifiable vegetable matter, and a few chitinous insect remains. Hantzsch (*loc. cit.*) lists a variety of vegetable and insect foods he took from nineteen stomachs, and adds that he found sand and small pebbles in many instances. Wheeler says that on Bart Island in Nain Bay, April 18, 1928, the Snow Buntings "were very busy running about on the bare patches of ground picking crowberries and bearberries. They chew the berry and spit out the skin, leaving at least some seeds still in it."

Hantzsch (*loc. cit.*) says, "The Eskimo hunters now and then shoot into the dense swarms and cook the fat birds as a delicacy." Cooke (*ibid.*) adds, "During the spring migration great numbers are killed for food, as many as twenty being taken at a single shot."

BIBLIOGRAPHY

ADAMS, CHARLES CHRISTOPHER.

1905   The Post-Glacial Dispersal of the North American Biota. *Biological Bulletin*, vol. IX, no. 1, June, 1905, pp. 53-71.

ALLEN, GLOVER MORRILL.   See Townsend and Allen.

ALLEN, JOEL ASAPH.

1893   The Geographical Origin and Distribution of North American Birds, Considered in Relation to Faunal Areas of North America. *Auk*, vol. X, no. 2, April, 1893, pp. 97-150, pls. III, IV.

AMERICAN ORNITHOLOGISTS' UNION.

1910   Check-List of North American Birds.   Third edition, New York, 1910. Pp. 430, map.

1931   Check-List of North American Birds.   Fourth edition, Lancaster, Pennsylvania, 1931.   Pp. xix, 526.

ANTEVS, ERNST.

1922   The Recession of the Last Ice-Sheet in New England. *American Geographical Society Research Series*, no. 11, 1922, pp. xiv, 120, pls. VI.

1925   Quaternary Climates. *Carnegie Institution of Washington Publication* 352, July, 1925, pp. 51-114, pls. I-III; pp. 115-153, pl. I.

1925a Retreat of the Last Ice-Sheet in Eastern Canada. *Canada Department of Mines, Geological Survey Memoir* 146, Geological Series no. 126, 1925, pp. iv, 142[=138], pls. IX.

1928   The Last Glaciation. *American Geographical Society Research Series*, no. 17, 1928, pp. x, 292, pls. IX.

AUSTIN, OLIVER LUTHER, Jr.

1928   Migration-Routes of the Arctic Tern (*Sterna paradisaea* Brünnich). *Bulletin of the Northeastern Bird-Banding Association*, vol. IV, no. 4, October, 1928, pp. 121-125.

1929   The Races of *Cepphus grylle* Linn. *Bulletin of the Northeastern Bird-Banding Association*, vol. V, no. 1, January, 1929, pp. 1-6.

1929a Some Labrador Banding Records. *Bulletin of the Northeastern Bird-Banding Association*, vol. V, no. 1, January, 1929, pp. 35-36.

1929b Labrador Records of European Birds. *Auk*, vol. XLVI, no. 2, April, 1929, pp. 207-210.

1929c Contributions to the Knowledge of the Cape Cod *Sterninae*. *Bulletin of the Northeastern Bird-Banding Association*, vol. V, no. 4, October, 1929, pp. 123-140.

BAIRD, SPENCER FULLERTON, THOMAS MAYO BREWER, and ROBERT RIDGWAY.
1874 A History of North American Birds. Land Birds. By S. F. Baird, T. M. Brewer, and R. Ridgway. Quarto, Boston: Little, Brown and Co., 1874, vol. I, pp. xxviii, 596, vi, pls. I-XXVI; vol. II, pp. [vi,] 590 pls. XXVII-LVI; vol. III, pp. [vi,] 560, [ii,] xxviii, pls. LVII-LXIV.

1884 The Water Birds of North America. By S. F. Baird, T. M. Brewer, and R. Ridgway. Memoirs of the Museum of Comparative Zoölogy at Harvard College, vols. XII and XIII, issued in continuation of the publications of the Geological Survey of California, J. D. Whitney, State Geologist. Quarto. Boston: Little, Brown and Co., 1884. Vol. I, pp. xi, 537; vol. II, pp. vi, 552. Many figures in text in each volume.

BANGS, OUTRAM.
1899 The Labrador Spruce Grouse. *Proceedings of the New England Zoological Club*, vol. I, pp. 47-48, June 5, 1899.

1900 A Review of the Three-toed Woodpeckers of North America. *Auk*, vol. XVII, no. 2, April, 1900, pp. 126-142.

1900a Occurrence of the Little Blue Heron in Labrador. *Auk*, vol. XVII, no. 4, October, 1900, p. 386.

1930 Types of Birds now in the Museum of Comparative Zoölogy. *Bulletin of the Museum of Comparative Zoölogy*, vol. LXX, no. 4, March, 1930, pp. 145-426.

BARNSTON, GEORGE.
1861 Recollections of the Swans and Geese of Hudson's Bay. *Canadian Naturalist and Geologist*, vol. VI, no. 5, October, 1861, pp. 337-344; also: *Zoologist*, series 1, vol. 20, 1862, pp. 7831-7837.

BELL, ROBERT.

1884 Notes on the Birds of Hudson's Bay. *Proceedings and Transactions of the Royal Society of Canada*, series 1, vol. I, section 4, pp. 49-54, 1883 [=1884].

1885 List and Notes by Dr. R. Bell of Birds of the Vicinity of Hudson's Bay and Labrador. *Report of Progress, Geological and Natural History Survey and Museum of Canada*, 1882-83-84, Appendix III, pp. 54DD-56DD.

BENDIRE, CHARLES EMIL.

1892 Life Histories of North American Birds with Special Reference to their Breeding Habits and Eggs. *Smithsonian Institution, United States National Museum Special Bulletin* 1. Washington, 1892. Quarto, pp. VIII, 446; pls. XII.

1895 Life Histories of North American Birds, from the Parrots to the Grackles, with Special Reference to their Breeding Habits and Eggs. *Smithsonian Contributions to Knowledge*, vol. 32, no. 985; also, *United States National Museum Special Bulletin* no. 3. Washington, 1895. Quarto, pp. IX, 518, pls. VII.

BENT, ARTHUR CLEVELAND.

1919 Life Histories of North American Diving Birds. Order Pygopodes. *United States National Museum Bulletin* 107, Washington, 1919. 8vo, pp. XIV, 245, pls. LV.

1921 Life Histories of North American Gulls and Terns. Order Longipennes. *United States National Museum Bulletin* 113. Washington, 1921. 8vo, pp. x, 345, pls. XCIII.

1922 Life Histories of North American Petrels and Pelicans and their Allies. Order Tubinares and Order Steganopodes. *United States National Museum Bulletin* 121. Washington, 1922. 8vo, pp. XII, 343, pls. LXIX.

1923 Life Histories of North American Wild Fowl. Order Anseres (part). *United States National Museum Bulletin* 126. Washington, 1923. 8vo, pp. x, 250, pls. XLVI.

1925 Life Histories of North American Wild Fowl. Order Anseres (part). *United States National Museum Bulletin* 130. Washington, 1925. 8vo, pp. x, 376, pls. LX.

1926 Life Histories of North American Marsh Birds. Orders Odontoglossae, Herodiones and Paludicolae. *United States National Museum Bulletin*, 135. Washington, 1926. 8vo, pp. xii, 490, pls. XCVIII.

1927 Life Histories of North American Shore Birds. Order Limicolae (Part 1). *United States National Museum Bulletin* 142. Washington, 1927. 8vo, pp. x, 420, pls. LV.

1929 Life Histories of North American Shore Birds. Order Limicolae (Part 2). *United States National Museum Bulletin* 146. Washington, 1929. 8vo, pp. x, 412, pls. LXVI.

BIGELOW, HENRY BRYANT.

1902 Birds of the Northeastern Coast of Labrador. Brown-Harvard Expedition of 1900, under the Leadership of Prof. Delabarre. *Auk*, vol. XIX, no. 1, January, 1902, pp. 24-31.

1902a Report on Ornithology, in E. B. Delabarre's Report of the Brown-Harvard Expedition to Nachvak, Labrador, in the Year 1900. *Bulletin of the Geographical Society of Philadelphia*, vol. III, no. 4, April, 1902, pp. 202-206. (This list contains a few additions to and corrections of the one in *The Auk*.)

BOULTON, RUDYERD.

1926 Remarks on the Origin and Distribution of the Zonotrichiae. *Auk*, vol. XLIII, no. 3, July, 1926, pp. 326-332.

BREWER, THOMAS MAYO. See Baird, Brewer, and Ridgway.

BREWSTER, WILLIAM.

1902 An Undescribed Form of the Black Duck (*Anas obscura*). *Auk*, vol. XIX, no. 2, April, 1902, pp. 183-188.

1909 Something More about Black Ducks. *Auk*, vol. XXVI, no. 2, April, 1909, pp. 175-179.

BROOKS, WINTHROP SPRAGUE.

1920 A New Jay from Anticosti Island. *Proceedings of the New England Zoological Club*, vol. VII, March 11, 1920, pp. 49-50.

BRYANT, HENRY.

1861 Remarks on Some of the Birds that Breed in the Gulf of St. Lawrence. *Proceedings of the Boston Society of Natural History*, vol. VIII, May, 1861, pp. 65-75.

CABOT, WILLIAM BROOKS.

1920 Labrador. Boston: Small, Maynard and Co., 1920. 12mo, pp. xiv, 354, pls. XLVII.

CARTWRIGHT, GEORGE.

1792 A Journal of Transactions and Events, during a Residence of Nearly Sixteen Years on the Coast of Labrador; Containing Many Interesting Particulars, both of the Country and its Inhabitants, not Hitherto Known. Newark [, England], 1792. Quarto. Vol. I, pp. viii, 287; vol. II, pp. x, 505; vol. III, pp. x, 248 [,15].

CHAPMAN, FRANK MICHLER.

1932 Handbook of Birds of Eastern North America with Introductory Chapters on the Study of Birds in Nature. Second revised edition. New York and London, D. Appleton and Co., 1932. 12mo, pp. xxxvi, 581, pls. XXIX. Many figures in text.

CLARK, WILLIAM EAGLE.

1907 Ornithological Results of the Scottish National Antarctic Expedition, III. Birds of the Weddell and Adjacent Seas, Antarctic Ocean. *Ibis*, ninth series, vol. I, no. 2, April, 1907, pp. 325-349, pls. VII.

CLARKE, JOHN MASON.

1913 The Origin of the Gulf of St. Lawrence. *Bulletin de la Société de Géographie de Québec*, vol. VII, no. 1, January and February, 1913, pp. 29-36.

CLEMENTS, FREDERIC EDWARD.

1920 Plant Indicators. The Relation of Plant Communities to Process and Practice. *Carnegie Institution of Washington Publication* 290, pp. xvi, 388, pls. A, I-XCII, figures in text.

COLEMAN, ARTHUR PHILEMON.

1921 Northeastern Part of Labrador and New Quebec. *Geological Survey of Canada Memoir* 124, 1921, pp. iv, 68, pls. X, maps 3.

1924 Ice Ages and the Drift of Continents. *American Journal of Science*, series V, vol. VII, no. 41, May, 1924, pp. 398-404.

1926 The Pleistocene of Newfoundland. *Journal of Geology*, vol. XXXIV, no. 3, April-May, 1926, pp. 193-223.

1927 Glacial and Interglacial Periods in Eastern Canada. *Journal of Geology*, vol. XXXV, no. 5, July-August, 1927, pp. 385-403.

COOKE, WELLS WOODBRIDGE.

1904   Distribution and Migration of North American Warblers. *United States Department of Agriculture, Division of Biological Survey, Bulletin* 18, 1904, pp. 142.

1906   Distribution of North American Ducks, Geese and Swans. *United States Department of Agriculture, Biological Survey, Bulletin* 26, 1906, pp. 90.

1910   Distribution and Migration of North American Shorebirds. *United States Department of Agriculture, Biological Survey, Bulletin* 35, October 6, 1910, pp. 100, pls. IV.

1915   Distribution and Migration of North American Gulls and their Allies. *United States Department of Agriculture, Bulletin* 292, October 25, 1915, pp. 70.

1916   Labrador Bird Notes. *Auk*, vol. XXXIII, no. 2, April, 1916, pp. 162-167.

COUES, ELLIOTT.

1861   Notes on the Ornithology of Labrador. *Proceedings of the Academy of Natural Sciences of Philadelphia*, vol. XIII, August, 1861, pp. 215-257.

DALY, REGINALD ALDWORTH.

1902   The Geology of the Northeast Coast of Labrador. *Bulletin of the Museum of Comparative Zoölogy*, vol. XXXVIII, no. 5, February, 1902, pp. 203-270, pls. I-XIII.

DAWSON, GEORGE MERCER.

1898   Summary Report on the Operations of the Geological Survey for the Year 1897 by the Director. *Geological Survey of Canada, Annual Report (New Series)*, vol. X, 1899 [1898], pp. 1A-156A.

DIONNE, CHARLES EUSÈBE.

1906   Les Oiseaux de la Province de Québec. Quebec, 1906.   8vo, pp. viii, 415, pls. VIII, figures in text.

DIXON, JOSEPH.

1928   Contributions to the Life History of the Alaska Willow Ptarmigan *Condor*, vol. XXIX, no. 5, September-October, 1927, pp. 213-223.

DUTCHER, WILLIAM.

1894   The Labrador Duck—Another Specimen, with Additional Data Respecting Extant Specimens. *Auk*, vol. XI, no. 1, January, 1894, pp. 4-12.

1894   In Re Dutcher on the Labrador Duck. *Auk*, vol. XI, no. 2, April, 1894, pp. 175-176.

DWIGHT, JONATHAN.

1925   The Gulls (Laridae) of the World; their Plumages, Moults, Variations, Relationships and Distribution. *Bulletin of the American Museum of Natural History*, vol. LII, article III, December 31, 1925, pp. 63-401, pls. V-XV, figures 1-384.

EAGLE CLARK, WILLIAM.   See Clark.

EIFRIG, CHARLES WILLIAM GUSTAVE.

1905   Ornithological Results of the Canadian 'Neptune' Expedition to Hudson Bay and Northward, 1903-1904. *Auk*, vol. XXII, no. 3, July, 1905, pp. 233-241.

FERNALD, MERRITT LYNDON.

1925   Persistence of Plants in Unglaciated Areas of Boreal America. *Memoirs of the American Academy of Arts and Sciences*, vol. XV, no. III, 1925, pp. 237-342.

1926   The Antiquity and Dispersal of Vascular Plants. *Quarterly Review of Biology*, vol. I, no. 2, April, 1926, pp. 212-245.

FISHER, ALBERT KENRICK.

1893   The Hawks and Owls of the United States in their Relation to Agriculture. *United States Department of Agriculture, Division of Ornithology and Mammalogy, Bulletin 3*. Washington, 1893. 8vo, pp. 210, pls. 26.

FLEMING, JAMES HENRY.

1906   Range of the Sharp-tailed Grouse in Eastern Canada. *Ontario Natural Science Bulletin*, no. 2, 1906, pp. 2-19.

FORBES, ALEXANDER.

1932   Surveying in Northern Labrador. *Geographical Review*, vol., XXII, no. 1, January, 1932, pp. 30-60, figures in text.

FRAZAR, MARSTON ABBOTT.

1887   An Ornithologist's Summer in Labrador. *Ornithologist and Oölogist*, vol. XII, no. 1, January, 1887, pp. 1-3; no. 2, February, 1887, pp. 17-20; no. 3, March, 1887, pp. 33-35.

GRIEVE, SYMMINGTON.

1885   The Great Auk or Garefowl. London, Thomas C. Jack, 1885. Quarto, pp. xi, 142, [ii,] 58, pls. IV, map, figures in text.

GRINNELL, JOSEPH.

1909   Birds and Mammals of the 1907 Alexander Expedition to Southeastern Alaska. *University of California Publications in Zoology*, vol. V, no. 2, February 18, 1909, pp. 171-264, pls. XXV, XXVI.

1909   (See also Hall and Grinnell.)

1928   Presence and Absence of Animals. *University of California Chronicle*, October, 1928, pp. 429-450.

GURNEY, JOHN HENRY.

1913   The Gannet. A Bird with a History. London, Witherby and Co., 1913. 8vo, pp. lii, 568, numerous plates, and figures in the text, most of the plates included in the pagination.

HALL, HARVEY MONROE, and JOSEPH GRINNELL.

1919   Life-Zone Indicators in California. *Proceedings of the California Academy of Sciences*, fourth series, vol. IX, no. 2, June 16, 1919, pp. 37-67.

HANTZSCH, BERNHARD.

1908   Beitrag zur Kenntniss der Vogelwelt des Nordöstlichsten Labradors. *Journal für Ornithologie*, vol. LVI, no. 2, April, 1908, pp. 177-202; no. 3, July, 1908, pp. 307-392.

1928-1929   Contribution to the Knowledge of the Avifauna of North-Eastern Labrador. *Canadian Field-Naturalist*, vol. XLII, no. 1, January, 1928, pp. 2-9; no. 2, February, 1928, pp. 33-40; no. 4, April, 1928, pp. 87-94; no. 5, May, 1928, pp. 123-125; no. 6, September, 1928, pp. 146-148; no. 7, October, 1928, pp. 172-177; no. 8, November, 1928, pp. 201-207; no. 9, December, 1928, pp. 221-227; vol. XLIII, no. 1 January, 1929, pp. 11-18; no. 2, February, 1929, pp. 31-34; no. 3, March, 1929, pp. 52-59. (Translated from *Journal für Ornithologie*, vol. LVI, 1908, by M. B. A. Anderson and R. M. Anderson.)

HARTERT, ERNST.

1903-1923   Die Vögel der Paläarktischen Fauna. Berlin, R. Friedlander und Sohn, 1903-1923. Large 8vo, vol. I, 1903-1910, pp. L, XII, 832; vol. II, 1912-1921, pp. XXIV, 833-1764; vol. III, 1921-1922, pp. XII, 1765-2328; supplement, 1923, pp. 92.

Howe, Reginald Heber, Jr.

1901   A new Subspecies of *Passerculus sandwichensis*. *Contributions to North American Ornithology*, vol. I, October 14, 1901, pp. 1-2.

1902   The Labrador Savanna Sparrow. *Auk*, vol. XIX, no. 1, January, 1902, pp. 85-86.

1903   A Further Note on the Subspecies of *Passerculus sandwichensis* Inhabiting Labrador. *Auk*, vol. XX, no. 2, April, 1903, pp. 215-216.

Hubbard, Mina Benson.

1908   A Woman's Way through Unknown Labrador. An Account of the Exploration of the Nascaupee and George Rivers. By Mrs. Leonidas Hubbard, Jr. New York, The McClure Co., 1908. 12mo, pp. xii, 305, pls. XXXIII, map.

Kendall, William Converse.

1909   The Fishes of Labrador. *Proceedings of the Portland Society of Natural History*, vol. II, part 8, November 15, 1909, pp. 207-243.

Kennard, Frederic Hedge.

1927   The Specific Status of the Greater Snow Goose. *Proceedings of the New England Zoölogical Club*, vol. IX, pp. 85-93, February 16, 1927.

Kindle, Edward Martin.

1924   Geography and Geology of Lake Melville District, Labrador Peninsula. *Canada Geological Survey Memoir* 141, 1924, pp. [iv,] 105, pls. I-XVII.

Koelz, Walter.

1929   On a Collection of Gyrfalcons from Greenland. *Wilson Bulletin*, vol. XLI, no. 4, December, 1929, pp. 207-219.

Kumlien, Thure Ludwig Theodor.

1897   Contributions to the Natural History of Arctic America, Made in Connection with the Howgate Polar Expedition, 1877-78. *Bulletin of the United States National Museum*, 15, 1879, pp. 179. (Birds seen along the Labrador coast, pp. 69-105.)

Lewis, Harrison Flint.

1929   The Natural History of the Double-crested Cormorant. Ottawa, May, 1929. Quarto, pp. [iv,] 94.

LINSDALE, JEAN M.

1928 Variations in the Fox Sparrow (*Passerella iliaca*) with Reference to Natural History and Osteology. *University of California Publications in Zoology*, vol. XXX, no. 12, September 28, 1928, pp. 251-392, pls. XVI-XX (included in the pagination).

LIVINGSTON, BURTON EDWARD, and FORREST SHREVE.

1921 The Distribution of Vegetation in the United States, as Related to Climatic Conditions. *Carnegie Institution of Washington Publication* 284, pp. xvi, 590, numerous maps (some in text).

LÖNNBERG, AXEL JOHAN EINAR.

1927 Some Speculations on the Origin of the North American Ornithic Fauna. *K. Svenska Vetenskapsakademiens Handlingar*, 3d series, vol. IV, no. 6, pp. 1-24, 1927.

LOW, ALBERT PETER.

1896 Report on Explorations in the Labrador Peninsula along the East Main, Koksoak, Hamilton, Manicuagan, and Portions of Other Rivers in 1892-93-94-95. *Annual Report of the Geological Survey of Canada*, vol. VIII, part L, pp. 387, pls. IV.

1906 Report on the Dominion Government Expedition to Hudson Bay and the Arctic Islands Aboard the D. G. S. 'Neptune,' 1903-04. Ottawa, 1906, pp. xvii, 355, pls. LXII, figures in text.

LUCAS, FREDERIC AUGUSTUS.

1892 The Expedition to the Funk Island, with Observations upon the History and Anatomy of the Great Auk. *Report of the United States National Museum for 1887-88*, 1892, pp. 493-529, pls. LXXI-LXXIII.

MACOUN, JOHN.

1900-1904 Catalogue of Canadian Birds. Geological Survey of Canada, Ottawa. 8ᵛᵒ, part I, 1900, pp. vii, 1-218; part II, 1903, pp. v. 219-413; part III, 1904, pp. iv, 415-733, i-xxiii.

MANNICHE, ARNER LUDVIG VALDEMAR.

1910 The Terrestrial Mammals and Birds of Northeast Greenland. *Medelser om Grönland*, vol. XLV, no. 1, pp. 1-200, pls. I-VII, figures in text.

MATTHEW, WILLIAM DILLER.

1915   Climate and Evolution. *Annals of the New York Academy of Sciences*, vol. XXIV, February 18, 1915, pp. 171-318.   (See also: Thomas Barbour, *ibid.*, vol. XXVII, January, 1916, pp. 1-15.)

MEINERTZHAGEN, RICHARD.

1925   The Distribution of the Phalaropes. *Ibis*, series 12, vol. I, no. 2, April, 1925, pp. 325-344.

MERRIAM, CLINTON HART.

1890   Results of a Biological Survey of the San Francisco Mountain Region and Desert of the Little Colorado, Arizona. *United States Department of Agriculture, North American Fauna* no. 3, Washington, 1890.

MILLER, GERRIT SMITH, Jr.

1924   List of North American Recent Mammals, 1923. *United States National Museum Bulletin* 128, pp. XVI, 674.   Washington, 1924.

MÜLLER, H. C.

1862   Faeröernes Fuglefauna med bemærkninger om Fuglefangsten. *Videnskabelige Meddelelser fra den Naturhistoriske Forening i Kjöbenhavn*, 1862, no. 1, pp. 1-75.   (Also review in *Ibis*, vol. V, 1863, p. 468.)

MURPHY, ROBERT CUSHMAN.

1914   Observations on Birds of the South Atlantic. *Auk*, vol. XXXI, no. 4, October, 1914, pp. 439-457, pls. XXXV-XXXIX.

NELSON, EDWARD WILLIAM.

1887.   Report upon Natural History Collections Made in Alaska between the Years 1877 and 1881.   No. III of *Arctic Series of Publications Issued in Connection with the Signal Service, United States Army*, Washington, 1887.   Pp. 337, pls. XXI.

NORTON, ARTHUR HERBERT.

1901   Birds of the Bowdoin College Expedition to Labrador in 1891. *Proceedings of the Portland Society of Natural History*, vol. II, article VIII, pp. 139-158, pl. II.

OBERHOLSER, HARRY CHURCH.

1902   A Review of the Larks of the Genus Otocoris. *Proceedings of the United States National Museum*, vol. XXIV, 1902, pp. 801-883, pls. XLIII-XLV, four maps.

1904   A Revision of the American Great Horned Owls. *Proceedings of the United States National Museum*, vol. XXVII, 1904, pp. 177-192.

1914   Four New Birds from Newfoundland. *Proceedings of the Biological Society of Washington*, vol. XXVII, March 20, 1914, pp. 43-54.

OSGOOD, WILFRED HUDSON.

1904   A Biological Reconnaissance of the Base of the Alaska Peninsula. *United States Department of Agriculture, Division of Biological Survey, North America Fauna*, no. 24, November 23, 1904, pp. 86, pls. VII.

PACKARD, ALPHEUS SPRING.

1891   The Labrador Coast. A Journal of Two Summer Cruises to that Region. New York, N. D. C. Hodges, 1891. 8vo, pp. 513, pls. X, many figures in text. (List of birds by L. M. Turner, revised by J. A. Allen, pp. 406-442.)

PALMER, WILLIAM.

1891   Notes on the Birds Observed during the Cruise of the United States Fish Commission Schooner 'Grampus' in the Summer of 1887. *Proceedings of the United States National Museum*, vol. XIII, no. 819, 1891, pp. 249-265.

PETERS, JAMES LEE.

1931   Check-List of Birds of the World. Cambridge, Harvard University Press. 8vo, vol. I, 1931, pp. xviii, 345.

PHILLIPS, JOHN CHARLES.

1922-1926   A Natural History of the Ducks. Boston and New York, Houghton Mifflin Co. Quarto. Vol. I, 1922, pp. ii, viii, 1-264, pls. I-XVIII, maps 1-27; vol. II, 1923, pp. xii, 1-409, pls. XIX-XLIV, maps 28-65; vol. III, 1925, pp. xii, 1-383, pls. XLV-LXX, maps 65-95; vol. IV, 1926, pp. xi, 1-489, pls. LXXI-CII, maps 96-118.

PIRSSON, LOUIS VALENTINE, and CHARLES SCHUCHERT.

1915   A Text-Book of Geology. New York, John Wiley and Son, 1915. Part II, pp. i-viii, 405-1026, map, many figures in text.

1930   A Text-Book of Geology. Third edition, revised. New York, John Wiley and Son, 1930. Part II, pp. i-x, 1-724, map, many figures in text.

PLESKE, THEODORE.
1928   Birds of the Eurasian Tundra. *Memoirs of the Boston Society of Natural History*, vol. VI, no. 3, April, 1928, pp. 107-485, pls. XVI-XXXVIII.

PRICHARD, HESKETH HESKETH.
1911   Through Trackless Labrador. London, William Heinemann, 1911. Small quarto, pp. xvi, 254, pls. LVI.

RAINE, WALTER.
1896   Nidification of the Dusky Horned Owl. *Auk*, vol. XIII, no. 3, July, 1896, p. 257.

REED, CHESTER ALBERT.
1904   North American Birds' Eggs. New York, Doubleday, Page and Co., 1904. 8vo, pp. x, 356, frontispiece, many figures in text.

RHOADS, SAMUEL NICHOLSON.
1893   The Hudsonian Chickadee and its Allies, with Remarks on the Geographical Distribution of Bird Races in Boreal America. *Auk*, vol. X, no. 4, October, 1893, pp. 321-333.

RIDGWAY, ROBERT.
1874, 1884   See Baird, Brewer and Ridgway.

1882   Description of Several New Races of American Birds. *Proceedings of the United States National Museum*, vol. V, pp. 9-15, June 5, 1882. (*Perisoreus canadensis nigricapillus.*)

1901-1919   Birds of North and Middle America. *Bulletin United States National Museum*, 50, parts 1-8.

SALOMONSEN, FINN.
1928   Bemerkungen über die Verbreitung der *Carduelis linaria* Gruppe und ihre Variationen. *Saertryk af Videnskabelige Meddelelser fra Dansk Naturhistorisk Forening i Kjøbenhavn*, vol. LXXXVI, 1928, pp. 123-202.

1930   Bemerkungen über die Geographische Variation von Charadrius hiaticula L. *Journal für Ornithologie*, vol. LXXVIII, pt. 1, January, 1930, pp. 65-72.

1931   On the Geographical Variation of the Snow Bunting (*Plectrophenax nivalis*). *Ibis*, thirteenth series, vol. I, no. 1, January, 1931, pp. 57-70, pls. I, II.

SCHUBERT, GOTTHILF HEINRICH VON.

1844   Correspondenz-Nachrichten aus Labrador. *Gelebrte Anzeigen heraus-
       gegeben von Mitgliedern der K. Bayerische Akademie der Wissenschaf-
       ten, München,* vol. XVIII, 1844.
          Verzeichniss der in Labrador befindlichen Landsäugethiere, no. 52
       (March 13, 1844), pp. 417-421.
          Verzeichniss der bekanntesten Wasservögel in Labrador. Pp. 422
       (no. 52, March 13, 1844)-424 (no. 53, March 14, 1844).
          Land- und Strandvögel. Pp. 424-430 (no. 53, March 14, 1844).

SHREVE, FORREST. See Livingston and Shreve.

SOPER, JOSEPH DEWEY.

1928   A Faunal Investigation of Southern Baffin Island. *National Museum
       of Canada, Bulletin* 53. Ottawa, 1928, pp. 1-143.

STEARNS, WINFRED ALDEN.

1882   The American Pipit: Its Habits in Labrador. *American Field,* vol.
       XVII, p. 35.

1883   Notes on the Natural History of Labrador. *Proceedings of the United
       States National Museum,* vol. VI, no. 7 (July 27, 1883), no. 8 (August
       1, 1883), no. 9 (September 20, 1883), pp. 111-137.   (Also, a reprint,
       New Haven, 74 pages.)

1884   Labrador. A Sketch of its Peoples, its Industries and its Natural His-
       tory. Boston, Lee and Shepard, 1884. 12mo, pp. viii, 295.

1890   Bird Life in Labrador. *American Field,* vol. XXXIII, 1890, p. 390;
       April 26; pp. 415-416, May 3; pp. 438-439, May 10; p. 463, May 17,
       pp. 486-487, May 24; p. 511, May 31; p. 535, June 7; pp. 559-560,
       June 14; 583-584, June 21; pp. 611-612, June 28; vol. XXXIV, 1890,
       pp. 6-7, July 5; p. 31, July 12; p. 55, July 19; p. 79, July 26; p. 104,
       August 2; pp. 128-129, August 9; p. 153, August 16; p. 176, August
       23; p. 191, August 30; pp. 223-224, September 6; p. 247, September 13;
       p. 271, September 20; p. 295, September 27; p. 319, October 4; pp.
       344-345, October 11.
       (There is a reprint, undated, octavo, pp. 100[=98], 7, one plate.)

STEJNEGER, LEONHARD.

1885   On the Alleged Occurrence of the Pacific Eider in Labrador. *Auk,* vol.
       II, no. 4, October, 1885, p. 386.

1901 On the Wheatears (Saxicola) Occurring in North America. *Proceedings of the United States National Museum*, vol. XXIII, pp. 473-481, February 25, 1901.

SUSHKIN, PETER PETROVICH.
1925 Notes on Systematics and Distribution of Certain Palaearctic Birds. *Proceedings of the Boston Society of Natural History*, vol. XXXVIII, no. 1, August, 1925, pp. 1-55.

1928 Notes on Systematics and Distribution of Certain Palaearctic Birds: Second Contribution. *Proceedings of the Boston Society of Natural History*, vol. XXXIX, no. 1, February, 1928, pp. 1-32, pls. I-III.

SWANN, HARRY KIRKE.
1922 A Synopsis of the Accipitres. Second edition. London, September 28, 1921—May 20, 1922. 8vo, pp. [xviii,] 233.

SWARTH, HARRY SCHELWALDT.
1920 Revision of the Avian Genus Passerella, with Special Reference to the Distribution and Migration of the Races in California. *University of California Publications in Zoölogy*, vol. XXI, no. 4, September 11, 1920, pp. 75-224, pls. IV-VII, 30 figures in text.

TAVERNER, PERCY ALGERNON.
1915 The Double-crested Cormorant (*Phalacrocorax auritus*) and its Relation to the Salmon Industries on the Gulf of St. Lawrence. *Canada Geological Survey, Museum Bulletin* 13, Biological Series no. 5, April 30, 1915, pp. 1-24, pl. I.

1929 A Study of the Canadian Races of Rock Ptarmigan (*Lagopus rupestris*). *National Museum of Canada, Annual Report for 1928*, 1929, pp. 28-38.

1931 A Study of Branta canadensis (Linnaeus), the Canada Goose. *National Museum of Canada, Annual Report for 1929*, 1931, pp. 28-40, pl. I.

1932 A New Subspecies of Willow Ptarmigan from the Arctic Islands of America. *National Museum of Canada, Annual Report for 1930*. Ottawa, April 4, 1932, pp. 87-88.

TOWNSEND, CHARLES WENDELL.
1907 Along the Labrador Coast. Boston, Dana Estes and Co., 1907. 12mo, pp. xii, 289, pls. 26, map.

1909 Labrador Notes. *Auk*, vol. XXVI, no. 2, April, 1909, p. 201.

1910 A Labrador Spring. Boston, Dana Estes and Co., 1910. 12mo, pp. i-xii, 11-262, pls. 32.

1913 Some more Labrador Notes. *Auk*, vol. XXX, no. 1, January, 1913, pp. 1-10, pls. I, II.

1914 A Plea for the Conservation of the Eider. *Auk*, vol. XXXI, no. 1, January, 1914, pp. 14-21.

1916 A New Subspecies of Hudsonian Chickadee from the Labrador Peninsula. *Auk*, vol. XXXIII, no. 1, January, 1916, p. 74.

1917 The Labrador Chickadee (*Pentbestes budsonicus nigricans*) in a Southward Migration. *Auk*, vol. XXXIV, no. 2, April, 1917, pp. 160-163.

1929 Breeding Range of the Northern Phalarope (*Lobipes lobatus*). *Auk*, vol. XLVI, no. 1, January, 1929, pp. 108-109.

TOWNSEND, CHARLES WENDELL, and GLOVER MORRILL ALLEN.
1907 Birds of Labrador. *Proceedings of the Boston Society of Natural History*, vol. XXXIII, no. 7, July, 1907, pp. 277-428, pl. XXIX.

TROTTER, SPENCER.
1909 The Geological and Geographical Relations of the Land-Bird Fauna of Northeastern America. *Auk*, vol. XXVI, no. 3, July, 1909, pp. 221-233.

1912 The Relation of Genera to Faunal Areas. *Auk*, vol. XXIX, no. 2, April, 1912, pp. 159-165.

1912a The Faunal Divisions of Eastern North America in Relation to Vegetation. *Journal of the Academy of Natural Sciences of Philadelphia*, series 2, vol. XV, pp. 205-218. (A summary of this paper appears in the Proceedings of the Academy for the same year, p. 142.)

TRUMBULL, JOHN.
1905 Notes on Land-Birds Observed on the North Atlantic and Gulf of St. Lawrence, 1904. *Zoologist*, series 4, vol. IX, no. 104, August 15, 1905, pp. 293-300.

TUCKER, EPHRAIM.
1839 Five Months in Labrador and Newfoundland, during the Summer of 1838. Concord, N. H., Israel S. Boyd and William White, 1839. 16mo, pp. 156.

TURNER, LUCIEN McSHANN.

1885 List of the Birds of Labrador, Including Ungava, East Main, Moose, and Gulf Districts of the Hudson Bay Company, together with the Island of Anticosti. *Proceedings of the United States National Museum*, vol. VIII, July 13, 1885, pp. 233-254. (For a revision of this List, *see* PACKARD, 1891.)

WALLACE, DILLON.

1902 The Lure of the Labrador Wild. New York, Fleming H. Revell Co., 1902. 12ᵐᵒ, pp. 339 [=335], pls. XVI.

1923 The Long Labrador Trail. Chicago, A. C. McClurg and Co., 1923. 12ᵐᵒ, pp. xii, 315, pls. XXVII.

WEGENER, ALFRED.

1922 Die Entstehung der Kontinente und Ozeane. Third edition. Braunschweig, Friedrich Vieweg und Sohn, 1922. 8ᵛᵒ, pp. VIII, 144, figures in text.

WEIZ, SAMUEL.

1866 List of Vertebrates Observed at Okak, Labrador, by Rev. Samuel Weiz, with Annotations by A. S. Packard, Jr., M.D. *Proceedings of the Boston Society of Natural History*, vol. X, pp. 264-277.

WHEELER, EVERETT PEPPERRELL, 2D.

1930 Journeys about Nain. *Geographical Review*, vol. XX, no. 3, July, 1930. pp. 454-468, pl. IV, figures in text.

WITHERBY, HARRY FORBES.

1928 A Transatlantic Passage of Lapwings. *British Birds*, vol. XXII, no. 1, June 1, 1928, pp. 6-13. (Reprinted in *Bird-Lore*, vol. XXX, no. 4, July-August, 1928, pp. 248-252.)

INDEX

In trinomial scientific names the middle term is omitted.
The principal reference to any subject is shown in heavy-faced type. A hyphen between two numbers indicates that the subject is mentioned on each of the included pages. A letter with a numeral denotes the position of a locality on the map.

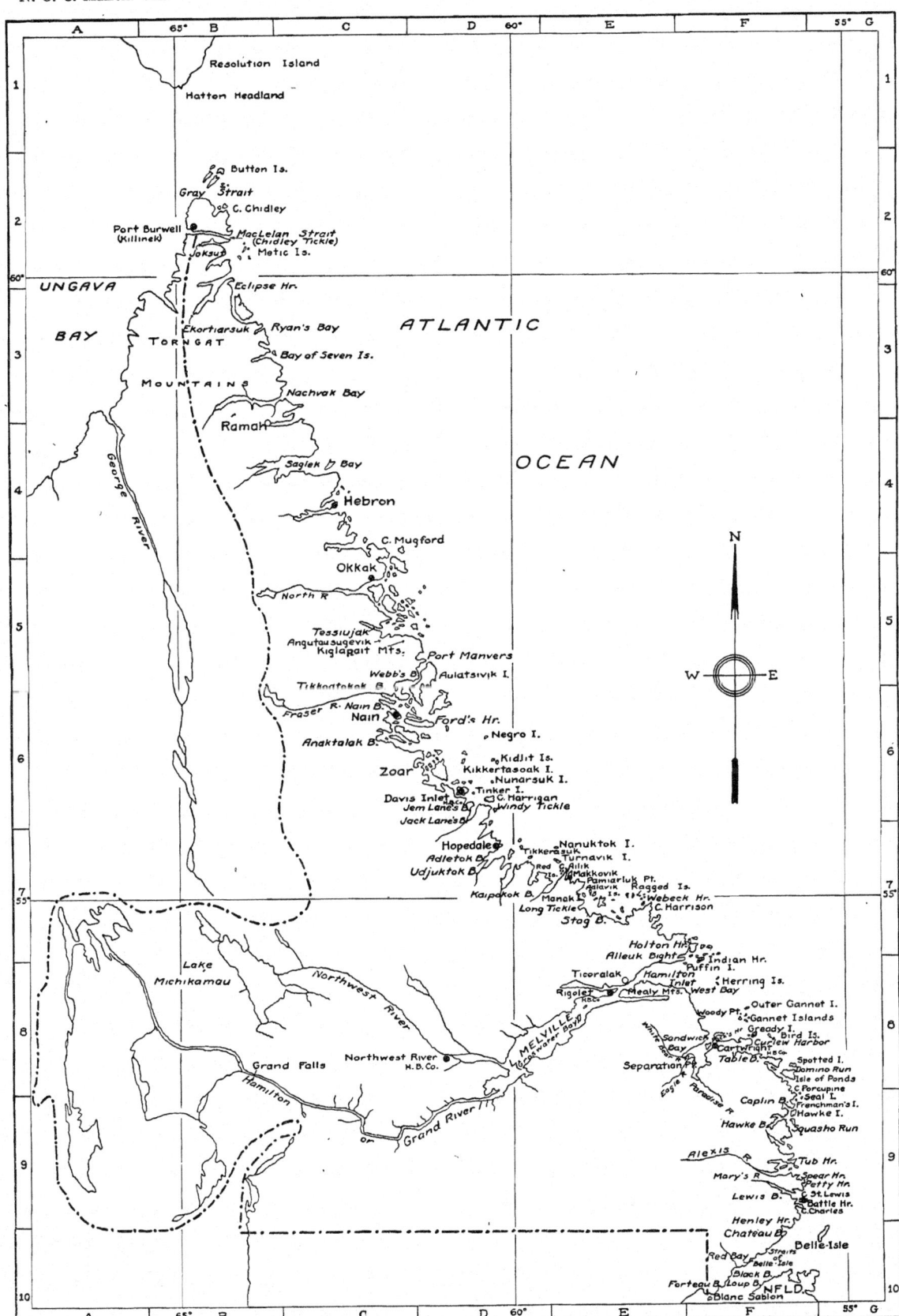

CPSIA information can be obtained
at www.ICGtesting.com
Printed in the USA
BVOW05s0603161216
470955BV00009B/103/P